Administration of
Special Education

Administration of Special Education

Clifford E. Howe
University of Iowa

LOVE PUBLISHING COMPANY
Denver · London

Copyright © 1981 Love Publishing Company
Printed in the U.S.A.
ISBN 0-89108-106-2
Library of Congress Catalog Card Number 81-81520
10 9 8 7 6 5 4 3 2 1

Contents

Figures

Tables

Acknowledgments

Major credit must be given to a number of my current and former students, who seemed to get more than the usual amount of enjoyment from critiquing the manuscript. Students who invested considerable time and made significant contributions include Carol Bradley, Gail Fitzgerald, Mary Green, Bill Kerfoot, Austin Mueller, and Alice Nelson.

Other colleagues — Bob Henderson of the University of Illinois, and Walt Foley and Willard Lane in Educational Administration at The University of Iowa — were encouraging and helpful. A special note of thanks goes to a former student, J. Donald Monroe of the University of South Dakota. His sense of humor combined with his skill as a writer kept steering me back on track regarding parallel structure and use of third person references. Thanks also to Bart Garvey, on the editing staff of the Iowa University Affiliated Facility, for his faithful and excellent job of textual editing. And last, thanks to my family, who kept redirecting me to the ping-pong table in the basement when I strayed from the task.

Preface

Not much has been published in the area of special education administration. Part of the reason is that the field has been so specialized and has used methods quite different from administrative practices in business or general school administration. In many respects, directing special education programs is now moving closer to mainstream administration as practiced by building principals. One argument made in this book is that a major role of the director of special education should be as a "teacher of other significant adults." Briefly, what this means is that whatever unique knowledge a special educator has about administration should be shared with the generalist. Of course, some of what a special educator considers unique is not really so at all, or at least not for very long. A current example is PL 94-142, the Education for All Handicapped Children Act. When it first became law in 1975, special educators were among the major interpreters of its meaning to general administrators. Now, five years later, the general administrator should be aware of the major provisions and assume major responsibility for its implementation.

This book is intended for two primary audiences: (1) experienced special educators training to be administrators of programs for handicapped children; and (2) general administrators and building principals either in training or working in the field. It is divided into two sections. In Part I, I have traced the development of the position of director of special education and then pointed out how the role is likely to change. In Part II, I've attempted to pull together a rather diverse set of readings that have been useful to students I've trained. Because the sources range from the *Harvard Business Review* and *Royal Bank of Canada Monthly Newsletter,* they are not readily accessible in a typical library. Putting them together may increase the likelihood of their being read. Last, this book is based on the premise that special education administration builds on the knowledge and practices used in the general field. It assumes that a major training component is with education administration and associated areas such as business and law.

C.E.H.

Iowa City, Iowa
January 1981

I

Administration and Special Education:
Its Changing Role

1

Current Administrative Arrangements
in Special Education

Who is responsible for managing special education programs in public school systems? This question, in various forms, has plagued general and special education administrators over the years. In the larger school districts the position of director of special education has typically been given staff status rather than being defined as a line position. Staff positions have historically had an "advise and consult" role, with little direct decisionmaking authority. Line positions derive their authority from delegation, such as that given principals by the superintendent. Line officers are usually responsible for serving children directly (Knezevich, 1975).

The staff and line concept is generally conceded to have originated in the military and has been borrowed by business corporations as well as school systems and other bureaucracies. Staff departments in the military are intended to support soldiers on the line. Similar positions in school systems provide assistance to the principal and teachers. Staff departments in corporations, such as the personnel department, are not in the mainstream of the organization but, rather, report to line executives at various levels of the hierarchy. "Support services" is one of the most common titles for special education departments, and that is probably not an accident.

When the position of special education director has been assigned line status, the model is often that of placing handicapped children in special classes or segregated facilities. A dual system of administration has resulted — one for the regular schools and another for special education. Reynolds (1978) characterized the practice as the "two-box" arrangement, whereby children are placed in either special or regular classes.

3

AGGREGATING SUFFICIENT NUMBERS OF CHILDREN

Another organizational complication in special education is the difficulty of aggregating numbers of handicapped children sufficient for group instruction. Before addressing this issue, however, let us review the relationship between enrollment and adequacy of instruction for regular students. The average school district in the United States has a low enrollment. As can be seen in Table 1, more than half (53.6 percent) of the operating school systems in 1977 had fewer than 1,000 pupils each. Studies over the past 30 years have recommended a basic enrollment of from 1,000 to 10,000 pupils, grades K through 12 inclusive (Knezevich, 1975), in order to provide a comprehensive program for regular pupils at a reasonable cost. Given the lower limit of 1,000 students, over half the school districts in the United States would have to be reorganized. Some consolidation of school districts continues to occur, but the rate is slow. According to the National Center for Education Statistics, the number of school districts declined by 4.1 percent from fall 1972 to fall 1976 (Foster & Carpenter, 1978). Local communities, especially in the more sparsely

TABLE 1
Distribution of Operating Local Public School Systems,
by Size of System, in the United States, Fall 1977

Size of System	Number of Systems	Percentage of U.S. Total	Number of Pupils	Percentage of U.S. Total
25,000 or more	187	1.2	12,162,027	28.0
10,000-24,999	530	3.3	7,686,162	17.7
5,000-9,999	1,104	7.0	7,703,873	17.7
2,500-4,999	2,067	13.1	7,222,844	16.6
1,000-2,499	3,463	21.9	5,669,588	13.1
600-999	1,864	11.8	1,464,788	3.4
300-599	2,323	14.7	1,018,759	2.3
Less than 300	4,296	27.1	516,013	1.2
Total operating systems	15,834	100	43,444,144	100

Source: Foster & Carpenter (1978).

From "Statistics of Public Elementary and Secondary Day Schools," by B. J. Foster and J. M. Carpenter, *Education Directory, Public School Systems, 1977-78 School Year (Final)*. Washington, DC: National Center for Education Statistics, U.S. Department of Health, Education and Welfare, 1978.

populated rural areas, continue to resist school reorganization. Reasons given include loss of local control, deterioration in community pride and business when the neighborhood school is closed, and increased bus riding time for pupils. In addition, the projected shortage of gasoline and its increasing cost will certainly cause a more determined resistance to the idea of moving pupils to larger centers. Thus, for the 1980s, the merger of school districts is not likely to be a major phenomenon.

If a hypothetical school district enrolled 1,000 pupils, the number of handicapped children probably would be somewhere around 115, as shown in Table 2. Note that these youngsters would be spread across eight to ten disability areas as well as distributed through the entire school-age range. A district of this size likely cannot program adequately for low-prevalence handicapped children and may or may not be able to do so for those classified in the mild and moderate ranges. We digress for a moment to comment on distinguishing between incidence and prevalence. As noted by Meyen (1978),

> The literature frequently incorporates two similar terms when describing population studies on exceptional children: prevalence and incidence. The two terms have different meanings but, unfortunately, often are used interchangeably, causing confusion for the person seeking accurate information. Simply stated,

TABLE 2
Approximate Numbers of Handicapped Children
in an Average School System of 1,000 Pupils

Handicapping Condition	Percentage of School-age Population	Number of Pupils
Visually Impaired (includes blind)	0.1	1
Hearing Impaired (includes deaf)	0.2	2
Physically Impaired	0.2	2
Mentally Retarded	2.6	26
Learning Disabled	3.8	38
Emotionally Disturbed	1.0	10
Speech Impaired	3.6	36
Total		115

Adapted from figures released by the Bureau of Education for the Handicapped, U.S. Office of Education, on May 14, 1980, "Number of Handicapped Children Reported Served Under P.L. 94-142 and P.L. 89-313 for School Year 1979-80."

prevalence refers to the number of exceptional children *currently existing;* incidence refers to the number of children who, *at some time in their life, might be considered exceptional.* Obviously, the latter figure would be much higher; it is also more difficult to substantiate. (p. 63)

Our hypothetical school district described above is not markedly different from the actual situation. Kohl and Marro (1971) surveyed all local administrators of special education in the United States who directed programs in three or more disability areas and spent at least 50 percent of their time in such efforts. The authors reported that few special education administrators were hired by school districts with enrollments smaller than 3,000 pupils. The largest numbers were hired by districts with enrollments between 8,000 and 15,000 pupils. Even then, the majority of the respondents (60 percent) directed programs that had fewer than 25 special education professional staff members. Such staff members were concentrated at the elementary level, and most worked with the speech handicapped and the educable mentally retarded. The average unit had fewer than 400 special education pupils enrolled in classroom programs. The smaller the program, the more likely the classes were to be basically self-contained rather than integrated. Kohl and Marro concluded that a unit should contain 8,000 to 10,000 regular pupils before a comprehensive specialized program can be developed and financial resources used efficiently. If a minimum of 10,000 students is taken as a base, only about 5 percent of the school districts in the United States meet this criterion.

From the foregoing discussion, most local school districts in this country clearly are not of a sufficient size to provide comprehensive instructional services to all their handicapped pupils. Realizing this, many states have developed some sort of cooperative arrangement among districts to provide for the handicapped. The best known are Illinois' joint agreement among districts, interdistrict cooperatives as in Minnesota, the old county school systems, and, more recently, the regional education service agency or intermediate education unit. Some combination of such consortia for provision of services to the handicapped has existed for almost 30 years. Even these joint agreement arrangements have been found to be too small for low-prevalence handicapping conditions, however, and some states, such as Illinois, have developed "super joint agreements," or regional programs, in addition to joint agreements.

Although these cooperative models aggregate sufficient numbers of handicapped children to provide more efficient instruction, they have also created management and ownership problems. An intermediate education unit includes a number of autonomous local school districts and usually has a board of its own with an administrative hierarchy.

Joint agreements and cooperatives often have separate administrative structures, although they are usually governed by superintendents of the constituent districts rather than lay boards. States with super joint agreements overlay a third tier of separate administration. All these arrangements have come under increasing criticism since passage of Public Law 94-142, the Education for All Handicapped Children Act of 1975. Local school districts tend not to view the pupils in regional special education programs as their responsibility. This makes it more difficult to return such pupils to the mainstream of regular classes or buildings and thus hinders the use of the least restrictive alternative as required by PL 94-142. Removing children from their local schools also makes involvement and communication with the parents more difficult.

Another aspect of the ownership question has been the continuing difficulty of maintaining stable sites from year to year in buildings in local school districts. As enrollment expands in a neighborhood school, local administrators may not be willing to provide the space for special education programs. Consequently, special classes often have been shifted yearly from building to building or even from one cooperating district to another, making it even more difficult to achieve a degree of integration and acceptance between regular and special education pupils. This problem is not unique to cooperative arrangements; it has also existed within larger school districts that manage their own special education programs. The situation may ease with the present trend of declining enrollments in the public schools.

Passage of PL 94-142 created a new set of conditions under which teachers and administrators must function. Special education administrators practicing in the field indicate (or lament) that the role of director is now "a whole new ball game." Reactions of regular administrators to PL 94-142 vary from cautious enthusiasm to feelings of resentment at being dictated to, and regulated by, agencies outside the school system.

DIRECTORIAL ROLES AND SKILLS

Perhaps, continuing to view the role of the special education director as independent of setting has been a mistake. It might be more profitable to look at the training and skills needed by a director from at least three viewpoints, and to consider three types of directorial roles. One is that of the special education leader and his or her management and supervisory team who run the majority of their own programs. This type occurs in the larger local school districts; those with total enrollments of 10,000 or more might be a reasonable benchmark. Although such districts represent only about 5 percent of the total in the United States, they have 45 percent of the enrollment. In such districts the special education director is employed by and accountable to the superintendent and the board of education. The director, then, is a part of the management team of the district and is not viewed as an "outsider" or agent of the state. This makes a subtle but important difference in the negotiations that take place regarding programming for handicapped children. Shared owner-ship is not assured, but the mechanisms are in place to promote the concept that all administrators and staff members are responsible for optimum education of the handicapped within the district.

The second type of directorial role is that found in joint agreements, cooperatives, and intermediate education units of some sort. This type of organization is superimposed over a number of school districts. The director is perceived as intrinsically different by administrators of local school districts. Although intermediate education units are intended to be service agencies to the local districts within their boundaries, a degree of confusion accompanies the role of the special education director and his or her management staff. The director may be viewed as an outsider and not part of the management team of the district. Legislatures and state departments of public instruction often assign monitoring, compliance, and advocacy roles to the position, and local school districts frequently view special education directors as "agents of the state." The state education agency often abets this view; communicating policy and regulations to 25 regional directors is more efficient and manageable than dealing directly with several hundred individual school districts.

A third type of administrative position in special education is that of staff member of the state education agency. Historically, most such personnel have been recruited from smaller school districts or inter-mediate education units, or are younger staff members moving up the career ladder. Salaries for staff in state education agencies have generally not been competitive with similar positions in the larger school districts of each state. Thus, state education departments tend to be staffed with people whose philosophy and understanding are more typical of the smaller districts and intermediate education units than of the larger urban school districts.

Staffs of state divisions of special education have been expanding rapidly in the past few years, principally because of the infusion of federal funds with passage of PL 94-142. People are more than half serious when they say that the "hard money" positions are now the federally funded ones, and the "soft money" positions are those funded by the state legislature. (The term "hard money" means local, stable, and enduring funds, and "soft money" means funds from outside grants of some type that may be here today and gone tomorrow.) The state-federal relationship for funding special education programs may still be in flux. During the 1960s a federal program under Title V of the Elementary and Secondary Education Act was enacted to strengthen state education departments. This and other federal programs have resulted in a situation in which from one-third to two-thirds of the operating funds of state education departments come from the federal government.

Illinois' chief state school officer, J. M. Cronin (1976) recently wrote an article with the intriguing title, "The Federal Takeover: Should the Junior Partner Run the Firm?" One of his points was that PL 94-142 may increase funds by 5 percent and federal regulation by 50 percent. State and local taxes still constitute about 90 percent of the revenues for the public schools in this nation. Cronin concluded that "the junior partner is taking over the firm through sheer aggressiveness, while the senior partners fret about additional paperwork but graciously accept the extra income" (p. 501).

State special education personnel must be able to administer federal as well as state funds. Federal programs such as PL 94-142 require comprehensive, written proposals and documentation to secure funds. Accounting practices must be consistent with federal practices. Skills in contract negotiation with the U.S. Department of Education are needed to come to agreement on how each state can best meet the needs of its handicapped pupils. Skills in interacting with state legislators becomes increasingly important, as do planning and evaluation. Sensitivity to local concerns and the ability to anticipate the capacity of a local district to institute change are needed skills.

Finally, developments during the past few years have brought about new demands on special education administrators at state, regional, and local levels. Principal among these is the need to understand, interpret, and implement legal requirements to assure that the rights of handicapped children and their parents or guardians are protected. In the past, most special education administrators have not been well trained in legal procedures and their nuances, as is now required by PL 94-142. "Due process" is a relatively new term in the vocabulary of special educators. In developing the PL 94-142 legislation, a Mr. Randolph (1978) addressed these rights:

> Another important feature of this legislation concerns the expansion of due process procedures in existing law. By building on those safeguards of due process in Public Law 93-380, we will assure handicapped children and their parents or guardian the right to have written prior notice whenever the educational agency plans to initiate, change — or refuses to change or initiate — the identification, evaluation, or educational placement of the child or the provision of a free

appropriate public education to the child; the right to examine relevant records; the right to have an opportunity to present complaints; and the right to have an impartial due process hearing. (p. S20427)

THE NEED FOR THEORY IN SPECIAL EDUCATION

The usefulness of theory in special education cannot be considered apart from its use in general education administration if one believes, as I do, that special education is a subsystem of the total education enterprise and should be integrated with it. Special education is, and will continue to be, a minority in numbers in the total system and is directly responsible to no more than 10 to 15 percent of the system's pupils. Current federal legislation such as the Education for All Handicapped Children Act of 1975 has redefined special education by emphasizing the least restrictive alternative and the inclusion of more handicapped students in regular classes and school settings. This should provide added impetus for making special education administrative practices consonant with the management models used in regular education.

Only recently has general education administration concerned itself with the development and application of theory. Before 1950, most administrative training programs were oriented toward skills and techniques, with the emphasis on acquiring a bag of tricks that worked but not much concern as to why they worked (Knezevich, 1975). In 1947 the National Conference of Professors of Educational Administration organized to improve preparation programs for school administrators (Morphet, Johns, & Reller, 1967). In 1957 a committee of 18 professors from this conference, led by Campbell and Gregg (1957), published a summary of research findings relevant to education administration. The report indicated quite clearly that many of the traditional views of leadership and leader behavior were not supported by current research evidence.

At about this time the University Council for Educational Administration was formed. Under the capable leadership of Jack Culbertson, the council devoted much effort in its early years to stimulating increased attention to theory in the preparation of school administrators. During the late 1950s and 1960s a number of departments of education administration added faculty members who specialized in theory. Often these persons had backgrounds in sociology, psychology, and other areas of the behavioral sciences and did not necessarily have long experience as administrators of school systems.

Several theories and models were examined during this period, with attempts to apply them to the field of education administration. The following were some of the more popular: mathematical models, adapted from the field of economics; the monocratic, bureaucratic model of Weber (1947); and McGregor's Theory X and Theory Y formulation as to what motivates human beings (1960). In the field of special education administration, Burello and Sage (1979) opted for the social system perspective of Getzel and Guba (1979) and the situational leadership theory of Hersey and Blanchard (1979). Burello and Sage viewed the duties of the special education administrator as including the roles of change agent, advocate, and even adversary.

Culbertson (1978, 1979) has reviewed the status of the so-called theory movement and concluded that, as defined in the 1950s, it has largely spent itself. He attributed this change in mood to disappointments over the past 30 years about what theory has produced and about its usefulness to practitioners. Halpin and Hayes (1977) remarked that, "because many of us had expected too much, too quickly, and too early, we foredoomed ourselves to disappointments. We became victims of our extravagant expectations" (p. 271). One problem theorists in educational administration encountered was in trying to apply the same methods as those used in the natural sciences. Natural sciences seek to explain and predict the physical world in a "value-free" climate, while human sciences are more concerned with ethical considerations, cultural impacts, and consequent interpretation and understanding. Culbertson (1979) argued for a "theory of practice" that "would inform management and leadership in educational organization; further, such a theory would necessarily encompass knowledge about both the 'is' and the 'ought' dimensions of school and society" (p. 4).

Considering the prevailing uncertainties about the usefulness of theory, as well as its most appropriate methods of inquiry, a theory of special education administration might be fraught with even more problems. The best approach may be for special education administrators to join with general administrators in a continuing effort to build a more useful theory of practice. What direction it will take is uncertain. Knezevich (1975) believed that general systems theory holds the most promise of fitting with education administration and being useful to practicing administrators. It is a way of thinking and can be used in performing functions of planning, organizing, and controlling operations. Open systems set up mechanisms to sense outside pressures and let the system adapt in order to survive. The systems approach views schools as a network of interrelated subsystems. Resources, including money, staff with varying skills, and so forth, are seen as inputs to be manipulated so as to maximize the outcomes, outputs, or benefits related to the goals of society. The systems concept would fit well with the perception of special education as just one subsystem in the total enterprise.

REFERENCES

Burello, L. C., & Sage, D. D. *Leadership and change in special education.* Englewood Cliffs, NJ: Prentice-Hall, 1979.

Campbell, R. F., & Gregg, R. T. (Eds.). *Administrative behavior in education.* New York: Harper & Row, 1957.

Cronin, J. M. The federal takeover: Should the junior partner run the firm? *Phi Delta Kappan,* April 1976, 57(8), 499-501.

Culbertson, J. *Educational administration: Where we are and where we are going.* Paper presented at the Third Phase of the Fourth International Invervisitation Program, University of British Columbia, Vancouver, May 1978.

Culbertson, J. *Some key epistemological questions about a "theory of practice."* Presentation at a symposium of the American Educational Research Association, San Francisco, CA, April 1979.

Foster, B. J., & Carpenter, J. M. *Statistics of public elementary and secondary day schools, 1977-78 school year (final).* Washington, DC: National Center for Education Statistics, U.S. Department of Health, Education & Welfare, 1978.

Getzel, J. W., & Guba, E. G. Social behavior and the administrative process. *School Review,* 1957, 65, 423-444. Cited by L. C. Burello & D. D. Sage, *Leadership and change in special education.* Englewood Cliffs, NJ: Prentice-Hall, 1979.

Halpin, A. W., & Hayes, A. E. The broken ikon, or, whatever happened to theory? In L. L. Cunningham, W. G. Hack, & R. O. Nystrand (Eds.), *Educational administration: The developing decades.* Berkeley, CA: McCutchan Publishing, 1977. Cited by J. Culbertson in *Educational administration: Where we are and where we are going.* Paper presented at the Third Phase of the Fourth International Intervisitation Program, University of British Columbia, Vancouver, May 1978.

Hersey, P., & Blanchard, K. *Management of organizational behavior: Utilizing human resources* (3rd ed.). Englewood Cliffs, NJ: Prentice-Hall, 1977. Cited by L. C. Burello & D. D. Sage, *Leadership and change in special education.* Englewood Cliffs, NJ: Prentice-Hall, 1979.

Knezevich, S. J. *Administration of public education.* New York: Harper & Row, 1975.

Kohl, J. W., & Marro, T. D. *A normative study of the administrative position in special education* (USOE) Project No. 482266, Grant No. (OEG)0-70-2467(607). University Park, PA: Center for Cooperative Research with Schools, Pennsylvania State University, 1971.

McGregor, D. *The human side of enterprise.* New York: McGraw-Hill, 1960.

Meyen, E. L. *Exceptional children and youth: An introduction.* Denver: Love Publishing Co., 1978.

Morphet, E. L., Johns, R. L., & Reller, T. L. *Education administration* (2nd ed.). Englewood Cliffs, NJ: Prentice-Hall, 1967.

Randolph. Congressional Record-Senate, November 19, 1975, p. S20427. Cited in *Developing criteria for the evaluation of due process procedural safeguards provisions.* Washington, DC: Bureau of Education for the Handicapped, 1978.

Reynolds, M. C. Basic issues in restructuring teacher education. *Journal of Teacher Education,* 1978, *29*(6), 25-29.

Weber, M. *The theory of social and economic organization.* (A. M. Henderson & T. Parsons, Trans., T. Parsons, Ed.). New York: Free Press, 1947.

2

The Legal Basis
for Educating the Handicapped

Decency cannot be legislated. Attitudes die hard. *Handicapped* has been associated with *inferior* in the mind of the American public for more than a century, and change will be slow. What the legislative process and the courts can do, and have begun to do recently, is invoke sanctions with strict and enforced penalties to protect minorities such as handicapped children from the possible or actual abuses of the majority (Weintraub, 1973).

Gunnar Dybwad (1973), who was trained as an attorney but devoted most of his time to advocacy for children's rights with groups such as the National Association for Retarded Citizens, saw early that professional groups would resist the impact of court decisions. He predicted that psychiatrists, psychologists, social workers, and educators would believe that their options were being restricted by lawyers and that they would ask what entitled the attorney to supersede their professional judgment with his or her legal opinion. The professional groups would of course not oppose changes when cases of abuse were clearcut, but for the majority of handicapped children, they would argue, the most appropriate program is a matter of judgment, and different persons come to different conclusions.

An example of such an issue is the recent ruling by a U.S. district judge in a Pennsylvania case, *Armstrong et al.* v. *Kline et al.* (1979), which would require school districts to provide some handicapped children more than the 180 days of instruction now called for in state law. Judge Newcomer ruled that Pennsylvania's refusal to provide this additional instruction violates a handicapped child's right to a free, appropriate education under PL 94-142. This view is based on the idea that some handicapped children may regress during the summer if their education is interrupted. An interesting sidelight of Judge Newcomer's ruling is his

15

opinion that the intent of PL 94-142 is to have these children be as independent as possible by the end of their schooling, but that the law does not intend the state to provide a program designed to allow each handicapped child to reach his or her maximum potential in every respect. What he meant is not fully clear, but the assumption is that the parent has some responsibility also. The State of Pennsylvania appealed the federal court ruling, arguing that the school system should not be required to assume total responsibility for the welfare of handicapped children.

Further examples of controversial change are the opinions handed down by some courts on the issues of suspension or expulsion of handicapped children (Lichtenstein, 1980). Each state has always had authority to suspend or expel pupils. Courts are now limiting this power based on PL 94-142. In *Stuart* v. *Nappi* (1978), the court ruled that a school may not apply its usual rules of suspension as a disciplinary technique if the child involved is handicapped. The reasoning was that suspension would deny the child access to the school and the most appropriate program — a requirement of PL 94-142. It was thought that the alternative program provided would be home instruction, which would be counter to the principle of the right to least restrictive environment. It does seem strange that a type of double standard can be endorsed by the courts.

Special educators have been critical of general educators for their assumed reluctance to endorse the right to equal education for all handicapped children, but special educators themselves have a history of varying philosophies. One classic example is that of the debate between Ignacy Goldberg and William Cruickshank (1958). Cruickshank, a national leader in special education, argued that the moderately retarded should not be the responsibility of the public schools. He based his view primarily on the definition of *education* and held that this group of children was trainable as opposed to educable. Now, just 20 years later, that argument is moot, and schools have the legal responsibility to "educate" not only the so-called trainable but the severely and profoundly retarded as well.

IMPACTS OF FEDERAL LEGISLATION AND OF THE COURTS

More than a dozen acts that relate specifically to the handicapped have been passed by Congress since 1954. Categorical federal funds for the handicapped were first appropriated in 1957, when monies were earmarked to be spent on research related to the education of the mentally retarded. Excepting Gallaudet College and the American Printing House for the Blind, both of which have been funded for over 100 years, this was the first evidence of Congress being willing to finance special education programs. The legislative history of these recent acts is well documented elsewhere (Martin, 1968; Weintraub, Abeson, Ballard, & LaVor, 1976; Turnbull & Turnbull, 1979).

The two pieces of federal legislation with a major impact on school systems today are PL 94-142 and Section 504 of the Rehabilitation Act of 1973. The unique aspect of Section 504 is that one of its statements extends to the handicapped those protections given to other minority groups by Title VI of the Civil Rights Act of 1964. Turnbull and Turnbull (1978) summarized the differences between PL 94-142 and Section 504: Section 504 defines the handicapped more broadly and includes persons who are addicted to drugs or alcohol. Both PL 94-142 and Section 504 require labeling of children by category of handicap, but Section 504 also uses a broader function definition. Section 504 does not require an individualized education program. According to Turnbull and Turnbull, it might be better to file suits for the handicapped under Section 504 rather than PL 94-142, because Section 504 does not include processes to be followed in due process appeals. PL 94-142 requires that the administrative due process procedure must be exhausted before a suit can be filed. Since Section 504 does not include such language, the parent may be able to avoid going through the administrative appeal system.

The next few sections focus on the principal components of PL 94-142 and of Section 504, where it applies. In 1988 the Bureau of Education for the Handicapped (now the Office for Special Education and Rehabilitative Services) published a series of commissioned papers intended to represent the most recent thinking of a number of qualified professionals regarding evaluation procedures for implementation of PL 94-142's major provisions. Prominent scholars in the fields of education and law gave their views on how best to achieve quality implementation. Provisions of PL 94-142 addressed were: (1) the least restrictive environment, (2) due process procedural safeguards, (3) protection in evaluation procedures, and (4) individualized education programs.

LEAST RESTRICTIVE ENVIRONMENT

The historical context and legislative history of PL 94-142 and Section 504, particularly in regard to the least restrictive environment or integration imperative, has been well documented by Gilhool and

Stutman (1978). They pointed out that when new procedures are directed by legislation, it becomes important for educators to be familiar with the intent of Congress, in order to interpret the law.

In *Brown* v. *Board of Education,* the Supreme Court in 1954 ruled against racial segregation in schools, and this was to have an impact later on handicapped children.

> Education is required in the performance of our most basic responsibility. . . . It is the very foundation of good citizenship. Today it is a principal instrument in awakening the child to cultural values, in preparing him for later . . . training, and in helping him adjust normally to this environment. In these days it is doubtful that any child may reasonably be expected to succeed in life if he is denied the opportunity of an education. Such an opportunity, where the state has undertaken to provide it, is a right which must be made available to all on equal time.

The late senator Hubert Humphrey of Minnesota addressed the topic of segregation of the handicapped as it related to Section 504 by introducing part of an article from the *Washington Evening Star* into the *Congressional Record* (Gilhool & Stutman, 1978).

> The lack of community resources is keeping institutions for the mentally retarded filled above capacity. . . . The new movement in other states of developing group homes — small living units in the community for the retarded — is just beginning in the Washington area.

> The deliberate segregation of the handicapped and their resulting invisibility have led to their traditionally low rating on the priority list of educational and community programs.

> Beyond the inadequate funding, the incomplete programs for the handicapped in public schools, and the sorely neglected state institutions, there is a larger issue at stake these days. It deals with the basic relationship between handicapped people and the so-called "normal society."

> So far, what has become known as the "normalization principle" is usually discussed when dealing with the retarded, the largest category of handicapped people, but its implications apply to other handicaps as well.

> The principle has been defined by Bengt Nirje, a specialist on the retarded in Sweden where the principle is being practiced, as "making available to the mentally retarded patterns and conditions of everyday life which are as close as possible to the norms and patterns of the mainstreamed of society."

> Many specialists in the field of educating handicapped children agree that children at the trainable or moderately retarded level do need *special classes. But . . . the traditional approach of segregating these children in separate schools or isolated classes within regular school buildings . . . is wrong* [emphasis added].

> The isolation of the moderately retarded dates from a time when educators felt that because children of this level of retardation often look and act differently from normal children they should be sheltered for their own good or the

"protection" of normal children. Specialists argue that if the objective of education for the retarded — or for the deaf, blind, and physically handicapped children — is to give them every chance to live as normal a life as possible in society, they must have early, frequent contacts with normal children.

Society has found it easy to segregate the handicapped because it does not view the hidden and invisible people as a direct threat. Handicapped children are unlikely to ever march on the school board, and retarded adults have never been known to stage a revolt in a state institution. (pp. 202-203)

Review of testimony on Section 504 makes it clear that the intent of Congress was to prohibit discrimination against the handicapped as well as to include a requirement of affirmative action.

By now the least restrictive environment provisions of PL 94-142 are well known to most educators. Section 612(5)(B) of the law requires placements that will, to the greatest extent appropriate, assure the handicapped an education comparable to that of their nonhandicapped peers (Morra, 1978). Regulations complementing the law require local education agencies to have various alternative placements available. For the least restrictive environment concept to be meaningful, a continuum of placements and services must exist. Many of the past abuses that led to legal action can be traced to a lack of available options. I was in charge of a special education program in a metropolitan school district in California during the early 1960s, and was amazed at the thinking of some of my colleagues in nearby districts. It went something like this: This child has a learning or behavior problem; all we have to offer is a regular class or a class for the educable mentally retarded; he will be better off in a smaller class with less academic pressure; if he is left in the regular class, he will be kicked out of school and turned loose on the streets; and so his best chance, and ours, is to find some way to qualify him for the EMR class. Such reasoning led to EMR classes in California and elsewhere that were populated by disproportionate numbers of children who were black, Mexican-American, or from impoverished or disruptive backgrounds.

The least restrictive environment provision should ideally be administered according to the following guidelines.

1. A school system should have at least four levels of programming options for handicapped children, which might include (a) an itinerant or consulting teacher helping the regular teacher, (b) resource programs with integration, (c) self-contained classrooms with some integration, and (d) self-contained classrooms. To be effective, each of these options must exist in sufficient magnitude to be available to handicapped children when they need it. In options (a) and (b), the handicapped child

is the major responsibility of the regular teacher and is carried on regular class rolls. For options (c) and (d), the major responsibility belongs to the special education teacher.

2.   Children should move up or down the continuum one level at a time unless there are compelling reasons to jump more than one level.

3.   Physical facilities for the handicapped should be equivalent to those provided for regular pupils in the district.

4.   Evidence collected over time should show that increasing percentages of children in each level of programming are being served in less restrictive settings.

5.   The term *mainstreaming* should be dropped because of confusion about its meaning, and terms such as *least restrictive environment* and *most productive environment* should be substituted.

DUE PROCESS PROCEDURAL SAFEGUARDS

A major purpose of PL 94-142 is to protect the rights of handicapped children and of their parents or guardians (Morra, 1978). Section 615 of the law coupled with the accompanying Bureau of Education for the Handicapped (BEH) regulations spells out procedures that must be followed by education agencies in order to guarantee a free, appropriate, public education to handicapped children. Central concepts of due process as it relates to this law are interpretations of the words *consent* and *notice.* State and local education agencies are currently struggling with issues such as what constitutes a reasonable amount of time for notice, and the meaning of *informed consent.*

According to Bersoff (1978), procedural due process has two basic elements: (1) the right to adequate notice and (2) the opportunity to be heard. Requirements for due process vary according to the situation, as has been noted by the Supreme Court (*Hannan* v. *Larche,* 1969):

> "Due process" is an elusive concept. Its exact boundaries are undefinable, and its content varies according to specific factual contexts. Thus, when governmental agencies adjudicate or make binding determinations which directly affect the legal rights of individuals, it is imperative that those agencies use the procedure which has traditionally been associated with the judicial process. . . . Whether the Constitution requires that a particular right obtain in a specific proceeding depends upon a complexity of factors. The nature of the alleged right involved, the nature of the proceeding, are all considerations which must be taken into account. (p. 68)

Although considerable dispute surrounds the meaning of *informed consent*, general agreement exists concerning its three basic characteristics.

1. *Knowledge.* The person seeking consent must disclose sufficient information in a manner that can be understood by the person from whom the consent is sought. The U.S. Department of Health, Education and Welfare has outlined in its regulations (Section 121a.505) what information it believes should be disclosed for a person or agency to be in compliance with PL 94-142. This includes stating actions proposed or reasons why the agency refuses to take action, describing each evaluation procedure to be used, and communicating the notice in an understandable way. The intent is that relevant information be communicated; every minute detail need not be dealt with in the process.

2. *Voluntariness.* The person giving consent must do so freely, and it must be obtained without coercion, duress, misrepresentation, fraud, or undue inducement. In relation to PL 94-142, the most likely abuse would be that of undue inducement, such as school personnel trying to convince parents of the wisdom of the school's recommendation. This certainly is a legitimate function of the school as long as the information is correct, parents are given time to think about it before responding, and they are not threatened with a loss of school rights if they do not agree. Parents are also to know that consent, even if freely given, is not permanently binding and can be revoked by them at any time.

3. *Capacity.* Persons giving consent must be competent to do so. By law, children are considered incapable of making most legally binding decisions. The law also presumes that all adults, unless proven otherwise, are competent, and school officials should be careful in challenging parents on this basis. If parents obviously cannot comprehend what is being asked, it would be acceptable to look for a surrogate who could represent the child's interests.

The notice requirements of PL 94-142 and its accompanying regulations apply both to children who have not yet been in special education programs but are being considered by the schools for initial identification and to children in special education programs who are being considered for reevaluation or a change of program. Thus, the principal notice requirements are keyed to major decisionmaking points by the school —identification, evaluation, placement, and program provision. Kotin (1978) observed that these notice requirements were derived primarily from judicial models of due process rather than from theory and educational practice within the schools. Typically, the courts apply the due process requirements to areas in which an individual's interests are threatened, as outlined in the 14th Amendment to the United States Constitution. Because of a number of documented cases of misclassification, segregation, and denial of services to the handicapped, Congress, through PL 94-142, expanded the concept beyond what the courts used, by requiring notice so that the parents can be actively involved in the decision process.

> In summary, the principal purpose of the notice requirements of PL 94-142 is to protect the civil rights of parents and children in the special education process. This purpose and most of the notice requirements which implement it are derived from judicial models of due process. A second purpose of the notice requirements, however, which has its origins in educational theory and practice, is to involve the parents and, "where appropriate," the child in making the initial placement decision. This purpose is best exemplified by the parental notice and involvement requirements which apply to the preplacement-decision stage of the process. A third major purpose of the notice requirements, also exemplified by the preplacement-decision notices, is the pragmatic one of minimizing future conflict and formal adversarial proceedings by maximizing mutual understanding and cooperation through parent notice and involvement requirements which apply early in the special education process. (Budoff, 1978, p. 153)

Budoff (1978) addressed these same due process issues from the viewpoint of a parent or guardian. He has been active in implementation of Massachusetts' special education legislation, Chapter 766, which is similar in its provisions to PL 94-142 but which has been in force several years longer. Reviewing the Massachusetts experience may allow us to anticipate issues that are likely to develop in the nationwide implementation of PL 94-142. One problem area has been parents' feelings of intimidation when they receive overlong notice statements phrased in legal language. Budoff noted also that school staff members became obsessed with meeting the legal requirements and had no energy left to develop meaningful programs. Several Massachusetts special education administrators estimated that one-third of the time of their staff was devoted to documentation.

Although due process requirements are rooted in the concept of procedural fairness, they have in fact tended to decrease trust between school and parent on the subject of long-term planning for the handicapped child. Budoff argued for a system that meets the due process requirements but at the same time focuses on the schools' being able to perceive the parent-school interaction in a positive way. If school personnel honestly believe that the parent should be an active member of the decisionmaking process, the notice and informed consent requirements can be used to initiate, cultivate, and develop this relationship with the home.

The provision should ideally be administered according to the following guidelines.

1.   Concede that times have changed and view parents as regular members of the decisionmaking process with as much to contribute as school professionals.

2.   Try to emphasize protecting the rights of handicapped children rather than the fear of being sued.

3.   Really work on developing an informal communication system with parents of handicapped children and emphasize the "no-fault" concept. Recognize that a school may end up in some adversary relationships but don't begin with them.

4.   Increase the number of visits with parents "on their own turf" rather than calling them into school.

5.   Work toward a process in which the hearing officer is truly impartial. This suggests eliminating as hearing officers members of the school board that employs the special education director, a colleague in another school district or intermediate unit, and employees of the department of public instruction or the state superintendent of education.

PROTECTION IN EVALUATION PROCEDURES

Because of reported abuses in the evaluation of handicapped children, Congress wrote into PL 94-142 a number of procedural safeguards regarding their testing and evaluation. These were augmented by regulations adopted by BEH that delineate specific evaluation procedures to be followed (Section 121a.532). Included are requirements that evaluation and test materials (1) be provided and administered in the child's native language or other mode of communication, if feasible, (2) be valid for the specific purpose for which they are being used, (3) be given in a standardized way by properly trained personnel, (4) include materials tailored to assess specific areas of ability rather than just those which provide a single general intelligence quotient, and (5) accurately reflect the factors that the tests claim to measure. The regulations also specify that the evaluation is to be made by a multidisciplinary team and not by a single examiner (Morra, 1978).

These rather restrictive regulations stem from a history of inappropriate labeling of some children as handicapped. One of the earliest cases to focus on the concept of discriminatory testing and consequent labeling was *Diana* v. *State Board of Education* in California (1970). The issues were fairly clear: (1) disproportionate numbers of Mexican-American children were being placed in special classes for the educable mentally retarded (EMR); (2) the principal method of identifying these children was through the use of individual intelligence tests in English, even though their primary home language was Spanish; and (3) the judgment prevailed that placement in an EMR class resulted in an education inferior to that of a regular class (Glick, 1973). At that time Mexican-Americans constituted 13 percent of the schoolchildren of California but represented 26 percent of the population of the EMR classes. In the *Diana* case, 12 of the 13 children enrolled in the EMR class were Mexican-American. The children were retested by a Spanish-speaking psychologist, whereupon higher IQ scores were reported. As the case was brought on behalf of every Mexican-American child in EMR classes in the state of California, negotiations began with state school officials and a settlement was reached. Retesting resulted in 4,000 Mexican-American children being taken out of EMR classes and placed in interim programs. Legislation was passed by the state requiring a series of protective evaluation procedures to be followed, similar to many of those later included in PL 94-142.

Following shortly after *Diana* was *Larry P.* v. *Riles* (1972), again in California. The challenge focused this time on disproportionate numbers of black children in EMR classes. At that time blacks represented 9 percent of the school population in California but made up 27 percent of the enrollment for EMR classes (Glick, 1973). The plaintiffs in this case were black children who resided in the San Francisco school district. The suit called for a moratorium on all individual intelligence tests used to place black children in EMR classes. Nondiscriminatory tests were to be developed. The case dragged on in the courts, but in October 1979 the U.S. District Court for the Northern District of California ruled that standardized intelligence tests cannot be used to identify and place black children in EMR classes without prior approval of the court. The state superintendent of education was ordered to monitor and eliminate disproportionate placement of black children in EMR classes and school districts in California must now reevaluate every black child who is currently an EMR pupil. No standardized intelligence tests can be used in this reevaluation unless the court has granted prior approval. The requirements set by the court for approving a test are comprehensive, and probably no current tests could qualify. The 131-page decision is highly critical of intelligence tests and of EMR classes, at least as far as their usefulness for black children is concerned.

Jones (1978) argued that PL 94-142 applies to group testing programs as well as to individual tests and assessment procedures. Jones based this opinion on the premise that group testing programs and individual testing procedures are interrelated, because results from group tests sometimes provide the first level of identification of children who may need specialized services. Also, any composite educational picture of an individual child includes group test results.

In his review of congressional testimony related to evaluation procedures, Ysseldyke (1978) concluded that the concerns were much broader than just the fairness of tests as used with minority groups. At issue were various abuses of assessment data throughout the whole process of making decisions about pupils. He summarized these abuses as including (1) inappropriate and indiscriminate use of tests, (2) bias in assessment of handicapped children, including the labeling as handicapped of those who are not, (3) bias through the entire decisionmaking process, and (4) bias following assessment.

Evaluation procedures should ideally be administered according to the following guidelines.

1. Whenever the percentage of minorities in special education programs exceeds their percentage of the community, the entire assessment and evaluation procedure should be reviewed to determine why it is happening. One should be particularly sensitive to overrepresentation in classes for the mildly retarded and the emotionally disturbed and underrepresentation in classes for the learning disabled.

2. The evaluation procedure should be balanced between formal assessments that yield numbers and informed judgments made by staff members who have observed the child for extensive periods in classroom settings. Neither part of the procedure should be allowed to dominate.

3. Some of the recent special purpose tests to be used with the handicapped should be viewed with extreme caution unless their standardization procedures can document acceptable reliability. The validity issue is even more difficult to resolve but should be addressed.

4. Presentations in placement conferences should be understandable by all present and should not be permitted to be forums for various professionals to promote the importance of their particular disciplines.

5.   So-called preplacement conferences should be avoided when the purpose is for the various professionals to "get their act together" and form a united front before meeting with the parents. Dress rehearsals should not be necessary if parents are being treated as real members of the team.

6.   Continual reemphasis and monitoring of the purpose of assessment should be undertaken. The reason for testing is to determine the child's present level of programming purposes and not to "qualify the child."

INDIVIDUALIZED EDUCATION PROGRAMS (IEPs)

Probably the most radical aspect of PL 94-142 as far as educators are concerned is the IEP. Although special educators have practiced some degree of individualized instruction over the years, most special education classes have been run on the model of small group instruction. The law requires that an IEP for *each* handicapped child is to be developed and reviewed jointly by a qualified school official, the child's teacher or teachers, the parents or guardian, and when appropriate, the child (Morra, 1978).

Torres (1977) interpreted the IEP requirement and its attendant regulations to mean that the program must be addressed to a single child rather than to a class or group of children; it is limited to aspects of the child's education that constitute special education and related services; and it is a statement of what will actually be provided for the child. Though the IEP is not a binding contract in the legal sense, failure to meet its provisions could form the basis for a parent complaint or hearing. Henderson (1979) saw the IEP as partly contractual — that is, to the extent that the IEP specifies the delivery of a certain quantity of services, the school district will be liable if those services are not delivered. Educational objectives stated in the IEP, on the other hand, specify desired levels of achievement but are not legally binding.

The IEP must include written statements regarding the child's present level of educational performance, annual goals and short-term objectives; specific educational and support services to be provided, including the projected date services will start and how long they will last; the amount of time the child will spend in regular classrooms, and annual criteria to determine whether the proposed objectives are being accomplished. Further, the IEP must be reviewed and modified, if necessary, at least annually.

Some expect the IEP concept to lead to an individualized program for all children; others view it as an exercise in paperwork for the special education teacher. The two major teachers' organizations, the American Federation of Teachers (AFT) and the National Education Association (NEA), have registered some complaints regarding PL 94-142. The AFT expressed reservations about the excessive amount of time required of teachers in preparing IEPs, giving them less actual time to spend in direct instruction of children (Rauth, 1979). At the 1979 AFT convention, the union passed a policy statement supporting the objective of providing effective educational services to handicapped children but listing weaknesses that must be resolved: (1) the federal mandate that requires the expansion of expensive services to handicapped students, (2) the increased paperwork involved in the IEP that reduces direct instructional time, and (3) the least restrictive environment mandate, which has led to wholesale mainstreaming without regular teachers being informed or receiving inservice training in how to work with the handicapped. The union intends, if corrective action is not taken by Congress on these issues, to work to suspend parts of PL 94-142.

The NEA, in testimony before a congressional subcommittee of the House Committee on Education and Labor, referred to the IEP as generating an intolerable amount of paperwork (Cameron, 1979). The NEA recommended that official policy should clearly state (1) that the IEP is not an instructional document, (2) that it should include only services planned in addition to the regular program, (3) that it should not be required for children with severe disabilities in custodial care, and (4) that teachers should be afforded release time to prepare IEPs.

IEPs should ideally be administered according to the following guidelines.

1. Do not assign the sole responsibility for developing the IEP to the special education teacher. This process should have significant input from the child's regular teachers and from the parents.

2. Avoid having regular teachers and parents initial or sign an IEP after it has already been developed by one person, who is usually the special education teacher. Tokenism can be lessened by not doing this.

3. Assign case management to one person who will coordinate the input of the various teachers and service providers.

4. Admit that the IEP is tentative — a "best guess" at the time it is written — and that it may well have to be substantially reviewed in less than a year.

5. In the IEP, emphasize behavioral components as well as the more traditional academic areas. Because writing objectives for an area like math, including numerical predictions of growth is easier, the more difficult but equally important area of behavior may be slighted or left out of the IEP.

REFERENCES

Armstrong et al. v. Kline et al. U.S. District Court for Eastern District of Pennsylvania, Remedial Order No. 2, September 1979.

Bersoff, D. N. Procedural safeguards. In *Developing criteria for the evaluation of due process procedural safeguards provisions.* Washington, DC: Bureau of Education for the Handicapped, 1978.

Brown v. Board of Education. 347 U.S. 483, 493 (1954). Cited by T. K. Gilhool & E. A. Stutman, Integration of severely handicapped students. In *Developing criteria for the evaluation of the least restrictive environment provision.* Washington, DC: Bureau of Education for the Handicapped, 1978.

Budoff, M. Implementing due process safeguards: From the user's viewpoint. In *Developing criteria for the evaluation of due process procedural safeguards provisions.* Washington, DC: Bureau of Education for the Handicapped, 1978.

Cameron, D. R. *Statement of the National Education Association on P.L. 94-142, The Education for All Handicapped Children Act.* Presented before the Subcommittee on Select Education of the House Committee on Education and Labor, October 9, 1979.

Diana v. State Board of Education. C-70, 37 RFP (N. D. California, 1970).

Dybwad, G. A look at history and present trends in the protection of children's right to education. In R. A. Johnson, J. C. Gross, & R. F. Weatherman (Eds.), *Leadership series in special education.* Vol. II. *Special education in court.* Minneapolis: University of Minnesota, 1973.

Gilhool, T. K., & Stutman, E. A. Integration of severely handicapped students. In *Developing criteria for the evaluation of the least restrictive environment provision.* Washington, DC: Bureau of Education for the Handicapped, 1978.

Glick, M. The California experience. In R. A. Johnson, J. C. Gross, & R. F. Weatherman (Eds.), *Leadership series in special education.* Vol. II. *Special education in court.* Minneapolis: University of Minnesota, 1973.

Goldberg, I. I., & Cruickshank, W. M. Trainable but noneducable. *National Educational Association Journal*, December 1958, *47*, 622-623. Cited by S. A. Kirk, *Educating exceptional children*. Boston: Houghton-Mifflin, 1962.

Hannan v. Larche. 363 U.S. 420, 442 (1969). Cited by D. N. Bersoff, Procedural safeguards. In *Developing criteria for the evaluation of due process procedural safeguards provisions*. Washington, DC: Bureau of Education for the Handicapped, 1978, p. 68.

Henderson, R. Personal communication, December 1979.

Jones, R. L. Protection in evaluation procedures: Criteria and recommendations. In *Developing criteria for the evaluation of protection in evaluation procedures provisions*. Washington, DC: Bureau of Education for the Handicapped, 1978.

Kotin, L. Recommended criteria and assessment techniques for the evaluation by LEAs of their compliance with the notice and consent requirements of P.L. 94-142. In *Developing criteria for the evaluation of due process procedural safeguards provisions*. Washington, DC: Bureau of Education for the Handicapped, 1978.

Larry P. v. Riles. 343 F. Supp. 1306 (N. D. California, 1972).

Lichtenstein, E. Suspension, expulsion, and the special education student. *Phi Delta Kappan*, 1980, *67*(7), 459-461.

Martin, E. W., Jr., Breakthrough for the handicapped: Legislative history. *Exceptional Children*, 1968, *34*, 493-503.

Morra, L. G. Introduction: Overview of the study. In *Developing criteria for the evaluation of the least restrictive environment provision*. Washington, DC: Bureau of Education for the Handicapped, 1978.

Rauth, M. Coping with public law 94-142. *Action* (American Federation of Teachers), September 1979.

Stuart v. Nappi. 443 F. Supp. 1235 (1978). Cited by E. Lichtenstein, Suspension, expulsion, and the special education student. *Phi Delta Kappan*, 1980, *67*(7), 459-461.

Torres, S. (Ed.). *A primer on individualized education programs for handicapped children*. Reston, VA: The Foundation for Exceptional Children, 1977.

Turnbull, H. R., & Turnbull, A. P. *Free appropriate public education: Law and implementation*. Denver: Love Publishing Co., 1978.

Weintraub, F. Court action and legislation. In R. A. Johnson, J. C. Gross, & R. G. Weatherman (Eds.), *Leadership series in special education*. Vol. II. *Special education in court*. Minneapolis: University of Minnesota, 1973.

Weintraub, F. J., Abeson, A., Ballard, J., & LaVor, M. L. (Eds.). *Public policy and the education of exceptional children*. Reston, VA: The Council for Exceptional Children, 1976.

Ysseldyke, J. E. Implementing the "protection in evaluation procedures" provisions of P.L. 94-142. In *Developing criteria for the evaluation of protection in evaluation procedures provisions*. Washington, DC: Bureau of Education for the Handicapped, 1978.

3

Financing the Enterprise

In most general administration and special education textbooks, comments on finances appear near the end of the volume. The subject is dealt with earlier in this book because of the major impact that securing funds has had historically on the operation of programs. Finances should not dictate programs but, unfortunately, programs are a function of finances. Special education has always had a heavier investment in ancillary personnel to back up the instructional program than has regular education. To the extent that psychologists, social workers, and audiologists provide identification and diagnostic information of direct use to instructional staff in programming for children, the use of funds for their services is legitimate and useful. To the extent that the major function of such identification practices is to label and to certify that handicapped children are eligible for additional state and federal funding, the use of scarce financial resources is questionable. Unfortunately, the history of special education indicates that such personnel have been used for the latter purpose.

Before states adopted criteria and definitions to identify handicapped children, administrators had the authority to assign children to special classes. This practice, followed until shortly after World War II, was considered a failure because any misfit in the school could be assigned to the "opportunity rooms." (For whom the opportunity was intended was never quite clear.) After this period, categories of eligibility were developed and had to be met in order for a program to qualify for state funds. School psychologists and physicians decided which children could be assigned to special education classes. This

I thank Dr. Francis Laufenberg, superintendent of the Long Beach Unified School District, Long Beach, California, for his review of and critical comments on this chapter.

practice continued until recently, when multidisciplinary teams began to determine eligibility. Whether this change has resulted in better educational programming for handicapped children continues to be debated, but the current practices clearly involve more professional staff time and increase costs. Meyen (1978) reported his experience as follows:

> Special education may be viewed from at least three primary perspectives: (1) determining the most appropriate instructional or curriculum program; (2) establishing the most accurate diagnostic base for programming; and (3) selecting the most efficient and economical administrative structure for delivering services. Obviously, [these perspectives all] relate to instruction; . . . instruction, to be effective, depends upon accurate diagnosis and effective administrative structures. After having reviewed a large number of public school programs over several years, however, this author believes that too many districts place primary emphasis on creating organizational structures which contribute to precise diagnosis and appropriate placement and not enough emphasis on what happens after a child is assigned to receive a particular service.
>
> Special education is not a placement process nor is it an evaluation system, even though both are essential to quality special education services. Special education in the true sense occurs only when a child or youth receives services appropriate to his or her needs. In this context, much of what is offered in the guise of special education services is not, in fact, special education. To assume that special education occurs automatically at the time a child or youth is placed or assigned to a service may be comforting to an administrator, but such placement provides no assurances of effective special education unless those responsible for delivering the services are competent and have access to the appropriate resources. (pp. 25-26)

In a recent study, Landau and Gerken (1979) reported that school principals preferred the major role of the school psychologist to be that of psychometrician doing diagnostic case studies. Teachers, however, gave this diagnostic/psychometric function lower rankings and preferred the consultant role, in which school psychologists would help them plan educational programs for children. Psychologists themselves prefer a consulting role and would do much less testing if they were not required to do so by administrators (Cook & Patterson, 1977; Manley & Manley, 1978; Waters, 1973).

Mercer (1976) recounted the dilemma in which special education finds itself by reviewing the history of funding of special education programs for the mentally retarded. The parents supported categorical aids (funds appropriated for specified restricted uses) and self-contained classes because it was a way to get their children admitted to the public schools. When these excess cost programs for the retarded were set up in the 1950s, they seemed reasonable to parents, who previously had to hound educators and legislators before they could even get their children inside the doors of the school. The use of categorical aids continued for

25 years but is now one of the major stumbling blocks to working with individual children in the regular school environment.

Jane Mercer (1976), a sociologist, has spent a number of years researching labeling practices in Riverside, California. For the past few years she has been working to develop a system of assessment that would control for cultural differences and not be radically or culturally discriminatory. This has resulted in publication of a set of instruments called the *System of Multicultural Pluralistic Assessment,* which is being used with increasing frequency throughout the United States. On the basis of her research, Mercer believes the following basic principles should be observed when developing and funding programs for special education.

1.   Minority group children who no longer qualify as handicapped under new assessment procedures — but who do have genuine educational problems — still need additional financial help. The funds that were available to them when they were labeled mentally retarded, however, may now be lost.

2.   Funding systems can be developed that do not require labeling or categorizing. What Mercer seems to be arguing for is some type of supplemental assistance similar to resource programs or the consultant model.

Many professionals in education undoubtedly share Mercer's views. Implementing new programs will, however, require substantial changes in various states' funding practices as well as the federal program under PL 94-142. Even though PL 94-142 is heralded as an endorsement of a mandate on behalf of a neglected minority, it does require that pupils be identified by the familiar categories in order to qualify for federal funds. The arguments that have been given to support "categorical funding" for handicapped children are that advocates for the handicapped demand accountability that the funds appropriated are truly being used for handicapped children. The Council for Exceptional Children opposes general funding procedures that would circumvent direct aid of a categorical nature until such time as all children are assured of adequate school programs (Thomas, 1976).

Involvement of the federal government in categorical aids has a long history. It began with the Smith-Hughes Act of 1917, which provided federal funds to support agricultural education in secondary schools. More recent examples are the National Defense Education Act of 1958, the Elementary and Secondary Education Act of 1965, and the Education for All Handicapped Children Act of 1975. Each of these pieces of legislation provided funds for very specific purposes.

Special interest groups such as special educators support the concept of categorical funding, but general school administrators usually do not. Such limited-purpose funding restricts their ability to use resources where they see the greatest need. Additional and separate accounting functions are usually required, and this adds to the paperwork and the red tape. Funds paid on a reimbursement basis require that managers use their own funds initially, and a year may elapse before the reimbursement. In these days of tight budgets and fewer discretionary funds, such delays may cause a cash flow problem.

Knezevich (1975) held that categorical aids are more compatible with regulatory functions than with leadership. Categorical aids imply that administrators and staffs at the local level are neither imaginative nor concerned with educational improvement. He suggested that the recent proliferation of federal funds calls for the abandonment of primary reliance on categorical aids and a move toward general support of education, with less restriction on how the funds are used at the local level.

Few well-designed research studies on the financing of special education are available in the literature. One of the most extensive is the study by Rossmiller, Hale, and Frohreich (1970) as part of the National Educational Finance Project. The design can be regarded essentially as a series of case studies of 24 school districts selected from five states thought by a jury of experts to be leaders in providing services to the handicapped. The five states were California, Florida, New York, Texas, and Wisconsin. Although each of these states was one of the most populous in the United States, there was considerable diversity in population density per square mile and in the percentage of the population that was urban. The sample of school systems included both public school districts and intermediate educational agencies. Data from these 24 school systems showed extreme variability in the costs of programs for special education and also in disability areas. The median cost index ranged from 1.14 for programs for the intellectually gifted to 3.64 in the program for the physically handicapped. The cost index was based on a ratio in which 1.0 represents the cost per pupil in a regular program. Thus, the median cost for programs for the physically handicapped was more than three times that for a regular pupil. Cost indices for individual districts ranged from 1.28 in the intellectually gifted category to a high of 11.64 in the area of emotional disturbance. High costs were associated with new programs, those with small pupil-teacher ratios, and those in which intensive and multiple services were provided.

Rossmiller et al. (1970) also analyzed costs by function and found that the largest single component was for instruction (salaries of teachers and teacher aides). Transportation, especially for the physically handicapped, was a disproportionately high cost in some districts. Costs for physical plant were higher for exceptional children, primarily because the number of pupils per classroom was smaller. The authors noted the extreme difficulty of identifying the costs of programs because virtually none of these systems had developed the concept of program budgeting so that inputs into each program could be pinpointed. Cost-benefit analysis is currently being advocated throughout the country. If such account-ability methods are to be used, accurate program budgeting is essential to identify input costs and program outputs. At least as of 1970, such fiscal, personnel, and pupil records were apparently not being kept on a program basis. This will be a necessary component of evaluation in order to develop a data base from which to study program effectiveness.

McLure, Burnham, and Henderson (1975) studied the needs, costs, and methods of financing used by the state of Illinois to fund programs for exceptional children. Instructional costs were analyzed for 23 Illinois school districts, but costs defined as public services and capital outlay were excluded. Items included under those headings were transportation, food service, community service, and tuition payments to other districts or to private agencies. Instructional expenditures studied included those for teachers and aides; academic support staff such as administrators, counselors, therapists, social workers, and psychologists; and auxiliary services such as clerks, custodians, and supplies. About 80 percent of all costs were in salaries for personnel.

Program costs were computed for 19 special education categories in Illinois plus 3 that were closely related (compensatory-Title I, bilingual, and gifted). Cost differentials varied widely among districts with the same program label. Interestingly, the authors' analysis revealed that the size of the instructional unit — the number of students assigned to a certified teacher — was the only important factor in examing cost differentials. In terms of finances, the disability label made no difference except in such areas as transporting the physically handicapped. Obviously, children with more severe disabilities were assigned in smaller numbers to self-contained classrooms and costs were higher. Costs for academic support personnel also depended on the number of students assigned to a teacher and were comparable regardless of disability label.

On the basis of these data, McLure et al. (1975) recommended that the pupil-teacher ratio be used as the measure by which to compute costs for exceptional children. Because education is such a labor-intensive enter-prise, instructional expenses represent from 70 to 80 percent of the total cost and account for nearly all of the cost differential between regular and special education. Figure 1 gives an indication of how numbers of children per teacher vary, nationwide, according to disability area.

The study also revealed the extent of nonteaching and auxiliary instructional costs. Personnel included are those mentioned earlier — psychologists, social workers, administrators, clerical staff, and the like. On the basis of a continuum-of-services model labeled "categories of intensity," handicapped children had backup costs ranging from 4 to 28 percent more than what was needed for regular students. Children categorized as high intensity had a total of 28 percent, groups with moderate and low needs each had 18 percent additional costs, and children identified as having mild needs had only 4 percent more than what was needed for regular students. This was one of the few studies that has addressed the issue of the cost of support services.

FIGURE 1
Average Number of Handicapped Children Served per Special Education Teacher[1] during School Year 1976-77

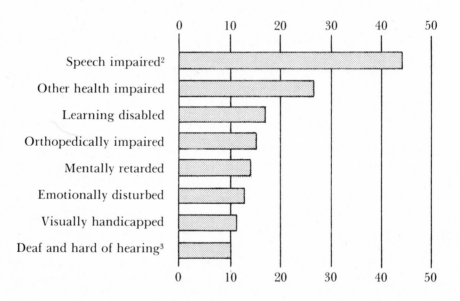

[1] The data include handicapped children counted under Public Laws 89-313 and 94-142 for FY 1977. (All learning disabled children were included in the data regardless of the ceiling placed on such children for allocation purposes.) Special education teachers include regular, special, and itinerant/consulting teachers.
[2] Speech pathologists are included in this category.
[3] Audiologists are included in this category.

Source: *Progress Toward a Free Appropriate Public Education* (1979).

In a study done for the Interim Study Committee of the House Budget Committee of the Iowa General Assembly, Howe (1978) looked at cost projections for special education funding for a 10-year period, 1975-76 through 1985-86. Iowa uses a modified continuum-of-services model in which funding is tied to the degree of integration in regular classes. This is accomplished by assigning additional "weightings" to handicaped children as a part of the regular State School Foundation Program. Current weightings include 1.7 for the mildly handicapped who are in regular classes for a major part of the school day, 2.0 for those needing an intensity of service using self-contained classes with little integration, and 4.0 for the severely handicapped, those with multiple handicaps, and the chronically disruptive. Pupils in the regular curriculum are assigned a weighting of 1.0.

Table 3 shows numbers of handicapped students weighted for instructional programs for a four-year period, 1975-76 through 1978-79. The number of handicapped children increased each year, while overall enrollment in Iowa declined. The major portion of the increase was in resource and integrated programs (1.7 weighting) for the mildly handicapped. This increase in special education enrollment during a period of declining general enrollment is expected. The goal of the Iowa Department of Public Instruction was to provide full service to all handicapped children in Iowa by 1980, and federal legislation through PL 94-142 had a similar timeline. Whether the goal would be reached remains uncertain. Factors likely to delay this full service goal were a shortage of special education teachers, negative community and school attitudes toward programming for the chronically disruptive and emotionally disturbed,

TABLE 3
Handicapped Students in Iowa Weighted for Instructional Programs from 1975-76 through 1978-79*

Year	Resource and Integrated		Self-Contained		Severe/Profound; Chronic Disruptive		Total Head Count	Percentage of State Public School Enrollment
	Head Count	% of Total	Head Count	% of Total	Head Count	% of Total		
1975-76	23,515	82	3,842	13	1,321	5	28,378	4.6
1976-77	26,853	80	4,689	14	2,107	6	33,649	5.5
1977-78	28,968	80	5,222	14	2,067	6	36,257	6.2
1978-79	31,052	80	5,423	15	1,897	5	38,372	6.7

*Does not include the speech handicapped or low-incidence programs served by itinerant teachers.

and continuing school dropouts in the sixteen-to-twenty-one age range. These figures do not include speech handicapped children. Speech and language clinicians, as well as support personnel and itinerant teachers for low-prevalence programs, are funded by a different mechanism through 15 area education agencies.

The Education Finance Center of the Education Commission of the States (1979) recently examined the development of state and federal financial support for special education. All states were surveyed, and in-depth analyses were made in Connecticut, Florida, Missouri, and Oregon, based on data from the 1975-76 school year. There were wide variations in the numbers of students served and in the amount of state support provided. Florida served 2.78 percent of the enrollment in special education, while Missouri served almost 13 percent. State aid per handicapped pupil ranged from $246 in Missouri to $2,615 in Florida. Numbers of handicapped students served and the outside financial support provided did not seem to be related to school district wealth. Urban districts and large school systems tend to serve a higher percent of handicapped students than do rural or small districts. The Education Finance Center report concluded that implementation of PL 94-142 is likely to place an increased burden on poorer school districts because state and federal aid in special education is not distributed on the basis of assessed wealth. The poorer school districts also tend to have higher percentages of handicapped children.

MAJOR FUNDING MODELS IN USE

Passage of PL 94-142 is also having an impact on state funding models. Ways in which different states fund special education programs have been summarized by several authors (Burello & Sage, 1979; Bernstein, Kirst, Hartman & Marshall, 1976; Rehmann & Riggen, 1977; Rossmiller et al., 1970). The difficulty with reviewing these models is that states frequently make adjustments and changes. This review, then, simply reflects the status as of this writing.

Summarizing funding models is difficult. There are 58 different state and trust territory methods of funding programs for handicapped or exceptional children. Some include the gifted; others do not. Some include portions of practically all the models. This should not surprise those who have had experience in developing state aid programs for regular or special education. State foundation aid programs, equalization aid formulas, and special education excess costs programs end up being political compromises. Special interest groups like those supporting rural schools introduce amendments in the state legislative process to meet specific needs of their constituents. Advocates for handicapped children do the same thing. With these shortcomings in mind, the next section summarizes the funding approach used for PL 94-142 and addresses the personnel and excess cost funding approaches of various states.

Federal Funding through PL 94-142

Although federal funding of special education programs has not usually been treated as one of the models, passage of PL 94-142 casts a different light on state funding practices. The amount of money flowing to the various states is not a significant percentage of the total state costs for handicapped children (Burello & Sage, 1979). Cronin (1976) estimated that less than 10 percent of state costs is federally funded for all programs, including the handicapped. Figure 2 shows that for 1978, according to U.S. Department of Education computations, PL 94-142 Part B funds contributed about 9 percent of the combined state and federal contributions to special education. What PL 94-142 has done, however, is to substantially increase the amount of discretionary funds available to the various state departments of education. This carries the effect of also increasing the amount of state control over local education agencies' use of these dollars. The novel component of PL 94-142 funding is that it is tied to a percentage of the national, yearly, average per-pupil costs of regular students. The Act itself authorized expenditures of 5 percent of average costs for 1978, 10 percent for 1979, 20 percent for 1980, 30 percent for 1981, and 40 percent for 1982 and each fiscal year thereafter. This is an authorization limit as the law currently stands and does not necessarily mean that Congress will pass appropriations at that high a level.

PL 94-142 is an advance-funded bill, so appropriations are determined by the current Congress for the next fiscal year. The program was funded at the maximum allowable level for the first two years (5 and 10 percent), but it was reduced for the 1980 fiscal year (1979-80 school year). Although the authorization for that year was 20 percent, funds were authorized for only about 12 percent, or roughly $211 per child. The authorization increases to 30 percent for the 1981 fiscal year. At the same 12 percent, that would translate to approximately $218 per child. Considering that costs for handicapped children are at least double those for regular students, the federal contribution to total costs for the handicapped is less than 10 percent. Programs for gifted students are not presently included in the definitions of PL 94-142, so states that include the gifted under the organizational heading of exceptional children have those costs additionally.

Funding from PL 94-142 is contingent upon certified counts of children provided by each state and requires that these figures be supplied according to the traditional categories defined in this law. Many professionals in special education think this is a mistake (Prehm & McDonald, 1979). They suggest that tying financing resources to categorical disabilities implies a state of the art that simply does not exist. The net effect of

FIGURE 2
Contributions of PL 94-142 Part B Funds Relative to State Funds for Education of Handicapped Children[1]

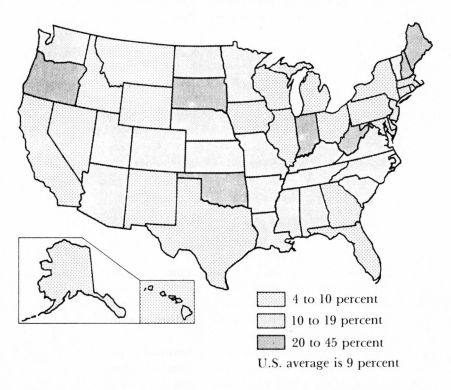

4 to 10 percent

10 to 19 percent

20 to 45 percent

U.S. average is 9 percent

[1] These estimates do not include contributions from sources other than PL 94-142, such as those from PL 89-313, and do not include local contributions. The PL 94-142 contributions reflect FY 1977 allocations, while state contributions reflect FY 1976 allocations.

Source: *Progress Toward a Free Appropriate Public Education* (1979).

PL 94-142's requirement of categorically labeling handicapped children is that it may prolong such labeling in states that are ready to move to another method of identification and funding. For example, Iowa's program is based essentially on a continuum-of-services-needed model and technically would not have to require labeling by category.

The Personnel Funding Model

The personnel funding model of state support to school districts and intermediate education agencies focuses on personnel rather than on the handicapped children. Special education teachers and aides are the principal staff members funded. Support or ancillary staff members such as school psychologists, social workers, speech therapists, physical or occupational therapists, consultants, and directors and supervisors are also included. Anderson (1976) estimated that 13 states basically used a personnel reimbursement system as of the middle 1970s. Illinois paid a flat amount, $6,250, for most personnel, and $2,500 for aides as of 1979. The state supplements this funding with other means to cover such things as private school placements and transportation. Minnesota pays a percentage of salaries up to a maximum amount. Wisconsin has a similar system; it reimburses 70 percent of salaries, and also of supplies and transportation. Other states — Colorado, Michigan, Vermont, and Oregon — have some variant of the personnel funding model.

Proponents of this model argue that it ties financial support rather directly to the continuum of services supplied (Burello & Sage, 1979), provides a fairly straightforward and easily understandable linkage between funds allocated and extra staff costs for special education, and lessens the need to label each handicapped child with a disability category in order to qualify for additional state funds.

Weaknesses of the personnel model include an inability, unless it is modified, to provide extra funds for specific children with multiple needs (such as tuition for private placement, high transportation costs, and so on); the inequity of paying a flat amount to districts with differing salary schedules; and the discrimination against districts employing or retaining experienced or advanced-degree personnel (Haarer, 1976). In addition, this system of funding requires considerable regulation at the state level to determine minimum number of children to qualify for an approved unit. Many of these minimum and maximum numbers are determined arbitrarily and are not based on systematic data. For example, deciding the number of students needed to justify the appointment of a school psychologist is not done on the basis of research data or agreement of role or function. State education departments also must regulate the new units that will be approved throughout the state each year. State legislators want some assurance that the escalation of costs from year to year is justified and can be anticipated so that large, unexpected increases in appropriations are not required.

The Excess Cost Pupil Funding Model

Some variant of the excess cost model has been used by many states to fund the difference in costs between regular pupils and the handicapped. The excess costs were generated by the smaller size of most classes for the handicapped and by the additional support personnel and services thought to be necessary to back up the instructional program. This excess cost model has waned in the past 10 or 20 years but is now reappearing, using a differential weighted index.

The advantages of the pupil funding model lie in the fact that individual handicapped children need specific intensities and amounts of special programming, with costs varying markedly from child to child. An individual accounting system reflects these costs more accurately, and resources per child are related directly to services needed.

Using the pupil unit in determining excess costs has many potential disadvantages. Usually, a fairly elaborate and separate system of accounting is required to reveal actual costs. This gets cumbersome when handicapped students are integrated into regular classrooms for a major portion of the school day. Some districts and teacher organizations are suggesting that regular class size be reduced whenever one or more handicapped pupils is integrated. If this were done, the instructional cost per pupil for that regular classroom would increase, and presumably that extra cost would be charged to special education. One frequently hears that a handicapped child integrated into a regular classroom should count as two pupils and that the overall class size should be reduced accordingly. If this concept were to take hold throughout the country, it would further complicate accounting procedures for costs.

Another disadvantage of the excess cost per pupil method is that many states set maximum amounts that can be reimbursed for a pupil in an exceptional category. These maximums must be revised upward frequently to reflect actual costs, but the process usually lags. Local districts are under pressure to keep class size at or near the maximum set by the state, because the excess cost allocation is a direct reflection of class size. Often, the maximum class size set by the state also becomes the minimum as the local districts perceive it. Because many handicapped youngsters do not clearly belong under a single disability label, the financial aspects may strongly influence the placement process, and marginal children may be placed in programs with low enrollment or in categories that provide higher state reimbursement.

Some states have recently gone to a variant of the old excess cost method by assigning differential weights to handicapped pupils either on the basis of disability labels or intensity of program needed, or a combination of both. Florida, using a full-time equivalency formula of student time, has adopted a system based on this combination. Fifteen different programs are authorized, with weighting factors from 2.3 to 15.0 (Burello & Sage, 1979). Indiana (Howe, 1976) counts the handicapped in the regular average daily membership (ADM) and then adds on additional ADM for 13 categories with weights from 0.57 to 2.73. Iowa (Howe, 1978) weights 1.7 for resource and integrated classes, 2.0 for self-contained classes, and 4.0 for the severely handicapped, those with multiple handicaps, and the chronically disruptive.

FACTORS TO CONSIDER IN FUNDING PROGRAMS FOR THE HANDICAPPED

In summarizing the preceding sections of this chapter, it becomes clear that two major approaches are used by most states to fund additional costs associated with special education programs. One approach uses the classroom as a unit to generate funds, usually a classroom with a special education teacher but also including support service personnel. The second employs the individual pupil as the base and figures excess cost for the handicapped in relation to costs for regular pupils. Different states use variations and combinations of these two models, but essentially the costs are computed on either a teacher or a pupil base. Costs are higher for special education because class size is from one-third to one-fifth as large as for regular classes. Also, more support services personnel are provided for handicapped children's programs than for regular class programs. The method of funding used by a state is decided on the basis of history, the method of funding regular programs, and political compromises among various special interest groups.

What, then, are some of the principal factors one should consider in working toward an ideal method of financing special education? This issue has been addressed by several authors in the past few years (Bernstein et al., 1976; Burello & Sage, 1979; Marinelli, 1975; McLure,

1976; McLure et al., 1975; Rehmann & Riggen, 1977). Their research indicates that the following should be considered.

1. Financing should be as simple as possible and require a minimum of resources to administer. Basing finances on a percentage of costs of regular education, a system similar to that used by PL 94-142, is attractive. When some states achieve full service for all handicapped, accurately computing the cost of special education relative to that of regular education should be possible. This would include some flexibility to take into account the varying concentrations of handicapped children, socioeconomic status of the community, and density of population. Parents with handicapped children will move to districts with good programs. Local school districts should not be financially penalized for conducting exemplary programs for handicapped children. Costs in addition to those of regular pupils will have to be borne by the state, to prevent inequities among districts within the state.

2. Revenues from the state should be provided on a current or advance funding basis. This will make funds available to finance program expansion and improvement and will prevent cash flow problems for districts with tight budgets.

3. Mechanisms for a clear audit trail should be built into the system to promote accountability for the actual use of funds. An audit would be conducted annually and the budget for the succeeding year adjusted up or down in relation to expenditures verified for the current year.

4. Funding should be integral with the regular state foundation and equalization aid program. Foundation aid programs are based on a combination of local property taxes and state funds. Equalization is accomplished by providing more state aid to poorer districts and should be realized through the general aid program. Educational opportunity should be equalized for all children in both rich and poor districts and this should be accomplished outside of the special education funding mechanism.

5. Options for private school and out-of-state placement should be integrated into the funding system. This aspect must be given careful attention to assure appropriate education for handicapped children who need a highly specialized program, although care must be taken that the public schools do not abdicate their responsibility.

REFERENCES

Anderson, R. Personnel reimbursement model. In A. M. Rehmann & R. F. Riggen (Eds.), *Special education leadership series.* Vol. V. *Financing of special education in the United States: Fiscal planning for programs for the handicapped.* Minneapolis: University of Minnesota, 1976.

Bernstein, C. D., Kirst, M. W., Hartman, W. T., & Marshall, R. S. *Financing educational services for the handicapped.* Reston, VA: Council for Exceptional Children, 1976, p. 12. Cited by L. C. Burello & D. D. Sage, *Leadership and change in special education.* Englewood Cliffs, NJ: Prentice-Hall, 1979.

Burello, L. C., & Sage, D. C. *Leadership and change in special education.* Englewood Cliffs, NJ: Prentice-Hall, 1979.

Cook. V. J, & Patterson, J. G. Psychologists in the schools of Nebraska: Professional functions. *Psychology in the Schools,* 1977, *14*(3), 371-376.

Cronin, J. M. The federal takeover: Should the junior partner run the firm? *Phi Delta Kappan,* 1976, *57*(8), 499-501.

Education Finance Center, Education Commission of the States. *Special education finance: The interaction between state and federal support systems* (Report No. F79-3). Denver: Education Commission of the States, 1979.

Haarer, D. Percentage of excess cost model: Michigan in transition. In A. M. Rehmann & R. F. Riggen (Eds.), *Special education leadership series.* Vol. V. *Financing of special education in the United States: Fiscal planning for programs for the handicapped.* Minneapolis: University of Minnesota, 1976.

Howe, C. E. Weighted per pupil reimbursement model. In A. M. Rehmann & R. F. Riggen (Eds.), *Special education leadership series.* Vol. V. *Financing of special education in the United States: Fiscal planning for programs for the handicapped.* Minneapolis: University of Minnesota, 1976.

Howe, C. E. *A cost projection for special education funding in the state of Iowa, 1975-76 through 1985-86.* Iowa City: University of Iowa College of Education, 1978.

Knezevich, S. J. *Administration of public education.* New York: Harper & Row, 1975.

Landau, S. E., & Gerken, K. C. Requiem for the testing role? The perceptions of administrators vs. teachers. *School Psychology Digest,* 1979, *8*(2), 202-206.

Manley, T. R., & Manley, E. T. A comparison of the personnel values and operative roles of school psychologists and school superintendents. *Journal of School Psychology*, 1978, *16* (2), 99-109.

Marinelli, J. J. Financing the education of exceptional children. In F. J. Weintraub, A. Abeson, J. Ballard, & M. L. LaVor (Eds.), *Public policy and the education of exceptional children*. Reston, VA: Council for Exceptional Children, 1975.

McLure, W. P. Unit support funding. In A. M. Rehmann & R. F. Riggen (Eds.), *Special education leadership series*. Vol. V. *Financing of special education in the United States: Fiscal planning for programs for the handicapped*. Minneapolis: University of Minnesota, 1976.

McLure, W. P., Burnham, R. A., & Henderson, R. A. *Special education: Needs, costs, methods of financing*. Urbana-Champaign: University of Illinois, Bureau of Educational Research, May 1975. (For the Illinois School Problems Commission and the Illinois Office of Education)

Mercer, J. Implications of funding practices for labeling and classification of children. In A. M. Rehmann & R. F. Riggen (Eds.), *Special education leadership series*. Vol. V. *Financing of special education in the United States: Fiscal planning for programs for the handicapped*. Minneapolis: University of Minnesota, 1976.

Meyen, E. L. *Exceptional children and youth: An introduction*. Denver: Love Publishing Co., 1978.

Prehm, H. J., & McDonald, J. E. *The yet to be served: A perspective*. Exceptional Children, 1979, *45* (7), 502-507.

Progress Toward a Free Appropriate Public Education. A report to Congress on the implementation of Public Law 94-142: The Education for All Handicapped Children Act (HEW Publication No. OE 79-050$3). Washington, DC: Department of Education, January 1979.

Rehmann, A. M., & Riggen, R. F. (Eds.), *Leadership series in special education*. Vol. VI. *The least restrictive alternative*. Minneapolis: Minneapolis Public Schools, 1977.

Rossmiller, R. A., Hale, J. A., & Frohreich, L. E. *Educational programs for exceptional children: Resource configuration and cost*. Madison: University of Wisconsin, 1970.

Thomas, M. A. Financing special education: From the perspective of the Council for Exceptional Children. In A. M. Rehmann & R. F. Riggen (Eds.), *Special education leadership series*. Vol. V. *Financing of special education in the United States: Fiscal planning for programs for the handicapped*. Minneapolis: University of Minnesota, 1976.

Waters, L. G. School psychologists as perceived by school personnel: Support for a consultant model. *Journal of School Psychology*, 1973, *11* (1), 40-46.

4

Organizing Instruction

The programming needs of handicapped children cannot be considered apart from the instructional system for regular students. The failure of educators to take this issue seriously has led to many of the difficulties involved in labeling children and to consequent lawsuits. Anyone who has spent some time working in the public schools knows that a child who is viewed as needing special education by the staff of one school may not be seen that way by the staff of another. It was always interesting to me to observe this variation in perception among the 80 schools included in the Long Beach Unified School District during the 1960s. The differences could not be accounted for by pupil-teacher ratios because these were almost identical among schools. Neither was the socioeconomic status of the neighborhood a factor, since schools with similar family and living constellations varied in the number of children referred for special education. One elementary principal referred almost half his total enrollment during one school year. This same principal was a strong supporter of special classes for the handicapped, provided they were housed in a building other than his!

This reminiscence is not intended to inpugn the school principal, but rather to make the point that identifying the handicapped is as much a function of the perceptions of the school staff as it is of the various criteria embodied in statutes that specify who qualifies for special education. As was noted in the previous chapter, the financing of programs for the handicapped also has an impact. The major purpose of legislation and state regulations as they relate to identification of the handicapped is to limit the number of children who qualify. A state legislature would not provide open-ended funding for exceptional children if the legislation were written in such a way that half the school population could qualify.

Thus there is the need to define who the handicapped are, and here many problems exist. The area of "behavior problems" is one of the most difficult to define in schools because the term has no universally accepted definition. Rubin and Balow (1978) conducted a longitudinal study of 1,586 children, following them from kindergarten through grade 6, to determine the prevalence and consistency of behavior problems as seen from the classroom teacher's perspective. No definitions were provided for the term *behavior problem;* the individual teacher was left to make the determination. Over this seven-year period the most striking finding was that more than half the children (58.6 percent) who received three or more teacher ratings were classified as a behavior problem at least once. A child identified as such by a teacher one year often was not so labeled by another teacher the next. Even with this high degree of inconsistency, 7.5 percent of the children were continually rated as having behavior problems. This is three times the prevalence figure currently used by the U.S. Department of Education. Although *emotional disturbance* may not be synonymous with *behavior problem,* children referred by teachers for special education programs under the former designation are quite often those who have been disruptive and difficult to manage.

Not only do regular teachers vary in their tolerance limits for some children in regular classrooms, but they are also affected by the disability labels others attach to particular children. Ysseldyke and Foster (1976) investigated the effects of labeling children *emotionally disturbed* or *learning disabled* on teachers' attitudes, even when they were confronted with behavior inconsistent with the labels. A videotape of a normal fourth-grade boy was shown to the teachers. Randomized groups of teachers were told different things about the child. Their ratings of him were lower if the experimenter told the teachers that the boy had been evaluated by a clinical team as either emotionally disturbed or learning disabled. This study demonstrated that deviancy labels do result in changes in teachers' expectations of children so labeled and that this can cause teacher bias.

One approach to dealing with the labeling of handicapped children would be to work with the adults who do most of the labeling — i.e., the regular classroom teacher and the principal. Such a tactic was reported by Beery (1972) in a study of ten schools, each of which had at least one class for handicapped children. A basic assumption was that the staffs of these schools already had the resources needed to solve most of their own problems if ways could be found to pool these resources. The emphasis was on developing ways of changing adult behavior — namely, that of the teachers and principals. Over a two-year period, the number of children placed outside the regular classroom for remedial instruction was reduced by 50 percent. The building principal was found to be the key to educational growth. These ten principals accomplished changes through a consortium; they met periodically to learn from and support one another in their efforts. They also met in pairs to observe one another in action at their respective schools.

INCREASING OPTIONS FOR CHILDREN

Obviously, no magical cutoff point separates the handicapped from the so-called normal child. Disagreements arise over children who are in the borderline areas, when it is unclear whether the most productive environment for them is the regular program or some form of special education. Fortunately, the dichotomy is not quite as much of a problem today as it has been in years past, largely because of the range of options becoming available in more schools. More choices are offered than the historical ones of regular class, self-contained special class, or expulsion from school. The greater use of options like the consultant and resource room models increases, in turn, the flexibility of school programs.

Nevertheless, ideological conflicts continue over the proper role of the schools. The schools' role is perceived differently by the community, by the school staff, and by the society as a whole. A recent report by the Carnegie Council on Policy Studies in Higher Education (1979), focusing on high schools, contended that one of every three youths is ill-educated, ill-employed, and ill-equipped to make his or her way in American society. The Carnegie Council, under chairman Clark Kerr, argued for a change in the way the "big, monolithic high schools and their deadly weekly routine" operate. The Council saw a need for basic changes, with more emphasis given to non-college-bound youth who are moving directly into the job market. New ways must be found to teach marketable job skills. The high school dropout rate is currently 23 percent and, additionally, 20 percent of the graduates fail to master basic work skills.

Reynolds (1979) held that rather substantial changes in teacher education are both necessary and inevitable because of changes occurring in the nation's schools in response to PL 94-142. Although his remarks focused primarily on preservice training of all teachers, the major ideas hold as well for practicing school personnel. He argued that PL 94-142 is the tip of the iceberg, that its major provisions must logically be extended to teachers of all children. Reynolds suggested the following ten items as domains of professional competence that are important for every teacher.

1. *Curriculum.* All teachers should be knowledgeable about the school curriculum from kindergarten through high school. They should observe instruction in various curricular areas at all grade levels.

2. *Teaching basic skills.* Every teacher, including secondary teachers, should be able to teach the basic skills. These include language arts skills like reading to at least fifth-grade level, life maintenance skills, and personal development skills.

3. *Class management.* Teachers should be able to apply individual and group management skills, including behavioral analysis procedures, to shape academic and social behavior.

4. *Professional consultation and communications.* Educators should know how to work together, to share the unique competencies they possess, and to take co-equal responsibility in building trust among themselves.

5. *Teacher-parent-student relationships.* Teachers should be sensitive in dealing with the parents of their students, especially the parents and siblings of handicapped and disadvantaged students.

6. *Student-student relationships.* Teachers should be skilled in teaching students to help each other. Peer and cross-age tutoring, for example, is a specific form of constructive relationship that can benefit the handicapped and all other students.

7. *Exceptional conditions.* All educators should have a rudimentary knowledge of all types of handicapping conditions, what additional help is available, how to get it, and how to use it. They should also know the functions of special educators so they will be prepared to establish team arrangements for the instruction of handicapped students.

8. *Referral.* Teachers should be taught to refer for special education children with whom they need help, without feeling that this is an admission of failure. At the same time, teachers should develop the attitude that referring a problem does not transfer sole responsibility to the specialist.

9. *Individualized teaching.* All teachers should be able to carry out assessments, identify different learning styles, vary instruction for individual students, and keep a record of learning outcomes. This would reverse past practices, in which teachers worked to make their classes and learning materials more homogeneous.

10. *Profesional values.* Educators should commit themselves to extending to all students the major provisions of PL 94-142 such as the right of due process in all school placement decisions, the right to education in the least restrictive environment, and the right to an individualized education program.

Training all teachers in these ten areas proposed by Reynolds is indeed a tall order. For the laudatory objectives to be achieved, several major changes are required that would affect administrators significantly. First, such training could not likely be accomplished in the traditional four-year baccalaureate program; it would require a fifth year of preparation or a master's degree. Second, average class size would surely have to be reduced, and the American public would have to be persuaded to commit relatively higher percentages of financial support to education. Third (although Reynolds is not clear on this issue), it would seem that what is sauce for the goose is sauce for the gander — that is, special education personnel should be competent in these ten areas also. This would undoubtedly displease college instructors and clientele who are specializing in such areas as school psychology, speech and language therapy, audiology, and school social work. The trend in recent years has been toward less, not more, training in regular teacher preparation. Few graduates of these training programs today could qualify for a regular teaching credential. Proponents of this so-called specialist approach are fond of comparing it to the medical model — yet physicians can specialize only after they have completed the basic coursework for a medical degree. As special educators clamor for regular educators to acquire more specialized skills, to what degree will they support basic training in general education for themselves before they specialize? I personally believe that such a move would be beneficial and would result in better acceptance of specialists by general educators.

CLASS SIZE AS A VARIABLE

One thing that clearly differentiates special from regular education is class size. Special education classes have fewer children than regular teachers usually have assigned to them. State regulations set maximum enrollments for special classes that are one-fourth to one-half those of regular classes. Smaller class size has always been a cornerstone of special education. For this reason, costs are usually at least double those of programs for regular pupils.

Research relating class size to pupil achievement has generally produced inconclusive results. Over half the studies reported in the literature were done prior to 1940, and much of this research was not well designed. Thus, not surprisingly, surveys of the literature prior to World War II typically reached the conclusion that reducing class size has no effect on achievement. Another factor contributing to this conclusion was that most of the studies compared class size in the range of 20 or larger. Many studies compared classes of about 26 pupils with classes of more than 30 pupils. Using a technique called "meta-analysis," developed primarily by Gene Glass and Mary Lee Smith of the University of Colorado, Cahen and Filby (1979) reported that in reanalyzing 50 years of data, they found that student achievement increases as class size is reduced and the advantage rises sharply for a class of 15 or fewer. Admittedly, these studies were not done using handicapped populations, but the class size of 15 or fewer is typical in special education.

It should also be noted that three-fourths of the children in special education programs are only mildly handicapped and should be candidates for some degree of integration into regular classes. Research on optimum class size in regular programs has been predicated on the belief that smaller classes enable the teacher to provide more appropriate, personalized instruction for each pupil. Although addressed to the regular teacher, these ideas sound familiar today in the special education language of PL 94-142, which emphasizes appropriate individualized programs in the least restrictive environment. The Glass and Smith data showed small differences in achievement between class sizes of 30 and 25, but fairly impressive differences between sizes of 30 and 15. Cahen and Filby (1979), of the Far West Regional Laboratory, San Francisco, are now involved in an intensive field study to examine systematically the question of how smaller class size influences student achievement. Achievement tests measure only one facet of instruction. Special educators frequently take the position that academic achievement is not necessarily the most important variable in educating the handicapped. For the mildly handicapped, who represent the bulk of special education pupils, the importance of academic achievement cannot be denied. The current study by the Far West Regional Laboratory also focuses on other variables that should be of interest to special educators, such as the numbers of slow learners and hyperactive children in the classes.

This current focus of research on class size should be of great interest to special educators. Teacher organizations are contending that class size must be reduced if regular teachers are to accommodate more handicapped students in their regular classes. The financial impact of reducing class size necessitates a substantial increase in spending for education, and the current political climate is unfavorable to such increases. One issue that will generate considerable debate is whether money is better spent in supporting special education programs for the mildly handicapped or whether these same dollars could more effectively be used to reduce the size of regular classes and pay salaries for personnel to aid the regular classroom teachers. One would hope that special educators would support such a concept if it were demonstrated to be effective. Whether special educators would participate in eliminating some of their own jobs is questionable.

TEAM TEACHING AS AN OPTION

Another alternative for the instruction of handicapped children is an increased use of team teaching. Although frequently used in the context of two special education teachers, the technique has not been employed much with a combination of a regular and a special education teacher. One reason is the restrictive way in which various state regulations are written. Again, the argument boils down to the financial one, because special educators and advocacy groups are afraid that "categorical special education money" will be used to finance a part of regular education. Such views are short-sighted, however; they escalate the need for labeling and sorting children into special education and regular education camps.

Marusek (1979) reported good success over 17 years of an Illinois high school program in math and science in which team teaching was used in classes for slow learners. Although these students were not labeled as handicapped, one can be fairly certain that the differences between teaching them and teaching the mildly disabled were not great. Advantages Marusek cited included more enjoyment in teaching, immediate assistance in case of trouble, the rapid accumulation of ideas during brainstorming sessions, observing others using successful techniques that could be copied, and taking advantage of each other's strengths. A three-member team of regular teachers seemed to work best.

The special education literature is almost devoid of data on the team teaching concept involving teams of regular and special education teachers. At present, special education resource teachers are limited in their ability to provide meaningful assistance to regular education faculty members because of the tutorial concept of resource program models, particularly at the secondary level (Armbruster, 1979). A team teaching model might provide an avenue for more effective use of the time a resource teacher is available. The instructional and management skills of the special education teacher in combination with the content expertise of the regular secondary teacher could be of real benefit to students with learning problems, including those labeled as handicapped. Such a team teaching effort has been employed on a trial basis by some midwestern secondary schools for the past two years. Preliminary results have been positive, as judged by school administrators, staff members, and participating students. Another advantage is the maintenance of accuracy of the course content taught. Most special education administrators who have spent time observing special education instruction at the high school level have had the uncomfortable experience of watching special education teachers who are not teamed with a regular teacher teach content in a subject in which they have had little or no training.

SPECIAL EDUCATION IN THE TABLE OF ORGANIZATION

Organization within a Local School District

The major focus of special education should be on instructional processes for the handicapped. One way to move toward this goal is to situate the program organizationally to be consistent with this purpose. The position of special education administrator should be a part of the management team of curriculum and instruction rather than categorized under ancillary or pupil services. The heart of power in a school system rests with the person or persons to whom the building principals are responsible. In small school districts, this is the superintendent. In larger school systems, assistant or associate superintendents have this line responsibility over principals. Sometimes the organization includes one assistant superintendent in charge of elementary schools and another for the secondary schools. In others, both levels are coordinated under one person. Additional positions are usually included in the table of organization at the assistant superintendent or director level. These include such functions as business and finance, personnel, public relations, and ancillary or pupil services. Although several assistant superintendents may be at the same level on a chart, they do not have equal responsibility or authority. The line managers (those in charge of building principals) are the key individuals.

Unfortunately, special education in the past has been linked most frequently to ancillary services such as health, guidance, pupil personnel, testing, child welfare, and psychological services. This, in effect, places the special educational program outside the mainstream of the school system's operation. In Kohl and Marro's nationwide study (1971), administrators of special education programs were asked what administrative changes they would make, if they could, in the structure of their organizations. Major responses included the following:

1. Change the special education line-staff placement from the traditional specialist-staff position to one directly connected to the superintendent in charge of school operations, so that the special education program would be more congruent with the regular education program.

2. Upgrade the position of the special education administrator to an assistant or associate superintendent so as to increase both authority and status. Respondents believed that their general responsibilities were far in excess of their authority, particularly in the areas of personnel and budget.

3. Integrate the special education administrator's position into curriculum and instruction — though opinion was almost equally divided between this response and attaching the position to a special services unit.

These reorganization ideas are easier said than done. The views summarized above are those of practicing special education administrators. Superintendents and general administrators were not asked for their opinions on the issue. Those who have worked in large school systems are painfully aware of the extreme difficulty in changing the relative status of a position in the hierarchy. The fewer the positions (directors/assistant superintendents), the more difficult it is to effect a change and the more competition there is from other special interest groups in the system to elevate their own status. Any superintendent of a large school system will acknowledge the consistent pressure from special interest groups for inclusion in his or her participating management team. Special education is only one of the groups arguing for admittance. But superintendents want to keep their cabinets at a moderate size for good reason — in order to have a manageable and efficient decision-making group.

If the position of special education administrator were to be integrated into the unit that directly manages school principals, the net effect might well be to dilute the authority of the director rather than to enhance it. Nevertheless, it would be worth the risk. Influence can be gained and change accomplished by the sharing of power. The times, and especially the passage of PL 94-142, suggest that separate administration of special and regular education is no longer feasible. If the principle of the least restrictive program is to be implemented, it can best be achieved through the organization of regular education, not separate from or in addition to it. Placing the special education program under the assistant superintendent for elementary and secondary schools would be a good place to start. However, such a plan would probably not have the full support of some current directors of special education.

Burello and Sage (1979) have addressed from a futures perspective the question of how best to organize special education within the total school system. They believe that all children would be best served through a dual authority arrangement. The matrix organizational model would fit this scheme in that it institutionalizes a system of shared responsibility and power. As conceived by Burello and Sage, the assistant superintendent in charge of elementary and secondary building administrators would have power and authority equal to another assistant superintendent in charge of support and specialized services. This has been a goal of directors of special education for many years. The problem has been, and will continue to be, that regular administrators won't buy the idea. Large school systems including Minneapolis, Long Beach, and Madison have tried for many years to elevate the special education administrator's status without much success.

Rather than continue to attempt to balance power through the dual system of support services, I believe a more reasonable approach would be to integrate the special education administrator into the instruction side of the table of organization, as shown in Figure 3. The chart itself is not significant, except insofar as it places special education in the mainstream of instruction rather than in auxiliary services in some other part of the organization. As Knezevich (1975) noted, "Frequently, the obvious facts that people rather than charts are being reorganized is overlooked. The personalities of the people holding the positions, rather than the best thought on administration, may dictate who reports to whom" (p. 52).

Regional Education Service Agency Organization

Although integrating special education into the instructional arm of regular education would not be too difficult organizationally for the large

FIGURE 3
Partial Table of Organization

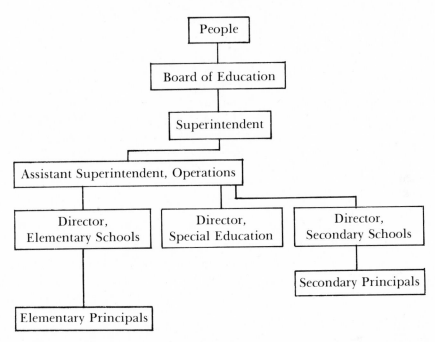

local education agencies, additional complications for such reorganization loom in intermediate units and special education cooperatives. Within these units, most of the larger school districts employ their own special education teachers. Staff members employed by the regional education service agencies (RESA) consist of ancillary personnel such as school psychologists, speech and language clinicians, school social workers, consultants, audiologists, and itinerant teachers in low-incidence programs in vision, hearing, and home instruction. Coordinators for the larger school districts or geographic sections of the area are employed by the RESA. Major functions provided by the RESA are not really instructional programs, but rather ones of sorting out students eligible for special education, monitoring local district programs for compliance with state and federal laws and regulations, providing consultative services to school districts, and administering directly some low-incidence programs for the area, such as those for preschool children, the severely handicapped, the visually impaired, and the deaf. Figure 4 is an example of an organizational chart for an area education agency special education program.

FIGURE 4
Organizational Chart for an Area Education
Agency Special Education Program

BOARD OF DIRECTORS

ADMINISTRATOR

Division Advisory Committee – – –DIVISION – – – – Special Education Division —
DIRECTOR   Dept. of Public Instruction
(1 FTE)

Assistant Director for   Coordinator   Assistant Director for Diagnostic-
  Instructional Support Services   for Special   Remedial Support Services
  (1 FTE)   Education   (1 FTE)
                                     Services
Supervisor for Mental Disability   within   Supervisor for Speech Services
  Services (1 FTE)   District   (1 FTE)

      Consultants (Mental   Speech Clinicians (38 FTE)
        Disabilities) (11 FTE)
                                                               Classified (Aides)
Supervisor for Learning   (19 FTE)
  Disability Services (1 FTE)
                                                         Supervisor for Hearing (Support)
      Consultants (Learning   Service (.5 FTE)
        Disabilities) (9 FTE)
                                                               Hearing Clinicians
Supervisor for Hearing   (6 FTE)
  (Instructional) Services*
  (.5 FTE)   Classified (Aides)
                                                                    (6 FTE)
      Consultant (Hearing)
        (1 FTE)   Supervisor for School
                                                          Psychological Services (1 FTE)
      Itinerant Teachers (Hearing)
        (6 FTE)   School Psychologists
                                                                (27 FTE)
      Consultants (Emotional
        Disabilities) (3 FTE)   Supervisor for School Social
                                                          Worker Services (1 FTE)
      Itinerant Teachers (Vision)
        (3 FTE)   School Social Workers
                                                                (18 FTE)
          Classified (Aides)
            (3 FTE)   Physical Therapists (6 FTE)

Supervisor for Preschool (1 FTE)   Classified (Aides) (7 FTE)

      Consultant (Preschool)   Occupational Therapists
        (0 FTE)   (2 FTE)

                                                               Classified (Aides) (0 FTE)

                                                        Special Education Nurse (2 FTE)

                                                        PL 94-142 Staff (39 FTE)
                                                          Psy 1   SC 6
                                                          SSW 2   OT 6
                                                          PT 3   SE Nurse 2
                                                          PST 6   Consult. PS 2
                                                          Comm. Aide 2   PT Aide 4
                                                          PS Aide 5

*Supervisor assumes responsibility for both instructional and support services.

A major criticism of intermediate units relates to their increasing bureaucracy. The largest school district in an area education agency usually wants to have control over its own special education personnel. It resents being given orders by an RESA 30 miles from its district. Local school districts argue that this concept violates good management practices of decentralization. Intermediate units are seen as useful, though, for small districts with insufficient numbers of children to hire specialized personnel. The arguments for decentralization of authority are almost identical to ones voiced in large urban school districts over the years.

Perhaps the time has come for decentralization with real delegation of authority as well as responsibility. The principle of the least restrictive environment as applied to administration argues for decisions to be made at the lowest possible level. This means that local districts or large attendance centers would participate in selecting and supervising personnel like speech clinicians and school psychologists. Special education administrators, polled in 1970, however, actually wanted more centralization of power, not less (Kohl & Marro, 1971). Decentralization of special education, although it is a sound organizational idea, may be achieved slowly.

SELECTING INSTRUCTIONAL MODELS

The bulk of special education programs has in the past been at the elementary school level. Part of the reason for this was the belief that early intervention with handicapped children would prevent later and more serious problems. Although few of us would admit thinking that early intervention will transform a handicapped child into a normal one, this assumption seems to be implied in much of what we do. Optimism is certainly preferable to pessimism, but we have tempered our views over the years to a more realistic outlook about what can be accomplished.

Until the past decade most of the interaction between regular and special administrators was at the elementary level. Because special education directors have been most familiar with teaching and class models at the elementary school level, we have tended to export these to junior and senior high schools. The self-contained classroom and remedial approaches are not so well suited to secondary schools, though, and we are now searching for more useful models.

Special education administrators can, and should, play a significant role in "showcasing" alternative instructional models and in helping procure a competent teaching staff. Beyond this point, the major influence on children passes to the administration and staff of the individual school building. If one were to write a definition of the special education director, it might well read "a teacher of significant adults in the school community." What the special education administrator can provide is a series of options through which good instruction can happen.

Schools over the years have tried a series of alternative instructional models to provide for the 15 to 20 percent of the children who cannot handle the regular curriculum (Wiederholt, Hammill & Brown, 1978). These have included special classes and schools, evaluation centers, homebound instruction, tutoring and remedial programs, vocational education, and alternative schools. Funding for some of the models came from special education; others were financed by school districts or special purpose federal programs for the disadvantaged. Until about 15 years ago, the predominant model in special education was the self-contained special class. Since the late 1960s, though, the resource program has become the most popular and will probably continue to be so for at least the next few years.

Criticism of the self-contained model culminated in the classic article by Dunn (1968). One of the earliest and best known alternatives offered was Deno's cascade system (1970), in which she proposed a continuum of services. Her conceptual model is shown in Figure 5. Meyen (1978) has compared Deno's model with others developed in ensuing years (Dunn, 1973; Chaffin, 1975; Adelman, 1970-71), and Reynolds (1978) has recast the cascade system as shown in Figure 6. Note that the schema emphasizes moving not only children toward the least restrictive environment, but specialized staff as well. Reynolds believes that teachers, psychologists, and other special education staff members lose touch with the mainstream and the normal educational world if they are left in self-contained and isolated settings. Fitting the isolated specialist into the mainstream of education may be just as important, and just as difficult, as mainstreaming the handicapped child.

Wiederholt, Hammill, and Brown (1978) believe that the resource program concept will continue to be the model of choice, at least for most mildly handicapped children. The resource program approach is meant to involve more than just a resource room. It may include one or several resource teachers; instruction may take place in the resource room or the regular classroom; and the resource teacher may provide direct instruction to children or may serve as a consultant to regular teachers. The resource teacher is viewed as a support person for the whole school, not just for the few students enrolled in the resource program. Wiederholt et al. described five of the types of resource programs currently operating in the schools.

FIGURE 5
Deno's Cascade System of Special Education Service

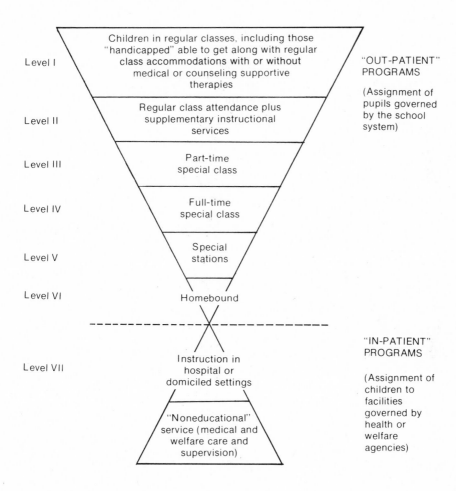

The tapered design indicates the considerable difference in numbers of students involved at the different levels and calls attention to the fact that the system serves as a diagnostic filter. The most specialized facilities are likely to be needed by the fewest children on a long-term basis. This organizational model can be applied to development of special education services for all types of disabilities.

From "Special Education as Developmental Capital," by Evelyn Deno, Exceptional Children, 1970, **37**(3), 229-237. Reprinted by permission.

FIGURE 6
The Changing Special Education Cascade:
Fewer Specialized Places, More Diverse Regular Places

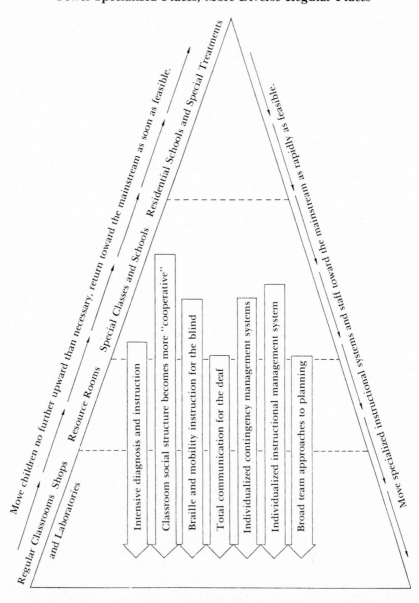

From "Basic Issues in Restructuring Teacher Education" by Maynard C. Reynolds, *Journal of Teacher Education*, 1978, *29*(6), 27. Reprinted by permission.

1. *Categorical resource program.* This model looks much like the traditional self-contained special education model except that children are integrated into some regular academic classes. To be eligible, a student must be labeled according to one of the traditional categories. One resource room serves only educable mentally retarded students; another serves only the learning disabled; and a third enrolls only emotionally disturbed youngsters. Some school districts have replaced their self-contained classes with these single-disability resource rooms. Others use a two-level approach, with resource programs for the handicapped who can succeed in regular classes on a part-time basis and self-contained classes for children who may require a more restricted setting for their management and education. Administratively, this categorical resource program is fairly easy to implement because it represents a minimum of change from the traditional bureaucratic mechanisms already in place. Children must still be categorized by disability. It fits with existing state regulations regarding funding and teacher certification. Parent groups such as the Association for Children with Learning Disabilities like it because it preserves the distinctiveness of the group of children for whom they advocate.

2. *Cross-categorical resource program.* This model resembles the categorical program in that it requires labeling children as a basis for eligibility, but mildly handicapped children with different diagnostic labels can be included in the same program. The most common mixing of children is among the areas of learning disabilities, emotional disabilities, and the educable mentally retarded. Some states refer to this arrangement as the multicategorical or multidisability resource model. An advantage to the resource teacher is that children, regardless of label, can be subgrouped on the basis of specific instructional needs. It is attractive to administrators in rural areas or in school buildings with low enrollments because it is financially feasible when the number of handicapped children is too low to justify separate programs for individual disability areas. On the other hand, this model creates administrative problems in states still using traditional funding and teacher certification approaches based on separate disability areas. Special education teachers often complain of duplication in college course content when they are required to go back to school to add a second disability to the certification one they already have. Some parent groups resist the idea because they do not want their children mixed with those who have presumably different disabilities.

3. *Special skill resource program.* In these programs, teachers provide help in one particular area, such as speech, reading, or mathematics. Some of the programs are organized under the heading of special education (such as speech therapy), and some are not (such as remedial reading programs). A school administrator faces the problem here of assigning children to appropriate programs within the guidelines of the particular funding sources. Often the criteria for funding special purpose programs prohibit a particular child's being served by more than one program, and this can be a headache for administrators.

4. *Itinerant resource program.* This model is usually a modification of any of the three already discussed. Its special characteristic is that the teacher travels to various school buildings rather than the child coming to the resource teacher. The program is popular in low density population areas and in schools with small enrollments. The major administrative problems with the itinerant program include teachers not being identified as part of a building staff, the possibility of confusion about where the teacher is on a particular day, the need to cart materials from school to school, lack of appropriate teaching space in each building, time wasted on the road between schools, and the teacher's inability to provide instruction to each child on a daily basis.

5. *Noncategorical resource program.* This model presents a more radical break with the traditional self-contained class, is designed for children with mild to moderate learning or behavior problems, and includes both "handicapped" and "nonhandicapped" students. It is grounded in the belief of many professionals that the present state of the art does not justify allocating funds for resources and support services based on categorical disabilities (Forness, 1974; Lilly, 1977; McDonald, 1968; Prehm & McDonald, 1979; Reger, 1972; Wiederholt, 1974). Tying money to categorical labeling requires making several assumptions that cannot be substantiated at this time (Prehm & McDonald, 1979), such as assuming that (a) the definitions of the different categories are functional, (b) each disability is homogeneous, with no overlaps between categories, (c) knowing a child's disability label is sufficient to select one instructional program over another, (d) diagnostic labeling interacts positively with the teaching program and changes in skill level, and (e) all children in need of special education will be identified and served appropriately by use of the categorical model.

Wiederholt et al. (1978) expressed a strong preference for this fifth model of the resource program but realized the difficulties in its current application in the schools. Major strengths of the noncategorical resource approach for the mildly handicapped are that (a) disability labels are not necessary for a child to be eligible; (b) children with learning or behavior problems from both regular and special education classes can be included; (c) more flexibility in instruction is possible; and (d) a child can attend the class without necessarily being labeled. This model is probably still ahead of its time, but it should be given extensive tryouts and evaluation. Certainly it is not appropriate for all handicapped children, particularly those with more severe levels of learning or behavior problems, but it seems useful for the mildly handicapped and for those children in the gray areas. These marginal pupils are the ones whose eligibility for special education regular and special educators now spend most of their time debating. Still, some or all of the other program models may be a better choice for a particular school system, and some large districts might well employ all five.

I opt for the noncategorical resource approach as the program of choice, but I would also integrate the component of team teaching. Using one or more regular teachers in combination with the special education resource teacher would surely provide great flexibility. The approach would lend itself more easily to secondary schools' subject-period organization, but it could also be applied in elementary schools using departmentalization.

Administrators' attempts to implement a noncategorical resource program will undoubtedly run headlong into a number of "sacred cows." Some sources of objection can be predicted, including the following:

1. *Watchdogs of categorical special education funds.* These include, among others, state departments of education, credentialling commissions, legislators, and parent groups. Such groups have fought long and hard to secure resources for handicapped children and may fear that money will be diverted and spent on the nonhandicapped. To legalize this model, most states would have to modify their current legislation and regulations. Current noncategorical programs are probably functioning thanks to the popular bureaucratic ploy of calling them "experimental."

Administrators will have to do cost-benefit studies to determine what the actual impact of this model will be. It could be argued that a tenth-grade science class made up of 20 "nonhandicapped" pupils and 5 "handicapped" pupils, team-taught by a regular and a special education resource teacher, would be an efficient use of special education funds. The resource teacher would probably not have more than the 5 "handicapped'' children at one time during a period in a traditional resource room.

2. *Special education administrators and staff concerned about losing control over a significant portion of the program.* This is what the least restrictive environment concept is all about, and this issue hopefully can be resolved amicably during the 1980s. One way to influence others positively is by giving up or sharing power. To practice this, one has to have authority to share. Some special education administrators still view their role as one of trying to obtain more authority.

3. *Those who have high confidence in their ability to make a differential diagnosis and to assign a categorical label to a child.* The noncategorical resource model would largely eliminate the need for extended formal assessments to qualify a child for a categorical special education program. The major functions of assessment would shift to educational and behavioral needs, rather than diagnostic or etiological considerations. In my opinion, many persons, such as psychologists, would welcome this change in role. Some, however, will probably see it as a threat to their livelihood or as a lack of appreciation for their psychometric skills. A state's requiring varying degrees of assessment over time might make sense. For example, a child assigned to a resource room for minimum amounts of time would require minimum amounts of time for formal assessment to "qualify." If this program were to work out well for the child, fine. If not, additional assessment would be brought into play. At present, educators appear to want to give the full treatment to everybody; the rationale is the fear of being sued. The thinking that leads to these practices is expensive and can be wasteful.

In summary, some form of resource model will continue to be popular, replacing many self-contained classes for the mildly handicapped. One would hope that decent evaluation systems will accompany this enthusiasm for a less restrictive alternative. As little evidence exists now to support the resource program concepts as was the case with the special class model from 1945 to 1965. Special education administrators should give a high priority to program evaluation this time around. A continuous investment of time and money will be required to collect significant data. Present methods of compliance evaluation will not yield information on quality of programs. Cost must become a variable to consider in evaluation; i.e., the benefits of a less expensive resource program should be weighed against those of a more expensive special class placement.

VOLUNTEER AND PEER TUTORING IN SPECIAL EDUCATION

Very little attention has been given in the literature to use of peers and adult volunteers in providing instruction to handicapped students. Paraprofessionals and teacher aides have been used most frequently in special education programs for the moderately handicapped. With the current emphasis on the least restrictive alternative, and on integrating the more mildly handicapped into regular classes, the volunteer and peer tutoring concept should be considered. Ehly and Larsen (1980) believe that peer tutoring can become a highly viable source of aid to the teacher.

Peer tutoring has been defined as one person providing instructional assistance and guidance to another (Cohen, Kirk, & Dickson, 1972). Ehly and Larsen (1980) indicated that the term is generally thought of in schools to mean children teaching other children. Older students teaching younger students is usually called cross-age tutoring.

Tutoring is not a new idea in education. Many societies expect older children to transmit information and skills to younger children. The one-room school concept incorporated older pupils teaching younger ones. Many studies on peer tutoring have been reported in the literature, but the majority have been anecdotal and descriptive and thus do not often appear in national journals emphasizing research.

In special education, relatively few studies have reported on peer or volunteer tutoring. Those that have seem to show that peer tutoring for the handicapped benefits both the tutor and the tutee. Principal benefits for the cross-age tutor are the acceptance of responsibility and improved self-concept, as well as the chance to review academic material presented at earlier grade levels. Several projects involving moderately retarded children tutored by educable retarded children reported positive results to both. These projects have been well reviewed by Ehly and Larsen (1980). They suggested that tutoring programs for handicapped children work better if particular attention is paid to specifying each component in considerable detail. Important factors to structure are selection, pairing, training, scheduling, creating tutoring space, materials, and monitoring.

The National School Volunteer Program, Inc. (NSVP) has initiated a new project, partly through funding by the Bureau of Education for the Handicapped, to help volunteers assist professional educators in implementing PL 94-142 (Cuninggim, 1980). Whitty Cuninggim, an NSVP board member, has been the driving force in developing this program. Most of the volunteers give direct services to children. Resource manuals have been developed to provide teachers and volunteers with information, ideas, and techniques.

Gray and Barker (1977) reported a study on the use of aides in the direct delivery of speech and hearing services. Aides were found to be able to work in certain areas of articulation training with efficiency and clinical impact comparable to that produced by speech and hearing clinicians.

In summary, no clear-cut evidence is available to either support or reject the increased use of volunteers or paid aides in special education. Much of the current information is based on anecdotal accounts or descriptive studies, but many of these support the idea of peer tutoring and adult volunteers. In terms of cost efficiency, an administrator of special education would be wise to explore this option to the fullest. Some professionals in special education resist the idea for purely mercenary reasons. Hopefully, fear of job loss or lowered status will not be the chief motivating factor for most of them.

INSTRUCTIONAL PROGRAMS FOR MODERATELY AND SEVERELY HANDICAPPED

Although large amounts of time and money are tied up in attempts to determine whether the mildly handicapped are eligible for special education, such is not the case for the more severely handicapped. Educators and parents generally agree that such children need a program considerably different from the regular curriculum. While the educational debate over the mildly handicapped has turned on the question of what is an appropriate program, the difficulty for the more severely handicapped has been to gain access to *any* type of public school program. This issue has largely been resolved in policy by passage of PL 94-142, which mandates educational rights for *all* handicapped children.

Negotiations between regular and special education administrators will continue on the subject of authority and responsibility for the mildly handicapped. For the more severely handicapped, though, special education administrators will probably be expected to provide more leadership. What seems to be happening now is a movement, using Reynolds' (1978) cascade, of moving up "one box" toward a less restrictive environment. Children who have traditionally been served by residential schools and treatments are now moving into special classes and schools in the public school systems. Pupils who have traditionally been housed in special schools in self-contained settings (such as moderately retarded or trainable children) are now in the process of being placed in self-contained classes in regular school buildings. The administrative model for the moderately mentally retarded looks much like the one of years past for the educable mentally retarded. One hopes that we won't repeat our earlier experience of having children housed physically in a regular school but having the program viewed as the responsibility of the special education administrator in the "downtown office."

Special educators in public school settings are now being asked to set up programs for children who, until recently, were largely seen as the responsibility of other community or state agencies — for example, secondary-school-age emotionally disabled or delinquent youth. Some of the most important elements of the programs may occur outside of the normal school day and be provided by a community agency other than the school. Community mental health services, therapeutic recreation, and vocational rehabilitation may be significant service providers. Done correctly, the individualized education program should define the critical elements of an arrangement in which the public school special class is only one element. Although interagency cooperation has been talked about for years, we still have a lot to learn in implementing a truly cooperative program for a child. Agency "turf protection" still seems to have a high priority.

With the movement toward a less restrictive environment for the moderately and severely handicapped, the following will be major issues that must be jointly resolved by regular and special education administrators:

1. The responsibility for selecting, supervising, and evaluating specialized personnel such as physical and occupational therapists must be spelled out.

2. The shorter length of the school day for severely handicapped pupils will be open for challenge. The old arguments of shorter attention span or longer transportation routes may not be sufficient justification.

3. Parents are pushing for, and courts are requiring, 12-month programs for some severely handicapped children. What evidence can be generated to indicate whether a particular child will regress if a summer program is not provided?

4. Developing appropriate instructional plans for students new to regular and special education will be a challenge. Autistic or autistic-like children present a good example in which questions about the extent of retardation or emotional disability still cloud professional thinking.

5. Schools will face increasing pressure to provide for youth who have been virtually incarcerated in the past. Fewer will be incarcerated and more will be eligible for special education and related services as defined by PL 94-142 (Johnson, 1979).

6. Will public-school-sponsored programs in segregated facilities and residential settings be challenged on the basis of the least restrictive environment concept?

These are but a few of the issues that will be contested in these changing times and from the mandate of PL 94-142. Their implications for the roles of the regular building administrator and the administrator of special education are explored in the next chapter.

REFERENCES

Adelman, H. S. Learning problems. Part 1: An interactional view of causality. *Academic Therapy*, 1970-71, *6*(2), 117-123. Cited by E. L. Meyen, *Exceptional children and youth: An introduction.* Denver: Love Publishing Co., 1978.

Armbruster, R. *Secondary resource and regular teaching team instruction in content areas.* Project proposal, Grant Wood Area Education Agency, Cedar Rapids, IA, 1979.

Beery, K. *Models for mainstreaming.* Sioux Falls, SD: Dimensions Publishing, 1972.

Burello, L. C., & Sage, D. D. *Leadership and change in special education.* Englewood Cliffs, NJ: Prentice-Hall, 1979.

Cahen, L. S., & Filby, N. N. The class size/achievement issue: New evidence and a research plan. *Phi Delta Kappan*, 1979, *60*(7), 492-495, 538.

Carnegie Council on Policy Studies in Higher Education. *Giving youth a better chance: Options for education, work, and service.* Berkeley: Carnegie Foundation for the Advancement of Teaching, 1979.

Chaffin, J. D. Will the real "mainstreaming" program please stand up! (or . . . should Dunn have done it?). In E. L. Meyen, G. A. Vergason, & R. J. Whelan (Eds.), *Alternatives for teaching exceptional children.* Denver: Love Publishing Co., 1975. Cited by E. L. Meyen, *Exceptional children and youth: An introduction.* Denver: Love Publishing Co., 1978.

Cohen, A. D., Kirk, J. C., & Dickson, W. P. *Guidebook for tutors with an emphasis on tutoring minority children.* Stanford, CA: Stanford

University, Committee on Linguistics, 1972 (ERIC Document Reproduction Service No. ED 084326). Cited by S. W. Ehly and S. C. Larson, *Peer tutoring for individualized instruction*. Boston: Allyn & Bacon, 1980.

Cuninggim, W. Citizen volunteers: A growing resource for teachers and students. *Teaching Exceptional Children*, 1980, *12* (3), 108-112.

Deno, E. Special education as development capital. *Exceptional Children*, 1970, *37* (3), 229-237.

Dunn, L. M. Special education for the mildly retarded — Is much of it justifiable? *Exceptional Children*, September 1968, *35.*

Dunn, L. M. (Ed.). *Exceptional children in the schools* (2nd ed.). New York: Holt, Rinehart & Winston, 1973. Cited in E. L. Meyen, *Exceptional children and youth: An introduction*. Denver: Love Publishing Co., 1978.

Ehly, S. W., & Larson, S. C. *Peer tutoring for individualized instruction*. Boston: Allyn & Bacon, 1980.

Forness, S. R. Implications of recent trends in educational labeling. *Journal of Learning Disabilities*, 1974, *7*, 445-449.

Gray, B. B., & Barker, K. Use of aides in an articulation therapy program. *Exceptional Children*, 1977, *43* (8), 534-536.

Johnson, J. L. An essay on incarcerated youth: An oppressed group. *Exceptional Children*, 1979, *45* (7), 566-571.

Knezevich, S. J. *Administration of public education*. New York: Harper & Row, 1975.

Kohl, J. W., & Marro, T. D. *A normative study of the administrative position in special education* (USOE Project No. 482266, Grant No. (OEG) 0-70-2467(607). University Park, PA: Center for Cooperative Research with Schools, Pennsylvania State University, 1971.

Lilly, M. S. A merger of categories: Are we finally ready? *Journal of Learning Disabilities*, 1977, *10*, 115-121.

Marusek, J. Team teaching: A survival system in teaching slow-learning classes. *Phi Delta Kappan*, 1979, *60* (7), 520-523.

McDonald, C. W. Problems concerning the classification and education of children with learning disabilities. In J. Hellmuth (Ed.), *Learning disorders* (Vol. 3). Seattle: Special Child Publications, 1968.

Meyen, E. L. *Exceptional children and youth: An introduction*. Denver: Love Publishing Co., 1978.

Prehm, H. J., & McDonald, J. E. The yet to be served — A perspective. *Exceptional Children*, 1979, *45* (7), 502-507.

Reger, R. Resource rooms: Change agents or guardians of the status quo? *Journal of Special Education*, 1972, *6*, 355-359.

Reynolds, M. C. Basic issues in restructuring teacher education. *Journal of Teacher Education*, 1978, *29* (6), 27.

Reynolds, M. C. *A common body of practice for teachers: The challenge of Public Law 94-142 to teacher education.* Unpublished manuscript, University of Minnesota, 1979. (National Support Systems Project)

Rubin, R. A., & Balow, B. Prevalence of teacher identified behavior problems: A longitudinal study. *Exceptional Children*, 1978, *45* (2), 102-111.

Wiederholt, J. L. Historical perspectives on the education of the learning disabled. In L. Mann & D. Sabatino (Eds.), *The second review of special education.* Philadelphia: Journal of Special Education Press, 1974.

Wiederholt, J. L., Hammill, D. D., & Brown, V. *The resource teacher: A guide to effective practices.* Boston: Allyn & Bacon, 1978.

Ysseldyke, J. E., & Foster, G. G. *Bias in teachers' observations of emotionally disturbed and learning disabled children.* Unpublished manuscript, 1976.

5

The Principal and the Special Education Director: Who Does What?

Reference has been made throughout this book to the role conflicts that frequently emerge between general and special education administrators. Where these conflicts come to a head is in the individual school building, with the principal. Principals have definite areas of authority derived from the central office and are responsible to the superintendent or an assistant superintendent. Major responsibilities include assignment, supervision, and evaluation of staff members within the school.

High school principals have more power than elementary school principals, partly because they serve larger attendance areas and partly because they manage larger buildings with larger staffs. The attendance area covered by a high school in a large district often includes two or more junior high schools and five to ten elementary schools. Salaries are usually linked to the size of staff supervised, and so secondary principals are paid more than their elementary counterparts. The influence principals have in the community is also related to whether they serve at the elementary or secondary level.

Special education administrators are central office personnel, but principals do not report to them. Often the principals are responsible to one assistant superintendent, and the special education director reports to a different assistant superintendent. Such a complex and frequently uncoordinated arrangement is fertile ground for conflict. Moreover, with the rapid increase in numbers of handicapped children served during the past few years and with the least restrictive environment ideology in vogue, it becomes all the more important to resolve the role conflict of who is responsible for what within a school building.

The extremes of the opposing positions often taken sound something like this:

Principal: I'm accountable and responsible for anything that goes on in my building, and that includes the special education program.

Special education director: I'm charged with the responsibility for special education in the district, and what goes on at the building level is a sharing of authority between the principal and me.

P: My role is based on the historical concept of authority by the nature of the position.

SED: My authority is based on specialized knowledge that the typical principal does not have.

P: The position of special education director is a staff position with a role of providing consultation to me, which I have the authority either to accept or reject.

SED: My role includes the responsibility of advocating for the handicapped and of monitoring the legality of programs within a building.

P: I'm accountable to the central office and the board of education.

SED: I'm accountable to the central office and the board of education and, in addition, to the state and its laws, rules, and regulations regarding special education.

P: Assignment of pupils to classes and teachers is my responsibility.

SED: I'm responsible for determining what children are eligible for special education and for their assignment within a building.

P: Special education teachers are part of my staff, and I'm responsible for directing their instructional programs.

SED: Special education teachers are accountable to me, and I have authority to assign tasks to them.

P: Itinerant personnel such as speech clinicians are accountable to me during the time they are working in my building.

SED: Itinerant personnel are central office employees and are assigned to buildings and tasks by the special education director.

P: My school doesn't have enough handicapped children to justify organizing a program. The eligible children we do have should be assigned to other buildings with existing programs.

SED: Part of my responsibility is to see that handicapped children are provided for to the extent possible, in their neighborhood school and in the least restrictive environment. I monitor school buildings to see that staff members don't dump children on other schools rather than changing their own program to acccommodate the handicapped.

P: Most of the handicapped in my school's low-incidence program come from other attendance areas. This is just the host school providing physical space and day-to-day maintenance of the program. The responsibility for staff, curriculum, and parent interaction rests with the special education director.

SED: While it is true that a building may serve a regional population for some low-incidence programs, the principal must be consistent in his or her views and not say, on the one hand, that all programs in the building are accountable to the principal and, on the other hand, abdicate responsibility because some students come from other attendance areas.

P: I have a shortage of physical space in my school and cannot justify the use of regular classroom facilities for programs with low student enrollment and/or part-time use.

SED: Part of my responsibility is to see that principals supply physical facilities equivalent to those given regular students. I guard against placing programs for the handicapped in basements, temporary buildings, or other substandard locations.

P: I'm responsible for evaluating all teachers in my building, and this includes special education staff member. They are to be evaluated using the same procedures as for all other teachers.

SED: Standard teacher evaluation procedures may not account for or acknowledge some of the key competencies and techniques used by special education teachers. Different procedures should be used.

P: The materials budget for special education should be decentralized for my school, just as it is for regular students. My staff and I should have control, without interference from the special education director.

SED: Although budget decentralization sounds good, I am accountable to the state for reimbursement for materials expenditures in special education. I need to monitor the principal's proposed expenditures to be certain they are appropriate and not used in the regular program.

Some of these positions may seem to border on the ridiculous, but persons working in the schools have encountered them and others as well. Mediating and finding compromises in such conflicts become major tasks of the special education director and of superintendents within the school system.

At the same time that special education programs are becoming more complex, the role of the building principal is being challenged by nearly all constituencies (Small, 1974). In the traditional chain-of-command model, the authority of the position of principal was consensually understood by all members of the hierarchy. Some dream of the good old days, but the time when the principal had unilateral authority is gone. Like it or not, most executives now operate in a climate of participatory management, and education is no exception. Decisionmaking and power are shared with teacher unions, teaching teams, concerned parent groups, and students. Many educators, of course, have welcomed this concept as a more humane way to administer an organization.

PARTICIPATORY DECISIONMAKING

Participatory decisionmaking is a technique used to negotiate differing views and arrive at a compromise. As usually practiced, it focuses on long-term planning and policy issues; it is not intended to be used for the daily decisions that must be made to "keep the store open." Foley (1980) has summarized research relating to participatory decisionmaking among teachers. The following claims have been made in its favor:

1.   Increased teacher participation in decisionmaking is accompanied by greater ego involvement, greater identification with organizational goals, and higher levels of motivation and satisfaction.

2.   Participative decisionmaking is democratically sound practice, in accordance with the principle that those affected by the decisions should have a voice in making them.

3.   Participative decisionmaking is organizationally sound in that, if decisions are to be effective, they should be made as close to the point of implementation as possible.

4.   The greater the expressed agreement in the decisionmaking process, the more likely will the decision be successfully carried through.

5.   Participation in the decisionmaking process allows for error correction and perception checks to improve understanding of the decision reached and of what lies behind its dissemination.

6.   Teachers are potential resource personnel whose contributions in terms of information and suggestions should be effectively utilized in the decisionmaking process.

7.   In general, joint contributions of group members and leaders facilitate generating better and more acceptable policies and decisions, ensuring their translation into concerted action.

On the other hand, a number of caveats are also identified in the literature. These may be summarized as follows:

1.   Training of both administrators and subordinates may be necessary for participative decisionmaking processes to be successfully implemented.

2.   Participative decisionmaking frequently takes a lot of time.

3.   The process may become an end in itself rather than a means to achieve organizational goals.

4.   Psychological costs (especially frustration) may be experienced by groups attempting to cope with greater decisionmaking autonomy.

5.   The formalities of consultation and delegation may cloud the realities of what is actually happening.

6.   Support for teacher participation in decisionmaking may weaken as the decisions encroach on the traditional territory of higher-level administrators.

7.   Teacher competence is limited in terms of access to information about resource allocation.

Conflict management as described by Knezevich (1975) fits many of the situations that occur in special education administration. The traditional approach of education administrators was to hide or deny conflict, but more recently conflict has been acknowledged as a fact of life in complex organizations. The concern now is how to deal with and manage divergent views held by various groups. Special education directors should feel comfortable in an organization using participatory management principles. The current changes in philosophy and imple-mentation of educating handicapped children cast special education administration more than ever into the role of conflict management.

SECONDARY SCHOOL PRINCIPALS

The National Association of Secondary School Principals (NASSP) recently completed a study of the senior high school principalship (McCleary & Thomson, 1979). These data are timely for special educa-tion, because programs for the handicapped in areas such as learning and emotional disabilities are just beginning to manifest themselves at the senior high school level. The lore of special education administration maintains that the high school principal has been the most difficult of all building administrators to deal with and to interest in comprehensive programs for handicapped children. The NASSP study was correlated with a similar one published in 1965, and the changes taking place over 12 years are interesting to note. The following items, with which the 1977 national sample of principals agreed, represent dramatic reversals of professional opinion from the 1965 group.

1.   Hostile or disinterested youth should not be required to attend school.

2.   Schools require too little academic work.

3. Schools should provide specific job training.

4. Schools should develop special programs for the talented.

5. Schools are not providing enough scholars in the fields of human needs, energy, environment, and medicine.

These views would probably meet with mixed reactions by special education administrators. Providing specific job training and developing special programs for the talented would be applauded, but eliminating hostile or disinterested youth from school seems to be at odds with the philosophy of special educators. Still, for principals, apathetic parents and problem students are serious difficulties that make increased demands on their time. Student rights required by federal legislation, as well as state compulsory attendance and categorical funding requirements, are perceived by principals as troublesome. They want more parental influence on student behavior but not more direct participation by parents in school affairs. Many tend to limit or even exclude parental involvement in program planning and other matters directly bearing upon the educational process. This appears to fly directly in the face of the PL 94-142 requirement for parent consent and involvement in planning individual educational programs for handicapped students.

Another part of the NASSP study that is instructive to special education administrators involved an in-depth look at 60 principals from the original sample of 1,600, who were judged as the most effective in each state. These 60 were selected through a nomination process on the basis of reputation as judged by the state education department, the executive secretary of the state association of secondary school principals, and an experienced professor of school administration. Four reference groups were interviewed to validate the perception of these principals as being the most effective. The group of effective principals differed from their colleagues in the following ways:

1. They controlled their use of time better and devoted it to personnel, program development, and school management. Less effective principals had the same priorities but let themselves get tied up in activities of low priority.

2. They attributed their ability to manage time well to their ability to delegate (having capable assistant principals), to trusting the competence of others, and to concentrating upon priority goals.

3. They considered district meetings, paperwork, and referrals to them of teachers' unresolved problems as their "biggest time wasters."

4. They perceived that they faced fewer administrative roadblocks and fewer constraints than their colleagues. Actually, the constraints were the same, but the effective principals had a more positive attitude.

5. They thought they had sufficient administrative staffs and regarded the central office as more supportive than their colleagues did.

6. They demonstrated better problem-solving abilities and exercised good timing in making decisions; they didn't perceive problems as terribly severe and thought they could be solved; they recognized that they could not solve problems by themselves, so they involved others; and they anticipated problems so they could be solved when they emerged.

7. They engaged themselves in developing curricula and improving instruction by supporting and encouraging innovation and flexibility on the part of their staffs.

8. They did involve parents in goal setting, policy advising, and curriculum planning. This was in direct contrast to their less effective colleagues.

9. They had no particular leadership style other than a desire to relate well to others. They worked through others, set standards, provided an example by their hard work, and made decisions at appropriate times.

10. They did not consider stress to be a major problem and handled it by keeping a good sense of perspective, by "getting away," and by involving themselves in recreation. They liked their jobs, were more mobile regarding job advancements, and did not take themselves too seriously.

Knowing about the leadership skills of today's effective high school principal can be useful to the special education administrator in two ways. First, it helps in understanding the principals when negotiating with them for special education programming. Second, it has been fairly well demonstrated that executive behavior is similar across a range of settings. Skills of the effective principal are probably not much different than the skills needed by the effective special education director.

A recent study done in Vermont (Nevin, 1979) looked at special education competencies that general education administrators thought they needed. The administrators named the same competencies that had been identified as important by special education administrators. The general administrators gave high priority to interpreting state and federal laws, using appropriate leadership styles, meeting record-keeping requirements, resolving conflicts among personnel, and determining staff functions and qualifications for education programs serving handicapped pupils.

ELEMENTARY SCHOOL PRINCIPALS

Wolcott (1973) employed the ethnographic approach to describe and analyze elementary school principalship. This fieldwork approach from methods used in cultural anthropology is unusual for education and provides a fresh look at the behavior of the elementary school principal. Wolcott's rationale was that the literature in school administration contains almost nothing about what elementary principals actually do, but, rather, focuses on what they ought to do. This rich case history is a fascinating portrayal of what was going on in a comfortable suburban elementary school in the late 1960s. The attendance area was a lower-middle to middle-class, predominantly white, American community.

Wolcott's observations have implications for special education administrators working with elementary school principals. He revealed the principal spending one-fourth of an average day attending formally scheduled meetings, being interrupted constantly during the day, attending to all types of minute problems, and having little time to spend in planning and improving instruction. Rather than serving the purported purposes of facilitating communication and reaching collective decisions, the meetings acted as definers of status and role. The real issue was not whether a meeting accomplished anything but whether the person who called it had the authority to obligate others to attend.

Wolcott concluded,

> It is ironic and even paradoxical that school administrators have been so touted in recent years as "agents of change." I believe that their contribution in education is quite the opposite of change, and although that contribution is equally essential to the institution, it happens to be an unheralded function both within the institution itself and in a society that reveres novelty and change. *School principals serve their institutions and their society as monitors for continuity.* Unlike the preliterate setting, where schools are introduced from outside to act as agents of directed social change, schools in complex, bureaucratically organized societies serve to maintain tradition and continuity. School administrators make a major contribution in maintaining this continuity. The real change agents of schools in modern societies are the young teachers, the young parents, and the pupils themselves.

Viable social systems need the stabilizing effect of a heavy load of "cultural ballast" if they are to maintain continuity with the past. Principals, though relatively few in number, have the considerable weight of authority and tradition on their side and an obvious personal commitment to keeping the system — including their own places in it — substantially intact. Insulated as they are within the layers of the educational hierarchy, with educators "above" them in the central office and educators "below" them in the classroom, they occupy an ideal position for acting as formal bearers of organizational and societal tradition. They are never acknowledged for this contribution to the stability of the institution they serve. More often they are indicted for their seeming resistance to change, for their predictable conservatism, for being constantly "behind the times" or "out of it." Their reaction to this perennial indictment has also been predictable. They have become ritually preoccupied with *talk* about change and expert at initiating continual minor reorganization within their own domains; one even hears them alluding to the danger of moving too quickly, leaving "others" behind. Since their positions require them simultaneously to present the appearance of change and to provide the stabilizing effects of continuity, their response has been to become agents of the rhetoric of change rather than agents of change itself. (pp. 321-322)

And finally:

Principals who find personal satisfaction in their work seem to lean toward one or the other of two different (but not necessarily antithetical) styles: those who create a mini-technology of their own, or those . . . who are attracted by the potential for human development and human interaction in an elementary school. The former develop skills at facets of management, such as efficiency in reporting and scheduling, craft in maintaining or developing the physical plant, adroitness in anticipating new curricular fads. Rather than complement the bureaucracy, they become part of it. The task they set for themselves is to maximize its (technical) efficiency so that the system can work for others as well as it has already worked for them. They serve the bureaucracy with special sensitivity to the expectations of those superior to them in its hierarchy.

The latter group work within the same institutional framework but find their purpose in a commitment to the promise of education and to the human aspects of the enterprise. Their inclination is to make the bureaucracy serve its clients rather than have clients serve the bureaucracy, and, as their patience and energy allow, they attend thoughtfully to ways in which the system can better serve everyone, especially those over whom they exert formal authority. They strive for quality in their interaction although usually they must content themselves with the quantity of it. They enjoy the responsibility of playing even a small part in so many lives and feel rewarded when either the position or their own unique personalities enables them to make a genuine and positive difference in the life of a child or another adult. (pp. 326-327).

The Philadelphia Public Schools, in conjunction with the Federal Reserve Bank, studied variables that relate to reading success in schools (Kean, Summers, Raivetz, & Farber, 1979). All fourth-graders in 25 elementary schools were included in the sample. Results of interest to us are the impact of principals' characteristics. Principals who were themselves professionals in the area of reading had fourth-grade students who achieved more reading growth. Other characteristics of principals —

previous administrative experience, the amount of consultation regarding reading received from publishers and the central office, length of time as a principal, highest degree, and amount of teaching experience — seemed to have little effect. Another interesting result reported was that the more a principal observed the fourth-grade reading classes, the better the students developed.

Caster and Brooks (1974) asked elementary principals and special education service personnel in Iowa to react to a series of statements on role responsibility. The special education personnel included directors, psychologists, speech and hearing clinicians, and consultants. Items were developed to obtain information on responsibilities of personnel, administrative practices, instructional practices, knowledge of elementary education, and pre-service preparation of personnel. Of the 42 items, special educators and elementary principals disagreed on half at a level that was statistically significant. This is not to say the differences were always in opposite directions on the agree-disagree continuum. Sometimes "the significance of the differences is an indication of the variation of the degree to which the two groups agree or disagree with the item content" (p. 12).

When responses were dissimilar in the two groups, they were centered in the following areas:

1.   The principal's role in supervising and evaluating special education personnel. A higher percentage of principals thought this was their responsibility and also expected consultants to provide principals with evaluations of special teachers.

2.   More principals than special educators viewing the director as a "central office" person having too little contact with principals.

3.   Principals feelings more strongly than special educators that work done within their building should be with their knowledge and consent.

4.   More principals than special educators believing that their regular teachers could work effectively with handicapped children.

5.   Principals believing that they knew more about special education than the special educators thought the principals did.

6.   Principals believing that special educators knew more about elementary education than special educators themselves thought they did.

SPECIAL EDUCATION DIRECTORS

Placing special education directly in the organizational hierarchy that manages the elementary and secondary schools, as suggested in Chapter 4, won't solve all the problems. It would be a step in the right direction in that it would acknowledge the major task of special education to be instruction in the classroom in regular school buildings. Note in Figure 3, Chapter 4, that the special education director has no buildings assigned to him or her. There are two reasons for this: (1) special, self-contained, segregated facilities operated by the school system should be administered by the regular director at the appropriate level, and (2) in the future, these self-contained facilities should disappear and become part, at least physically, of regular elementary and secondary buildings.

This absorption will take some time, and not only because of negative attitudes toward "different" children. Many school systems throughout the country have built edifices for the handicapped of which the school board and community can be very proud. For example, consider a school for the physically/orthopedically handicapped, specially constructed with ramps, railings, resilient flooring, and facilities for therapy, among other things — expensive to build and still in good repair. Because of its special construction, it is not easily adaptable to some other use by the schools. What happens, then, is that the district has a "white elephant" on its hands and will continue to use it as a center for severely handicapped children, for economic reasons.

The traditional separate facility concept is sometimes encouraged by special education staff members themselves. They become comfortable over time with the concentration of specialized staff in one place. Most likely, the principal has training in, and sensitivity to, special education, understands the problems, and may report administratively to the director of special education for the district. This dual system has operated for many years and will change slowly.

Brighi (1978) studied the effects of integration on the attitudes of elementary school children toward the physically handicapped in a midwestern school system. The results are of interest because the facility for the physically handicapped was constructed as part of a neighborhood elementary school that provided a typical education program to some 400 nonhandicapped students in kindergarten through sixth grade. Also, 60 to 75 physically handicapped children attended the school. The regular elementary principal is in charge of the rehabilitation unit, and handicapped students are integrated to the fullest extent possible. The assistant principal is a qualified special education administrator. The school has been in operation since 1973. Brighi compared the degree of acceptance of the physically handicapped in this integrated school with that of another building that did not have physically handicapped students enrolled. Both male and female students in the integrated school had significantly more positive attitudes toward the physically handicapped than did their control group counterparts.

The position taken here, then, is that the special education director should not be in the business of line management of any specialized settings. To the extent such special schools or centers endure, they should be under the management of the appropriate director of elementary or secondary principals.

Besides the existence and operation of segregated special facilities, another issue revolves around the type and number of specialized personnel working out of the central office. Should these staff people be directed by the "downtown office" or should they be assigned to, and under the control of, the building principal? The personnel involved are often ones whose assignment to an attendance center is less than full-time — for example, home teachers, speech and language clinicians, supervisors, consultants, and itinerant teachers of the visually or hearing impaired. Ancillary staff members such as school psychologists and social workers are sometimes assigned to special education, or they may be in another division of support services.

How these personnel who serve multiple attendance centers should be organized has no easy answer, but to decentralize them to the maximum extent possible makes sense. If two principals share a staff person, they should be able to work out a system of shared responsibility. Success in such a cooperative venture could open the way for further sharing of materials, equipment, and in-service activities. For staff people serving several attendance areas, though, there probably is no best way. In large urban districts, decentralization has taken the form of appointing an assistant to the superintendent for an area or zone of the district. In this model many of the special educational personnel could be "spun off" from the central office and assigned to the area superintendents. The other type of organization with greater numbers of centralized staff members is the regional education service agency or cooperative. In this case the superintendents of each of the districts within the intermediate unit represent the level at which some decentralization of staff management could take place.

At this time most directors of special education are resisting the decentralization of some or most of their staff members. This includes urban directors as well as those in intermediate education agencies. One would hope that the perceived loss of power and control is not the sole reason, but it seems to be a good part of it. With the implementation of

PL 94-142 and the principle of the least restrictive alternative, the old concept of centralized and "legislated" authority in special education will come under increasing pressure to change.

Raske (1979) looked at the roles being performed by general school administrators since passage of PL 94-142. He found that they now spend 14.6 percent of their total time in special education duties. The special education tasks performed and percentages of time spent on each are shown in Table 4. General and special education administrators were viewed as performing essentially the same administrative tasks in special education. The major difference lay not in what they did but in how much of their time they spent doing it. While superintendents, assistant superintendents, directors of general education, and principals spent 14.6 percent of their administrative time on special education, approved directors of special education in two intermediate school districts in Michigan spent all their time performing the same duties. Raske recommended that all general school administration students be required to include special education administrative components in their training programs.

Supervision of Staff Members and Delegation

Staff members supervised directly by the special education administrator are usually those assigned to the central office. Most are non-teaching personnel — supervisors, coordinators, and consultants. A few instructors may also be involved, such as itinerant teachers of the low-incidence handicapped who work in students' homes or supplement instruction in areas like vision or hearing impairment. Directors of special education have never really had much direct supervisory responsibility in most teaching programs for the handicapped conducted in regular school attendance sites. With the move toward less restrictive environments as a result of PL 94-142, central office staff members will have fewer segregated settings to supervise. The majority of staff directly responsible to the director, then, will themselves be in quasi-administrative or leadership roles in the system.

Delegation as Related to Power and Authority

Before one can delegate authority, one must have authority. Special education administrators have thought for years that their general responsibilities were far in excess of their authority to do a good job (Kohl

TABLE 4

Time Spent by General Education Administrators on Special Education Administrative Duties, in Percentages

Duties Performed	Percentage of Time
1. Participating in individual education planning meetings	18.2
2. Filling out forms	16.7
3. Reviewing referrals for special education services	8.3
4. Supervising and coordinating the annual review, individualized education plan, and follow-up system processes	8.1
5. Communicating either in written form or by telephone	7.3
6. Attending staff meetings outside the local school district	6.8
7. Attending staff meetings within the local school district	5.9
8. Preparing and monitoring the budget	5.1
9. Observing instruction in the entire local school district	5.0
10. Interviewing prospective personnel	3.8
11. Developing the curriculum	3.8
12. Reviewing purchase orders, conference and field trip requests, and so forth	3.7
13. Arranging transportation	3.7
14. Evaluating the staff	2.2
15. Arranging in-service programs	1.4

From "The Role of General School Administrators Responsible for Special Education Programs" by D. E. Raske, *Exceptional Children*, 1979, *45*(8), 646. Reprinted by permission.

& Marro, 1971). Special educators are probably not the only ones who feel this way. Since many of the skills of administration are common across settings and specialties, studying the authority system in the larger context of the school executive seem reasonable.

Sergiovanni and Carver (1980) have described the authority of a school executive as a situation in which there is the capacity to effect movement toward goals. Many models have been developed over the years to explain the nature and source of authority in organizations. Most of those that apply to schools seem to have in common the idea that power for school managers comes from several different sources. Peabody's (1962) formulation, for example, suggested several bases for authority. They translate to the position of special education administrator roughly like this:

1. *Authority based on legitimacy.* This source of authority is based on laws and regulations. State codes and regulations and federal law (PL 94-142) are examples. Special education probably has more of this authority than does any other area of education. But conflict arises when part of a director's job description is written into state law or regulation. Iowa, for example, has such a situation for its 15 area education agency (AEA) directors of special education. A state code section specifies that the director shall determine the appropriateness of each handicapped child's program. Each director is employed by an AEA board and is responsible to the AEA administrator. Conflicts ensue when the AEA special education director points to this section of the code as authorizing his or her power and contends that it is not under the authority of either the administrator or the board. The question raised then is whether the director is an employee of the board or an agent of the state. The issue becomes clearer in a confrontation between the board and the director. When the votes are counted for contract termination, the state department has not voted.

2. *Authority based on position.* Authority here is associated with the historical understanding of the role — that is, the administrator has the right to act by virtue of being "the boss." Authority depends further on what the superintendent delegates. In the case of the position of director of special education in the central office, there is no long history to define the role and subsequent job description, as is the case, for example, for the school principal.

3. *Authority based on competence.* This source of authority is based on specific knowledge and skills. As related to the administrator of special education, knowledge of the field of handicapped children is the

major feature. Little evidence supports the idea that the administrative skills, in themselves, are much different from those employed by any other administrator.

4. *Personal authority.* The basis for authority in this case is the individual's personal characteristics. The ability of directors of special education to effect movement toward goals relates to their charisma and powers of persuasion.

Authority in special education administrative positions, using Peabody's classification, is probably chiefly based in the areas of legitimacy and competence. A major part of a director's job description is drawn from the specific laws and regulations governing education of handicapped children in that state (legitimacy factor). The director is expected to know what can and cannot be done to keep the district or agency in compliance. Of no small importance is the need to be certain that the district receives the maximum categorical funding to which it is entitled, in both state and federal appropriations.

Nearly all school programs are under some degree of state control because education is constitutionally a function of the state. Special education, though, has more outside restrictions imposed upon it. The effect is that the director's role in part becomes one of monitoring state laws and regulations to see if the district is in compliance. This regulatory "agent of the state" status may not endear the director to the building principals of the district. But the director is not the only one performing this role. Central office special education staff members have these same monitoring, regulatory duties assigned to them by the director.

Since monitoring rules and enforcing compliance are not exciting or rewarding experiences for most education professionals, a good approach is to try to determine the reasons the regulations were written and to persuade colleagues to comply on this basis. Presumably, regulations are written with the purpose of helping ensure better programs for handicapped children. The director ought to use logical persuasion (authority of person) to train the central office special education staff to work for compliance, and to minimize the impression of wielding the heavy hand of authority (authority of position).

REFERENCES

Brighi, R. *The effects of integration on children's attitudes toward the physically handicapped.* Unpublished education specialist thesis, University of Iowa, 1978.

Caster, J. A., & Brooks, R. D. *The interfacing of elementary education and special education: The views of elementary principals and special service personnel.* Study sponsored by Drake University College of Education and Iowa State Department of Public Instruction, Division of Special Education, 1974.

Foley, W. J. Personal communication, February 1980.

Kean, M. H., Summers, A. A., Raivetz, M. J., & Farber, I. J. *What works in reading?* (The results of a Joint School District/Federal Reserve Bank Empirical Study in Philadelphia). Philadelphia: Office of Research and Evaluation, School District of Philadelphia, May 1979.

Knezevich, S. J. *Administration of public education.* New York: Harper & Row, 1975.

Kohl, J. W., & Marro, T. D. *A normative study of the administrative position in special education* (USOE) Project No. 482266, Grant No. (OEG) 0-70-2467 (607). University Park, PA: Center for Cooperative Research with Schools, Pennsylvania State University, 1971.

McCleary, L. E., & Thomson, S. D. *The senior high school principalship. Vol. 3. The summary report.* Reston, VA: National Association of Secondary School Principals, 1979.

Peabody, R. L. Perceptions of organizational authority: A comparative analysis. *Administrative Science Quarterly*, 1962, *6*, 463-482.

Raske, D. E. The role of general school administrators responsible for special education programs. *Exceptional Children*, 1979, *45*(8), 645-646.

Sergiovanni, T. J., & Carver, F. D. *The new school executive: A theory of administration.* New York: Harper & Row, 1980.

Small, J. F. Initiating and responding to social change. In J. A. Culbertson, C. Henson, & R. Morrison (Eds.), *Performance objectives for school principals: Concepts and instruments.* Berkeley, CA: McCutchan Publishing, 1974.

Wolcott, H. F. *The man in the principal's office: An ethnography.* New York: Holt, Rinehart, & Winston, 1973.

6

Selection and Development
of Staff Members

Most large school systems have a separate personnel department to coordinate recruitment, employment, and upgrading of staff members. In many ways the role of personnel administration is similar to that of special education. Both are traditionally thought of as staff functions supporting the operations of schools. But each is beginning a new era in the 1980s. For special education, the focus will shift to providing appropriate education for all handicapped children, and in the least restrictive environment. For personnel administration, the role will change from recruiting new staff people for expanding enrollments to dealing with staff reduction and upgrading the quality of teachers already employed by the system. The major exception will be for special education personnel; these staff positions will have growth and changing needs for at least several more years.

Since both special education and personnel administrators are faced with changes in role, how can each function in a way to secure the best special education staff for a school system? Although an oversupply of teachers exists in most fields of regular education, a shortage of special education personnel continues, except in the area of the educable mentally retarded at the elementary level.

It seems trite to repeat the often-heard opinion that the quality of the teacher makes the difference, but it is all too true in special education. If you were to ask general administrators who have been in the business since World War II, most would say that the quality of teachers of the handicapped has not been equivalent to that of regular teachers. For one thing, because of the historical shortage of trained personnel, school systems have not had the luxury of being able to choose among several candidates for an opening. In addition, many employers were not clear about the qualities they were looking for in a special education teacher.

Too often, words like "patience" and "sympathy" seemed to embody the major qualifications. Many special educators, including myself, believe that the efficacy of the special class model was never really tested because of a shortage of high-quality teachers in the field (Goldstein, Moss, & Jordan, 1965; Brown, 1968). Some of us are still living with mistakes we made 20 years ago when we employed someone on the assumption that any teacher is better than no teacher.

HOW TO GET THE BEST OF WHAT'S AVAILABLE

What have we learned in the past 30 years that will help us select special education staff members in the decade ahead? How can we avoid hiring the poor teacher, especially with the added burden of new staff needs as a result of PL 94-142? Harris, McIntyre, Littleton, and Long (1979) made an important point with reference to all professional personnel in education when they wrote, "neither can basically weak personnel be 'in-serviced' out of their ineptitude. The notoriously disappointing records of many training programs are probably due as much to limitations in the trainability of the personnel as to inadequacies in the training" (p. 147).

My intention is not to indict special education support staffs and teachers. There have always been many outstanding persons in the field, and there will continue to be. The job of personnel and special education administrators is to attract and retain those top-quality people and to avoid employing marginal people. But several factors contribute to the difficulty of recruiting and retaining top-quality teachers in special education. Teachers in such areas as emotional disabilities and severe retardation seem to suffer a high degree of "burn-out" after a few years and either leave the field or seek some other type of teaching. And not all regular teachers are interested in being recruited to teach the handicapped.

Recruiting from the Pool of Regular Teachers

Because school enrollment will continue to decline for at least the next five years, special education does have an opportunity to recruit regular teachers into special education. This includes teachers currently employed who are being cut, as well as beginning teachers who cannot find jobs. Negotiated agreements between teacher unions and administrations usually base staff reduction on some form of seniority. This practice provides a pool of relatively younger teachers who may consider working with handicapped children an attractive alternative for their endangered careers. The emphasis on least restrictive environment and increased use of the resource model may be more attractive than the traditional self-contained model to this group. Experience in the regular classroom should provide credibility among special education colleagues for those teachers who become resource teachers.

Now is the time to increase efforts to recruit personnel from the ranks of regular teachers. Because of the way certification is set up in most states, the regular teacher will be required to add training of from 15 to 30 semester hours in special education. To the extent that tight finances and master contracts permit, school systems should look for ways to assist these regular teachers in meeting the additional training requirement.

Attracting Student Teacher and Practicum Students

Another powerful recruiting method is to maximize the number of sites available to colleges and universities for placing their students for practice teaching, practicum experience, and internships. The school system that adopts a passive attitude toward this form of recruitment is being short-sighted. Having a "blue-chipper" attend summer sports camp before signing a letter of intent is a technique used effectively by college coaches. Working in a school system before deciding where to teach has advantages for both parties. The prospective teacher sees the school system and community as they really are and can make a more intelligent decision about teaching there. The school system has an opportunity to observe the candidate on the job, giving a solid basis for evaluation.

As soon as the student teaching or internship experience indicates that the person has high potential, the school system should commence an aggressive procedure to "sign the prospect." Although offering early contracts has its risks, especially when actual vacancies may not yet be known, the advantages tend to outweigh the risks.

Using One's Own Staff as Recruiters

The best way to attract new staff members, of course, is to have a reputation as a school system with an outstanding special education program. One way to encourage this reputation is through "advertising" one's own teachers by encouraging them to participate in state and regional professional activities. And, of course, that "pool" contains special education teachers who may be interested in moving from their

93

current employment in other districts. For example, you might send one of your best teachers to a regional special meeting, with staff recruitment as one of his or her objectives. You, the director of special education, stay home and act as the substitute teacher. This has the added advantage of giving you some "renewal" — fresh and direct contact with teaching in the schools. That certainly won't hurt the director's image in the eyes of prospective staff either!

Many reasons can be conjured up to declare an approach like this unworkable, but if the personnel and special education administrators want it to work, it will. Special education directors need not be the only ones who recruit at meetings. And using some of the best teachers as emissaries for the district can provide additional benefits in terms of their morale.

University and College Placement Services

Nearly all colleges and universities maintain placement offices, which represent a source of potential candidates. The usual procedure with placement offices — simply listing vacancies — provides no competitive edge in obtaining more than one's share of top-quality candidates. Rather, the procedure should be used to its maximum but should not be relied on as the exclusive method of recruitment. To increase the probabilities of positive results, one should get to know the placement director on a first-name basis, be honest about the strengths and weaknesses of one's school system, try to get the director to do some initial screening, be on time for and stay on time with the interview schedule, and follow through on any commitments made to candidates or to the placement director.

Other Recruiting Techniques

Although the three approaches just discussed should form the core of a recruiting effort, some additional methods are worthwhile. Some are short-term; others will produce several years in the future. They include encouraging the best staff members in their first few years of service in the district to write to colleagues with whom they went through training. They probably still have fairly close ties with some former classmates who may not be happy with their first job and are looking for another position as well as a more suitable community in which to live.

Another source of professional staff members several years in the future are classroom aides. Special education programs are making increased use of aides, both paid and volunteer. They may be adults or high school students considering special education teaching as a career. Top-quality aides, given encouragement, may decide to complete professional requirements and qualify as teachers of handicapped children.

Promotional materials about the school system and special education program might be developed by professionals. These should be of a quality comparable to those used by major corporations in the community. Commercial advertising in professional journals is judged effective by some administrators, although I have never had much success with this technique. Still, some regions seem to rely heavily on classified ads in newspapers that have statewide or regional readership. Advertising becomes a necessity with affirmative action requirements.

In summary, the purpose of recruiting is to increase the candidate pool so the local system has some choices in selecting new personnel. One should invest as much in securing top-quality personnel in the first place as is likely to be spent in terminating or trying to upgrade mediocre or incompetent staff members already employed because they were assumed to be all that was available.

USUAL TECHNIQUES FOR EVALUATING PROSPECTIVE STAFF MEMBERS

Education has had a fairly standard set of procedures over the years to accumulate data on prospective teachers. These have included application forms, letters of recommendation, telephone checks, rating scales, transcripts, interviews, and standardized tests (Harris et al., 1979). Each method contains enough problems of validation to make one cautious about putting too much faith in any one of them. Some of the techniques that have been employed routinely for years have little hard evidence to support their use.

Research related to the appraisal of teaching has focused principally on teachers after they are hired, although some work has been done on what Borich (1977) has called the preoperational stage of appraisal. An interesting question is whether items used in selecting personnel are similar to items used in evaluating personnel after they have been on the job for a few months. Variables studied in the evaluation of prospective personnel have included personality, attitude, achievement, and aptitude, but little evidence suggests that higher ratings in any of these areas will assure meaningful pupil improvement (that is, effective teaching). Relationships between attitude and teacher performance in the classroom have been low and nonsignificant. Of the attitudes studied, Borich reported that motivation to teach and positive attitude toward children seem the most promising. Achievement and aptitude variables such as grade point average have also been of little value, mainly because the spread in grades earned by teachers has not been large enough to permit discrimination. The common practice in grading student teaching, for example, is to award As and Bs, with a preponderance of As.

Before looking at the research to get an idea of what variables may indeed have promise in selecting personnel, let us review the frequently used techniques. Both the procedures used and the research done to date on appraising teacher performance have concentrated on regular teachers; no comparable body of literature exists for special education. For now, then, the best advice for special educators is to learn from the experience of regular education and to apply those findings in the area of special education.

Letters of Recommendation

What little evidence there is suggests that letters of recommendation are practically worthless as a tool for selecting teachers (Harris et al., 1979). Nonconfidential letters of recommendation, widely used by college placement offices, contain comments that are so laudatory and inflated that they provide little in the way of discriminating insight to prospective employers. The occasional straightforward letter that does suggest weaknesses or problems in a candidate may result in the removal of that teacher from the eligible pool. Letters of recommendation written for special education candidates would have no reason to be any more valuable than those for general education candidates.

The Telephone as a Tool for Gathering Information

Telephoning someone who has written a letter of recommendation about a teaching candidate is always interesting. One frequently has the feeling that the person being discussed must be someone different than the person named in the letter. Although not much research has been done on this question, most recruiters in personnel administration believe they are more likely to get an honest, detailed evaluation of a candidate by telephone than through letters of recommendation. Knowing the person on the other end of the line helps, of course. It brings the obvious advantage of two-way communication in which issues other than those usually included in letters can be explored. The discussion can also focus on a particular position and the candidate's strengths and weaknesses as they relate to a specific job description. Skillful telephone inquiry, which is a difficult technique to master, often turns up the name of another person who can be called for specifics that will add to the body of pertinent information.

Frequent and consistent use of the telephone enriches the data base and reduces the number of mistakes made when employing new personnel. To the extent that this technique eliminates the pain of later going through termination procedures with an unsatisfactory employee, it is a small price to pay. Like any other procedure, telephone follow-up should not be relied on by itself. It may be more useful as a way of eliminating a candidate than as a way of deciding which of several is the best.

Interviews

The personal interview with a prospective staff member is one of the most heavily relied on methods of personnel selection. It is also time consuming and expensive. But choosing among applicants is only one of two purposes for interviewing. The second and equally important purpose is to interest a pool of applicants to explore the school system further as a place they might like to be employed. This must be done carefully and in a way that is credible. Everyone has endured the high-pressure sales approach of a representative from some school system. More constructive is to have some data to support the view that one's system is operating a top-quality special education program that is engaged in recruiting top-quality teachers.

Although interviewing is a widely used procedure, Harris et al. (1979) reported on a series of studies that suggested not much is learned about interviewees from the process. They attributed this largely to subjective practices in which usable records of impressions are seldom kept to compare later with subsequent performance of the staff person. Recently, however, groups using highly structured interview procedures have made claims of success. In these interviews specific questions are asked of the candidate, and responses are scored according to a predetermined scale. These packaged approaches are most often used as a gross screening method to sort candidates and establish those to be considered further. Some reported difficulties with the technique include candidates knowing the test questions and how they should respond, as well as candidates who are so talkative that the interviewer cannot ask all the questions in the allotted time.

Rating Scales

Rating scales as they are currently used for selection of new personnel suffer from some of the same flaws as do letters of recommendation. Borich (1977) has summarized the difficulties with these forms of measurement.

1. Many scales lack unidimensionality and ask questions over a broad range of behaviors. When such multifaceted characteristics are rated, interpreting the results becomes difficult.

2. The shades of meaning of response alternatives are often confusing. For example, the Likert scaling technique usually includes response choices like "very often," "fairly often," "sometimes," and so on, and the user is never certain what sort of difference is intended between "fairly often" and "sometimes." Other descriptions, such as "outstanding," "adequate," and "poor," create the same difficulty in interpretation. Moreover, raters consider judgments on the negative end of the scale so detrimental to the teacher that they usually use only the positive end, regardless of how inadequate they may think the candidate is.

3. Rating scales may be difficult to interpret because the responses are made relative to other teachers, and the user doesn't know what characteristics were used as anchoring points.

4. Responses rely largely on the rater's memory, perceptiveness, and bias. Although extensive efforts often are made to train raters, every teacher rating is susceptible to such bias.

In summary, little conclusive evidence can be offered to guide administrators in selecting special education staff members. Research done in regular education raises questions about the usefulness of several of the most commonly used techniques. One should always be aware of the limitations and not fall into the trap of thinking one particular measure is foolproof. Using several sources of information is prudent, as is having more than one person interview prospective candidates. Congruent with the idea of shared decisionmaking, the building principal and the director of special education should each interview candidates and compare judgments. Some of the more gross screening methods usually eliminate marginal applicants. Unfortunately, collecting relevant information to help decide who is the best prospect is the more difficult challenge. The next section explores current efforts in the appraisal of regular teachers, to seek techniques that might be useful in evaluating special education personnel. Particular attention is given to studies focusing on the teachers of poor learners and children from lower socioeconomic backgrounds.

PROMISING VARIABLES IN TEACHER APPRAISAL

Special education must ultimately face the issue of assessing the quality of programs for handicapped children. Much effort is now being devoted to monitoring the due process requirements of PL 94-142 and state law. But even with programs conforming to the letter of the law, whether the children are really making appropriate gains because of the teaching they have received remains untested and unknown (Arp, 1978). Borich's statement of the purpose of teaching in general is appropriate to special education: "Since the business of teachers is in the promotion of pupil growth, the product stage of appraisal assesses teacher effectiveness by measuring changes in pupil achievement, both affective and cognitive, over a prespecified period of instruction" (p. 25). His statement fits well with some of the language in PL 94-142 as it relates to the individualized education program and the annual review and evaluation requirements.

As one input variable, examining actual behaviors of teachers may provide some clues about how to proceed with instruction for the handicapped. Several studies have related teaching variables to pupil achievement. But when the results are spread across grade levels, subject areas, socioeconomic status, (SES), student prior achievement, and geographic setting, many blank spaces remain. Rosenshine (1977) reviewed six major studies on selected variables, conducted with children from low socioeconomic schools. The research was done in primary grades in reading and mathematics. Because disproportionate numbers of handicapped children come from low-SES homes, some of these variables relating teacher behavior to student achievement may have meaning for special education. At least they provide a place to begin exploration.

1. *Time a teacher spends on direct instruction.* Rosenshine found that the amount of time spent directly on reading and mathematics was related to student achievement. Effective teachers in these low-SES schools with students of limited ability spent more time on these two subjects. Activities were more highly teacher-directed, and time was structured by the teacher. Questions asked by the teacher were narrow, direct, usually had a single answer, and were structured to obtain a high percentage (80 percent) of correct answers. Less time was spent on activities like dramatic play, games, or questions about home and family. Students worked in groups, and deskwork was done under supervision. Independent study correlated negatively with achievement.

2. *Teacher as the dominant leader.* Effective teachers for low-SES schools were direct and businesslike in manner. They controlled the activities and decided what activities would take place. Systematic instructional patterns were used, with more emphasis on programmed materials. Questioning techniques were direct, and the teacher made sure to get some kind of response from the student, even if that response was "I don't know." Flanders' concept of indirect teaching seemed to be especially inappropriate for these lower-ability students. The dominant characteristics of the effective teachers should not be construed to mean that they were cold or uncaring, though. They combined their directiveness with warmth and encouragement. Interestingly enough, warmth seemed to have no effect on achievement for students in high-SES schools.

3. *Enthusiasm as an important variable.* Successful teachers in low-SES schools had a general attitude of warmth and encouragement, as noted above, and expected the students to be able to do the work — but also expected to help them do it. Interestingly, verbal praise, a variable considered tremendously important by special educators, was not of particular importance — at least that was the case for student-initiated contacts when students brought their work to the teacher and appeared to be seeking praise.

These variables may or may not be the crucial ones in relating teacher performance to student gains in special education. Nearly all of this research has been done at the elementary school level, and the product outcomes measured have usually been some form of academic achievement as measured by standardized achievement tests. Although many educators point to the importance of measures of change in affect, these studies did not really deal with this variable. This is an important subject for future research in special education.

Whatever variables are the most important ones, the special education administrator must begin to address the issue of what constitutes effective teaching in special education. As the key variables are identified, they will provide a more reasonable basis both for the selection of new staff members and the in-service training needs of existing staff members.

HOW TO KEEP GOOD PEOPLE ONCE YOU HAVE THEM

Selecting special education staff members for school systems should be a joint effort of the principal, the personnel department, and the special education department. If a system really works hard to acquire the best staff available, it then becomes doubly important to provide a climate in which these good people can grow, feel challenged, and have experiences that make them want to remain with the system. Providing these opportunities along with those for the improvement of instruction involves a shared role of building principals and the special education administrator.

One frequently hears from top-quality teachers who have been on the job a few years that they are getting bored and are thinking of leaving the system to seek new opportunities. This in itself is a healthy sign. What should be disturbing to the special education administrator is that the system has not had the flexibility to offer a variety of satisfactory options for personal growth from this staff person's point of view. There must be some ways to increase the career satisfaction of staff members.

Options to Transfer Within the System

Large school districts and intermediate units have various types of special education programs for different age levels. In most systems, procedures for transfer give staff members first priority when they apply for positions in the district for which they are qualified. Assignment, transfer, and promotion have increasingly become mandatory items in collective bargaining agreements. Most of the conflict over transfers involves involuntary transfers initiated by the administration.

Transfers of special education personnel are not always easily accomplished. Denials of transfer requests frequently are based on the argument of the specialty of the position and the difficulty of finding an adequate replacement. This is a short-sighted view and can lead to deterioration of morale, plus the eventual departure of the staff member from the district. Options for transfer should include new opportunities within special education, but also within the larger framework of the whole school system. A staff member should not hold a contract or have tenure as a special education teacher but, rather, as a teacher in the school system. The same opportunities should exist for a resource teacher in an elementary school and for anyone else in the system to apply for, and be assigned to, a regular fifth-grade class. What better way for such people to enhance credibility with their regular colleagues than to demonstrate their interest and ability to teach a regular class? This might be one of the best ways to practice the least restrictive environment concept. Special education teachers, along with handicapped children, may well need to be integrated into the mainstream.

The degree to which this approach can be implemented depends upon several factors, not the least of which is a state's certification patterns and its teacher training institution's ideology. If basic certification as either a regular elementary or secondary teacher is prerequisite to additional certification in some area of special education, special teachers could be assigned to regular settings. If, on the other hand, the college program promotes the ideology of training only specialists, it may train teachers who cannot qualify for regular elementary or secondary credentials.

Considerable debate has continued for years among college and university staff as to whether basic training as a teacher should precede training as a special education teacher. As far as I have been able to determine, the issue has yet to be settled, with little or no convincing evidence either way. A person's point of view seems to reflect his or her own background of training and experience. Considering that 80 percent of the handicapped children being served are in the "mild" category, assigned to resource or integrated programs (Howe, 1978), seeking people who are trained both as regular educators and as special education teachers seems reasonable to me for the decade ahead.

Trainers of support service personnel such as school psychologists and speech and hearing clinicians have opted for the specialist model. They argue that basic training as a teacher is not critical to their functions in the school. Given the certification patterns existing in most states, these staff members would not be qualified as regular teachers, and that option would not be open to them.

Certification and training patterns, then, constitute one variable that impinges on the degree to which job transfers can be used to enrich the experience of special education personnel and to forestall feelings of stagnation. Another factor is the attitude of building principals and central office administrative staffs toward teachers of handicapped children. If they consider such teachers to be as competent as regular teachers, the idea of a switch in assignment from special education to a regular first grade or to twelfth-grade English will probably be supported. If principals regard them as second-rate teachers, good enough for special education but not for a regular class, they will resist appointing the special teachers to regular positions. These attitudes are a result of recruitment, selection, and in-service shortcomings that have permitted such circumstances to develop.

One weakness of the intermediate unit is its inability to take advantage of the option to transfer special education teachers into regular teaching assignments. Regional education service agencies hold the contracts of their special education and support staffs and are not tied to the regular elementary and secondary schools of a school district. This problem could be circumvented to some extent if intermediate units were to negotiate with the large school systems so that the local districts might hold the contracts of some of these teaching and support personnel. Local superintendents of these large systems would welcome this decentralization and increase of local control. But fear of losing power and control seem to be the major reason why intermediate education agencies resist the idea.

If special educators are serious about wanting to integrate programs for the handicapped into the mainstream of regular education, this should be pursued at more levels in the education system than those of the child and teacher. Special education administrators might well assume other roles for periods throughout their careers. After a few years on the job, a special education director might welcome the idea of serving as a building principal for a couple of years. One of the best ways to understand another person's role is to "walk in his or her shoes."

Graduate training programs in special education administration today have larger concentrations of study in general school administration. Several programs, including the one at the University of Iowa, require completing the requisites for the superintendent's credential in order to be certified as a special education director. Nonetheless, while the director may have had academic training for the role of the principal, he or she probably has not had any real experience in the position.

No research literature in special education reports on staff satisfaction and morale as related to administrative practices. Some work, although not recent, has been done with regular teachers, finding that teachers relate job satisfaction to the leadership qualities of the principal. Interestingly, however, the work of Herzberg, Mausner, and Snyderman (1959) and their motivation-hygiene theory, while controversial, has had an impact on education. (The theory is discussed further on page 114.) Sergiovanni and Carver (1980) believe that Herzberg et al.'s research in business is applicable to educational organizations, and Sergiovanni (1967) found support for that theory using teachers and other educators. Achievement and recognition represented 58 percent of the job satisfactions that produce good attitudes and high performance in teachers. Sergiovanni and Carver believe much can be done to increase motivation in teachers by expanding the reward system through:

— providing opportunities for teachers to advance within the ranks of teaching;

— altering responsibilities among the various teaching roles and keying advancement to responsibility; and

— eliminating elements of the work itself that are sources of dissatisfaction for teachers, thereby salvaging teaching itself as a motivator. Using paraprofessionals would be helpful in this effort.

103

In summary, a flexible system of new responsibilities both within special education and in general education increases the competence of special education staff members and broadens their career objectives. To be successful, such a system must be endorsed and supported by general administrators. An inherent objective would be to break down the barriers between general and special education. This system could provide some alternatives to teachers who feel they are "burning out" or stagnating in their present job and need a fresh perspective.

Employing Associates Who Have Skills Different from Yours

Administrators quite naturally surround themselves with associates having skills, leadership styles, and points of view similar to their own. Thus, they tend to employ colleagues who share their biases. This is comfortable, prevents dissonance in the system, and adds stability. Staff members continue on their jobs, with little turnover. But the practice can be bad for an organization.

Consider a scenario in which the group is made up largely of innovative program developers; the system is under constant stress from change. These persons are much like the "cosmopolitan empire builders or outsiders" described by Gouldner (1957). During periods of growth and mobility, they are happy and motivated. Upwardly career oriented, though, they are willing and eager to move for more money and increased prestige (Sergiovanni & Carver, 1980). Highly committed to change, to improvement, their loyalties lie outside the school system, with other reference groups.

Although the above researchers were describing regular teachers, anyone who has worked in special education can recognize in the description many of his or her colleagues. Partly because special education has been a high growth area for the past 30 years, it has attracted a number of such cosmopolitan empire builders in both the teaching and adminis- trative ranks. They usually enter the system from other districts or other states and are committed to change in programs for handicapped children. The advocacy or change agent role recommended by many in special education fits them perfectly. Parent groups love them in the beginning as they work to institute new programs or improve existing ones, and much of the credit for bringing groups of formerly unserved or poorly served handicapped children into public schools must be given to these cosmo- politans. Nevertheless, problems begin after a few years when program initiation and growth begin to level off and the school system has reached a tolerance level for change. At this point the innovators tend to move to other settings where they can continue to initiate new programs. If trapped in their original district, they tend to treat the necessities of program maintenance with muted enthusiasm.

To continue this scenario using Gouldner's framework and Sergiovanni and Carver's enrichment, special education has also attracted many teachers and administrators who may be classified as "locals." Locals identify with the values of their school system and are deeply committed to the community. Although they may not have intended to do so originally, they are now committed to remain with their particular school system for the rest of their careers. Typically older and tenured, they often identify with an informal peer group of colleagues who came into the organization about the same time they did. They evaluate the present in terms of this earlier time when they were fairly new in the schools. These are the special education administrators who look with fondness on programs they initiated 10 or 20 years ago, and they are frustrated by many of the new requirements of PL 94-142. They long for the "good old days" and view collective bargaining and adversary proceedings as leading to the ruin of special education. Moreover, they prefer in new staff members people having value systems similar to those persons already employed in the district.

Such locals are subtyped by Gouldner as "the true bureaucrats." A director of special education who holds these values doesn't want interference or new ideas from outsiders, thinks primarily about the security of the organization, and worries about loss of power or control. Such administrators formalize procedures and see PL 94-142 as a reason to centralize authority in the name of uniformity. They tend to be viewed by their staffs as obsessed with having a policy to cover every detail, trying to run everything from their office, and employing assistants who have little authority of their own. Locals run special education programs that are stable and highly predictable from year to year.

Obviously, these two descriptions are extreme. Any school system with an exclusively local or an exclusively cosmopolitan approach would likely have problems. Most special education staffs are a combination of both types, although the overall programs usually are slanted in one direction or the other. To attach the labels of liberal and conservative to these organizations might be tempting, but the differences go beyond that. For example, during periods of enrollment stability or decline, most schools strongly favor the local orientation.

Because a local type of organization is easier to operate, the director of special education should not succumb to the path of least resistance and should make sure that some cosmopolitans continue to be brought into the system. If nearly all promotion comes from within the system, the organization can become inbred. A pattern of dependency develops under such a special education director, and authoritarianism can flourish. New ideas and different ways of doing things are approached with much skepticism, if at all. Program evaluation is viewed with disfavor because the results might generate ideas the director doesn't want to hear. At the other extreme, cosmopolitans ought to be made to stay on the scene long enough to deal with the outcomes of some of their "grand schemes." Even though trying to achieve a mix between locals and cosmopolitans in a leadership team can be frustrating, it is worth the pain.

Special education has too brief a history for much confidence to be placed in one set of its techniques and methods. The field is also fertile ground for new discoveries that are ballyhooed as "the answer to education's problems." Until special education has matured and built a better data base to guide decisions, it seems wise to work toward a balance between innovation and tradition.

GET OUT OF THE OFFICE AND INTO THE SCHOOLS

What administrator doesn't lament being "chained to a desk" and want to spend more time in the schools? The general uncertainty about what directors of special education actually do may be all the more reason for them to be highly visible in the schools. As the position was described in Chapters 4 and 5, the director operates principally in a staff role in relation to directors of elementary and secondary programs and to their principals. Actually, the position has always been primarily one of consultation rather than of line responsibility, and maybe it is time just to accept the role and proceed to maximize its impact. Thus, the director will encourage change through persuasion and discussion.

Another major function of the special education administrator might well be as a teacher of significant adults, such as principals. The individual building administrator is, of course, one of the most important adults affecting programs for handicapped children. In the 15 or more school systems for which I have acted as a consultant or evaluator during the past decade, the most frequent suggestion of building administrators and their staffs is that the special education director should come to their schools more often. They want the director to spend time in their buildings (as much as half a day at a time) discussing special education and observing the programs.

Principals frequently say they value an opportunity to share ideas and possible solutions to problems. They report a desire for equal-status discussion rather than dictates delivered from the downtown office. Staff members and teachers say they are not necessarily interested in technical help, but rather in having the director see what they are doing and getting reactions to their efforts and programs. Actually, they are asking for "positive strokes," and they openly concede this.

Principals usually report a preference for interacting one-to-one in their own building instead of attending group meetings of principals in which the director appears on the agenda. My evaluation data from more than 200 principals support the data from the nationwide senior high principalship study (McCleary & Thomson, 1979), which show that effective principals consider district meetings one of their biggest time wasters. Yet, special education directors often appear on the program of the regularly scheduled meetings of principals. A much more effective approach would be to conceive in-service training of principals by special education directors as a one-to-one interaction between equals at the school building level.

Townsend (1970), in *Up the Organization,* gave some funny and at the same time sage advice to corporation executives: "When you get right down to it, one of the most important tasks of a manager is to eliminate his people's excuses for failure. But if you're a paper manager hiding in your office, they may not tell you about the problems only you can solve" (p. 41). I have observed this sort of phenomenon when evaluating leadership styles in Iowa area education agencies. Directors of special education frequently expressed surprise at the views and feelings of staff members in the field. Subsequent leadership staff meetings with the directors and management staff revealed that the managers thought the "boss didn't want to hear bad news." If the directors stayed in their offices, followed the chain of command, and obtained their information about what was going on out in the schools from the management staff, they often received "filtered" information. It is fascinating to sit with such a leadership group, watch the degree of trust grow, and finally see people level with one another about what is really happening. When this occurs, a group is ready to face its problems, honestly consider alternatives, and begin planning for long-term change and improvement. One way for the director to make a "reality check" is, as Townsend suggested, to get out in the field and ask what he or she can do to help.

One goal a leadership group in special education might set for itself is to spend half its time out of the office and in the schools. I observed an interesting variant of this in a midwestern school district in the early 1950s. The superintendent said he would be unavailable for meetings for two weeks because he would be teaching in one of the schools. Each member of his central-office certificated staff was committed to teach for that length of time each year. The purpose, of course, was to provide a kind of renewal and to find out what was really going on in the classroom. When one first proposes this idea to a principal, the initial reaction is usually one of incredulity. But when it becomes a reality, it represents a quantum jump in communication and relationships with the personnel of that school. It goes a long way toward breaking down the stereotyped field comments like "staff people in the downtown office haven't been in a classroom or seen a kid in 10 years!"

A former student of mine wrote this account after such an experience (Monroe, 1975).

During my training to become an administrator, I was told that the director of special education should leave his desk, stop counting paper clips, stop philosophizing on the telephone, and find out what handicapped kids look like. I also learned there were other Howisms,[1] such as, look out for who is shooting at you, find out who has the real bullets, and do not chase every fire truck that goes by. Brimming with such adages, I left my training behind, and at my first job, bushy tailed and full of bursting enthusiasm as a director of special education, I established a policy of substituting for my special education teachers. It had many benefits. For example, I learned the names of selected students in various classrooms and could then have discussions with the teachers regarding their problem students and use the student's first name. The teachers appreciated that, for if I knew the name of the students, I surely knew what was going on, and was probably on top of everything.

One of the classes in which I substituted was for profoundly deaf students. An oral day school for the deaf was part of the special education program and for years there had been a steady accumulation of nonlearning deaf students who caused the oral oriented teachers no end of frustration. My first step was to stop exempting the normal kids from school and the next was to involve everyone in a meeting to discuss what to do. Well, eventually a class for eight nonoral students was established, which was called a multiplex classroom — called that because they must have had a multitude of complex learning problems if they could not learn to speak. All of the multiplex students were profoundly deaf and three were brain injured — maybe. All had been in the oral school for at least six years, were very active, had no speech, and a minimum of language. The day I substituted, my manual alphabet had a workout. Very quickly I learned the signs "stop," "look" (at me), "sit," and "no!"

Thankfully the teacher's aide, a trained interpreter for the deaf, was frequently able to rescue me and I completed the day. Sweaty, near hysterics, sour stomached from the hot dog, Boston bean, strawberry jello, and milk lunch, I returned to the office at four o'clock to check for messages, wanting to put in a full day to demonstrate how long and how hard the administrator works. However, I was forever uncomfortable after that whenever I met the teacher of the multiplex children, remembering how small her salary was and how large her task, both of which I had so comfortably recommended for her.

Another classroom in which I substituted was one for the intermediate educable mentally retarded. The teacher was a retread, the straw hat and tennis shoes type, who was having management and control problems. The twelve students in the

---

[1] Howe, Clifford E., personal communications, Iowa City, Iowa, 1965-1968.

class were the usual variety — mainly boys from lower income families, aggressive, nonverbal, and uninterested in school. Jimmy was their leader, a nonreader whose social skills with the opposite sex were in the gifted range. On the day I substituted, Jimmy, smirking, began by rattling his desk, then progressed to talking in a stage whisper, making faces (at the Administrator, no less), saying "no" to all instructions or requests, and throwing the paper to emphasize his position. He would not work. Remembering positive reinforcement, the theory of which I had so recently reviewed with the teacher of that class, I smiled, then patted a shoulder, ruffled his hair, and finally ignored him. Nothing worked. Since the class was deteriorating anyway, the lesson plans were discarded. We sang songs, had free time, quiet time, early playground time — still Jimmy disrupted.

Finally, the day ended and I dismissed class while keeping Jimmy's row for last. As Jimmy walked by, I held him, smiling. Firmly and reasonably I stated how important it was for him to cooperate, and to accentuate the point, I furiously but lightly kicked him in the seat of the pants. His mother reported the incident to the superintendent before I returned to the office. Thereafter, the boss took great delight in asking me about my management and control techniques with special education students.

Still another adventure was with a preprimary group of seven hyperactive, nonverbal, very low functioning kids aged 6 to 8. Their teacher was a saint —optimistic, quiet, and thoroughly dedicated. She had a great technique in handling the group, which was unusual. If someone were out of his desk, she would look at him, smile, and quietly say, "I like the way Dougie (or whoever) is sitting at his desk." And Dougie would sit. She never had to say it twice. It was magic, and I observed her class several times with fascination. She never raised her voice and could effectively halt the contamination of hyperactivity with a smiling word.

One day she was ill and I substituted. Everything went well: roll call, pledge to the flag, calendar time, job assignments, show and tell. They liked the way I talked, and sat quietly. Come language time in the magic circle, I liked the way they sat listening while only having to put my hand on one or two shoulders, but the fire alarm was not in the lesson plans. It was thoughtlessly fire prevention week and the firemen had come to inspect the school's fire drill. The alarm in our wing of the two storied, wooden structure school stuck out over the preprimary door and was a red trumpeted siren which could make the deaf hear and the crippled walk. The kids jumped, screaming and grabbing each other, then shrieked and began running in circles. Then there was a scramble for the door, and I won, blocking the way. However, while one crowded under my legs, two went around, opening the door as they went. There stood Miss Ruddles, the sixth grade teacher, who was waiting for my class to pass, and who observed while they screeched down the hall and gushed out the doors toward the awaiting, austere, black uniformed firemen who were standing next to a bright, shining red fire truck. Wondering if the kids would stop at the river and whether or not I could use the fire truck to catch them, I followed, grabbing one and then clutching two. I finally got my seven lined up in front of the entire elementary school, smirky teachers, somber faced principal, and all.

The school passed the fire inspection, getting a deficiency for only one room. It was at that point that a call was made to procure a substitute and I left for my paper clips and telephone and later for the rarefied life of a professor, where I tell my students: Get your administrator out of the office and into the classroom. (cover page 3)

109

Special education consultants usually operate out of the central office of a school district or intermediate education agency. They are selected because they are thought to be master teachers. The problem is how to keep needed competencies up to date once consultants have left full-time teaching in the schools (Zinser, 1979). Zinser proposed retraining and renewal through firsthand experience by periodically returning the consultant to the school classroom for a nine-week stint. The concept is being inaugurated in a regional education service agency. An alternate consultant is employed to fill in while the regular consultant is teaching.

In sum, I am arguing for a different set of relationships between directors of special education and the staffs in the schools. Communication, public relations, in-service training, and improved morale can be accomplished in many ways. As Townsend (1970) noted, "What should happen in organizations and what does happen are two different things and about as far apart as they can get . . . The keys that will accomplish this are justice, fun, excellence" (cover).

EVALUATION OF STAFF MEMBERS

Earlier in this chapter, we examined the reliability and validity of teacher appraisal systems as they are used in the initial selection of staff members. Careful initial selection should diminish the likelihood of later conflicts between administrators and teachers over evaluation of the teachers' performance. If a teacher receives high ratings from the administrative staff, all is well and good. But problems arise with that small percentage of staff members (one could argue that it should be greater) who receive low ratings, are considered to need improvement, or may be in the process of being dismissed. This section looks at some of these issues and at changes occurring in the domains of evaluation, tenure, and dismissal.

Impact on Administrative Behavior of
Collective Negotiations and Tenure

The more populous states, and those with strong labor unions, have for years had some form of collective bargaining for teachers. In more rural states, this may be a rather new and unsettling experience for many administrators. Harris et al. (1979) summarized this feeling among administrators in stating: "Of all the changes that have recently taken place in education, many administrators would select collective bargaining with employees as the most dramatic and often the most traumatic" (p. 271). Collective bargaining is undoubtedly with us to stay. Originally fueled by the American Federation of Teachers and now also by the National Education Association, most states currently have laws permitting or requiring collective bargaining for public employees. Special education administrators are no more experienced, and perhaps less so, in this arena of labor-management relations than are other educators. Attitudes of directors run the gamut from Chicken Little's "the sky is falling" pessimism to the optimism of those who see this new era as an opportunity to develop a more humane and fair system of participatory decisionmaking in education.

Special educators are no more and no less involved in collective bargaining than are any others in the school system, but certain issues have particular significance for special education administrators. Some of these are outlined below:

1. Setting limitations on class size. If this were linked, as some have suggested, with some "double counting" for handicapped children who are integrated into regular classes, it could have significant impact on instructional practices and finances for handicapped children. If the number of mildly handicapped pupils who could be integrated into a particular regular classroom were limited because of union contracts, such children might be placed because of a "quota" and not according to the appropriateness of a regular teacher's classroom.

2. Determining what is to be included in the in-service training program. States and school systems are under pressure to provide much more in-service training to implement the PL 94-142 requirements.

3. Setting limits in terms of time, frequency, or length of faculty meetings.

4. Controlling innovations or experimental programs. Attempts to provide special education instruction through team teaching, more use of volunteers and paid aides, or use of federal or state grant money that is guaranteed only for a limited number of years, among other things, could be items of conflict.

5. Limiting parental conferences in terms of frequency, purpose, time, and so on. This seems to work against the intent of parent participation and shared decisionmaking as directed by PL 94-142.

111

6. Designating student discipline procedures. To the considerable extent that special education is involved with socially maladjusted, emotionally disturbed, and chronically disruptive youth in its programs, negotiated discipline procedures could radically affect instructional programs for these pupils. A case is currently on appeal to the Iowa Supreme Court as to whether a learning disabled student can be expelled because of repeated instances of smoking on school grounds. He clearly could be expelled if he were not labeled as handicapped. Also, his smoking and learning disability have been established as unrelated!

7. Mandating referrals of students to other personnel. To the degree that this negotiated item relates to the degree and amount of aberrant behavior to be tolerated in a regular classroom, this could lead to more restrictive settings for handicapped children (self-contained classes, for example).

8. Determining the ratio of support personnel to teaching staff or dictating their modes of operation within the school.

These, then, are some of the items that have already been negotiated, and indications are that the number of negotiable issues will continue to increase each year. Of course, in relation to the special education items enumerated above, one must remember that items contrary to state or federal law cannot be negotiated.

Sergiovanni and Carver (1980) have made some interesting observations about the collective bargaining process in teacher organizations. They presented their data using Herzberg's motivation-hygiene construct and classified staff members as either motivation or hygiene seekers. Motivation seekers are task-oriented, like their work, realize great satisfaction from accomplishments, and have positive feelings toward work and life. Hygiene seekers, on the other hand, are motivated by salary as a way of achieving goals not related to their jobs, do a day's work for a day's pay but no more, and think of their jobs primarily in terms of salary, working conditions, supervision, status, and job security. Using these labels, Sergiovanni and Carver speculated that administrators should:

— open and expand reward systems for motivation seekers;

— avoid pushing hygiene seekers into activities they don't like but that motivation seekers want, such as participatory decisionmaking involving long-range planning, creative problem solving, and curriculum evaluation;

— improve teacher-selection procedures to achieve a balance so that a system doesn't end up with a majority of low-commitment hygiene seekers; and

— avoid elevating hygiene seekers to administrative or supervisory positions.

Whether or not one agrees with Herzberg's formulations, the interpretations of characteristics related to organization success as presented by Sergiovanni and Carver merit consideration.

Evaluation Integrated into the Total System

Except for special purpose organizations such as intermediate units or cooperatives that employ only special education personnel, teacher evaluation procedures are similar for the entire professional staff in a school system. But this system of single evaluation is being challenged by some who think it has created problems in personnel evaluation. Glass (1974) attributed past failures to rate teacher behavior reliably to the vague terms that have been used, such as "openness," "professional manner," or "sensitivity." He proposed that no teacher behavior be included in rating scales until we can demonstrate that it can be reliably observed and that it is related to desired pupil learning, either cognitive or affective. Glass argued against using either standardized achievement tests of pupils or performance tests of teaching effectiveness as ways to evaluate teachers. He based the objection to using standardized tests in this way on reviews of past studies that showed the approach had contributed little. His proposal to include as ratable behaviors only those characteristics known to make a difference could mean that teachers of different subjects or different age levels would not be evaluated on the same things.

A question special education administrators will have to address is whether significantly different skills and behaviors are required for teaching handicapped children as compared to teaching regular classes. Regular education has yielded little research evidence to document competencies that really make a difference in student learning, and special education has produced even less evidence. So special educators would probably be judicious in evaluating teacher effectiveness as regular educators do unless it is demonstrated at some point that different behaviors are important for teachers of handicapped learners.

Shavelson and Atwood (1977) reported some consistent effectiveness of teachers' skills across various types of students, although none of the students was identified as handicapped. Two studies (Wallen, 1968; Campbell, 1972) used subjects from the inner city and/or with low achievement levels. But looking at the stability of teacher behavior over time and type of student, both Wallen and Campbell found that most behavior is not consistent from lesson to lesson. Global ratings like "warm and friendly" seem to be the most stable, which is interesting because that has been the direction personnel rating systems have taken in the past. Only four clusters of teacher behavior remained fairly stable: teacher presentation, positive and neutral feedback, probing, and direct teacher control (classroom management). Perhaps the best special education can do right now is look for ways to include these four variables in observation systems used to evaluate teachers.

Kounin (1977) reported on some work that focused on teachers' management of groups of children within their classrooms, emphasizing classroom discipline techniques. What works appears to depend partly on the setting in which it occurs. Using the term *desist* to designate a teacher doing something to stop a behavior, Kounin found that desists effective in a regular classroom were not equally useful if applied at home, in an experimental classroom, or in a camp setting. Other results Kounin reported that should be of interest to special educators related to managerial techniques effective for emotionally disturbed children mainstreamed in regular classes. These included handling two things simultaneously and communicating a knowledge of what is going on; managing movement during recitations and transition periods; maintaining everyone's focus of attention; and managing variety and challenge.

How to Fire Someone

Employers, and educators in particular, would rather not deal with the issue of dismissing personnel. It is unpleasant, can be threatening to all involved, and is time consuming. In an adversary hearing, all the weaknesses of the present teacher evaluation practices are held up to the light for inspection. Educators like to believe that dismissal will be rarely necessary if we tighten up the initial selection practices and provide good in-service training procedures to improve instruction. Collective bargaining contracts increasingly stipulate procedures that must be followed for assignment, transfer, and dismissal of employees. A fairly extensive set of due process steps is now required. All these factors tend to cause an administrator to conclude that the better part of valor is to "live with it" rather than institute dismissal proceedings against an employee who is judged marginal or even flatly incompetent.

We all know, though, that dismissing a teacher or other professional employee is occasionally necessary. To do otherwise is to abdicate the role of leadership and accountability expected of administrators by their colleagues, the board of education, and the community. In dealing with the prospect of dismissing someone, special education administrators might consider the following suggestions:

1. Become completely familiar with every detail of due process in the state, school system, and master contract as it relates to dismissal of employees. Follow it to the letter. When dismissal procedures are overturned, the reason most often is sloppy adherence to due process rights, such as missing notification deadlines and so on.

2. Be certain that the employee is not in a situation in which no one could succeed. Sometimes a particular constellation of children and circumstances in a classroom produces a nearly impossible situation. Special education classes for the emotionally disturbed, chronically disruptive, or socially maladjusted have been prime sites for such situations in the past.

3. Keep an open file, one to which the employee has access. Make sure material included is factual and signed with dates. Don't write complimentary evaluations unless they are warranted. Encourage persons who complain about the employee to put it in writing.

4. Involve several observers in the evaluation process. This should include the principal, special education director, and his or her boss. Getting the latter involved is important, because the special education director will need his or her support before the process of dismissal is over.

5. Hold the employee to whatever the requirements are for the position. Document any variance from the job description, including absences and tardiness, as well as the whole range of instructional processes subject to evaluation in the system. Generally, transferring the employee because of poor performance is not a good idea. This wastes time and requires starting the whole procedure over in a new setting and with a different principal. Some due process procedure or master contracts, however, may require a transfer, and if that is the case, of course it should be done.

6.   Have staff members — ones who are competent to pinpoint the major problems and to suggest and demonstrate solutions — observe and work with the employee in question. Be certain that the following things are done:

a. Schedule the observation in advance, arrive on time, and observe the entire activity. The employee deserves a fair and reasonably lengthy observation. Some research suggests that a minimum of 120 to 150 minutes a week are required to obtain an adequate sample of a teacher's behavior.

b. Write up the results of the observation immediately, meet with the employee to discuss it, and both sign the written document. If the employee disagrees with the report, he or she should sign it acknowledging that he or she has read it but does not agree.

c. Don't begin the conference with the typical education approach of a series of compliments unless they are truly warranted.

d. Specify shortcomings and be explicit about suggestions for improvement.

e. Set a fairly short time for accomplishing agreed-upon changes and try to get the employee to agree to this.

f. Decide upon the next observation time.

g. Observe the employee in different job functions and at different times of the day and week.

h. Don't drop in for informal, unannounced visits, and don't socialize with the employee.

7.   Continue the observation-evaluation-conference process, putting outcomes in writing, signed and dated.

8.   Don't make any threats that can't be backed up by the system.

9.   If the employee offers to resign, have him or her put it in writing immediately and sign it. Do not make a commitment as to whether or not the resignation will be accepted, but as soon as the resignation is tendered, take it to superiors and the board with a recommendation for

acceptance. Don't stand on the formality of allowing the employee to complete the contract for the year; let the employee quit immediately.

10. If the employee opts to take the dismissal through administrative hearings and civil court action, do not back down; carry it through to the end.

The Exit Interview as an Organizational Evaluation Practice

Answers to the question, "Why do employees leave your organization?" should provide useful information to special education administrators. The exit interview has been widely used in industry for years (French, 1970). Companies utilizing this technique have experimented with interviewing employees not only when they are leaving but also at some time after they have left. Reviewing the literature in education administration leads one to believe that this is less common in schools, if infrequent discussion of the topic is an indicator.

Because most special education personnel are in short supply and will continue to be so for at least the next few years, directors should be concerned about the rate of and reasons for turnover as indicators of potential problems in an organization. Having a competent staff member decide to leave because the job holds no more challenge is an expensive and wasteful situation.

To develop a systematic procedure for evaluating one's organization, using exit interviews as one variable, the following questions should be considered.

1. *Who will do the exit interview?* Usually this is done by a member of the personnel department who does not have a direct investment in the employee's work. Someone in the central office special education unit also could do it if the employee is identified with a specific school attendance site. Otherwise, objectivity is contaminated by what the employee is willing to reveal and by the defensiveness of the central-office interviewer.

2. *How should the interview be structured?* Determining what information is truly useful is plagued with some of the same problems discussed earlier in this chapter in relation to teacher evaluation. Vague, general questions probably won't elicit much. Unless the employee already has another job, he or she may not want to be too frank in

disclosing the real reasons for leaving. The importance of having a good recommendation from one's previous employer is well recognized. Two questions that have proved useful to me are: Would you recommend this district to a colleague as a place to work? What are some things this district could have done to increase your interest in continuing to work here?

3. *When should the exit interview be done?* Sound information to answer this question is not available, but certain evidence suggests that a follow-up some time after the employee has left (six months or a year, for example) may produce information that is more objective and useful for an organization. The emotionality that can manifest itself at the time of departure will have waned, and more candid responses are possible because the ex-employee doesn't have to worry about the effect on his or her chances for the next position. I have had some success in using a structured interview format via long-distance telephone calls.

In summary, a certain amount of turnover in an organization is inevitable. Some turnover is healthy in that it provides an opportunity to bring in staff people with new ideas and perspectives. Staff members do leave for legitimate reasons unrelated to the organizational climate, such as spouse transfer, health conditions, promotion not available within the existing district, and so on. And a number of superintendents have indicated particular difficulty in keeping new special education staff during the first few years of their careers. I believe, however, that too little attention is given to staff turnover. In special education, with its shortage of personnel, it is particularly important not only to work to get the best individuals available but to keep them by paying attention to ways to provide job enrichment.

REFERENCES

Arp, M. N. *Special education teacher evaluation.* Paper prepared for Seminar: Current Issues in Special Education, Division of Special Education, University of Iowa, May 1978.

Borich, G. D. *The appraisal of teaching: Concepts and process.* Reading, MA: Addison-Wesley Publishing Co., 1977.

Brown, L. F. The special class: Some aspects for special educators to ponder. *Education & Training of the Mentally Retarded,* 1968, *3*(1), 11-16.

Campbell, J. R. A longitudinal study in the stability of teachers' verbal behavior. *Science Education*, 1972, *56*(1), 89-96.

French, W. *The personnel management process: Human resources administration*. Boston: Houghton-Mifflin, 1970.

Glass, G. V. A review of three methods of determining teacher effectiveness. In H. J. Walberg (Ed.), *Evaluating educational performance*. Berkeley, CA: McCutchan Publishing, 1974.

Goldstein, H., Moss, J., & Jordan, L. *The efficacy of special class training on the development of mentally retarded children* (Cooperative Research Project No. 619). Urbana, IL: Institute for Research on Exceptional Children, 1965.

Gouldner, A. W. Toward an analysis of latent social roles, I and II. *Administrative Science Quarterly*, 1957, *2*; 1958, *3*. As summarized by T. J. Sergiovanni & F. D. Carver in *The new school executive: A theory of administration* (2nd ed.). New York: Harper & Row, 1980.

Harris, B. M., McIntyre, K. E., Littleton, V. C., & Long, D. G. *Personnel administration in education: Leadership for instructional improvement*. Boston: Allyn & Bacon, 1979.

Herzberg, F., Mausner, B., & Snyderman, B. *The motivation to work*. New York: John Wiley, 1959.

Howe, C. E. *A cost projection for special education funding in the state of Iowa; 1975-76 through 1985-86*. Iowa City: University of Iowa College of Education, 1978.

Kounin, J. S. *Discipline and group management in classrooms*. Huntington, NY: Robert E. Kreiger Publishing Co., 1977.

McCleary, L. E., & Thomson, S. D. *The senior high school principalship. Volume 3. The summary report*. Reston, VA: National Association of Secondary School Principals, 1979.

Monroe, J. D. On an administrator as a classroom teacher. *Teaching Exceptional Children*, Winter 1975, *7*(2), cover 3.

Rosenshine, B. Review of teaching variables and student achievement. In G. D. Borich, *The appraisal of teaching: Concepts and process*. Reading, MA: Addison-Wesley Publishing Co., 1977.

Sergiovanni, T. J. Factors which affect satisfaction and dissatisfaction of teachers. *Journal of Educational Administration*, 1967, *5*, 66-82.

Sergiovanni, T. J., & Carver, F. D. *The new school executive: A theory of administration*. New York: Harper & Row, 1980.

Shavelson, R., & Atwood, N. Generalizability of measures of teaching process. In G. D. Borich, *The appraisal of teaching: Concepts and process*. Reading, MA: Addison-Wesley Publishing Co., 1977.

Townsend, R. *Up the organization: How to stop the corporation from stifling people and strangling profits.* New York: Fawcett World Library, 1970.

Wallen, N. E. *Sausalito teacher education project: Annual report.* San Francisco: San Francisco State College, 1969.

Zinser, C. R. *Retraining and renewal of special education consultants.* Project proposal, Area Education Agency 15, Ottumwa, IA, 1979.

7

Evaluation of
Special Education Programs

Evaluation has progressed to a point at which at least we aren't spending most of our time arguing about what it is and how it can be differentiated from other forms of research (Guttentag & Saar, 1977). The accountability movement, grant funding requirements, and a questioning public have emphasized the need to have better data for making decisions about program alternatives. Passage of PL 94-142 and its accompanying regulations mandate that each state funded under this act must provide for evaluation procedures that ensure the effectiveness of educational programs for handicapped children (including evaluation of individualized educational programs). Evaluation must be done at least annually.

Whelan (1979) defined evaluation as follows:

> Evaluation is a set of observable, sequential procedures used to determine if a planned program is functioning below, at, or above expectations. Proper application of evaluation procedures enables detection of gaps between what is and what should be. These gaps may not be negative, in that a program can exceed planned objectives — a positive gap. The word *program* can be used to refer to an administrative group, an entire classroom, or a piece of instructional material used with only one child. Program evaluation is a varying and critical responsibility for all educators who arrange means to ends. The classroom teacher, the supervisor, and the administrator cannot avoid evaluation. They can only determine to do it well or poorly. Doing it poorly victimizes children; doing it well benefits children. (p. 349)

Evaluation involves setting a standard that a person or a program is expected to meet. Determining this benchmark and ways to measure it represent one of the largest challenges in special education. Despite the ambiguities involved, several models focusing on evaluation in education have promise for evaluation of special education programs.

EVALUATION MODELS

CIPP Model

The CIPP model was developed by Phi Delta Kappa's Research and Advisory Committee under the authorship of Stufflebeam, Foley, Gephart, Guba, Hammond, Merriman, and Provus (1971). It views the components of evaluation as *context, input, process,* and *product* (CIPP). The outcomes of evaluation are seen principally as providing useful information for making decisions about program alternatives.

MacMillan and Semmel (1977) applied the CIPP model to special education, specifically to mainstreaming handicapped children, as follows.

1. *Context evaluation.* The focus is on specifying objectives to be realized. Agreement must be reached, in this case, about the anticipated outcomes of mainstreaming handicapped children in regular classes. Perspectives may differ as to what is important, "as mainstreaming is of interest to many persons and groups — administrators, teachers, parents, school boards, legislators, child advocate groups, researchers, and others —each of whom may be interested in different kinds of information" (p. 8).

2. *Input evaluation.* The purpose is to consider alternative ways of using resources to achieve objectives of the program. Input evaluation as it relates to mainstreaming might be concerned with the costs of various staffing patterns, with in-service needs of regular teachers, and with estimating costs for the program.

3. *Process evaluation.* The major concern is with monitoring the ongoing program on the basis of the input evaluation to see whether it is achieving the objectives set. Process evaluation provides a description and record of what is happening and is intended to give information to decisionmakers if changes need to be made. If certain objectives selected for the mainstreaming program are not being achieved, attention can be given immediately to the problem and other alternatives tried.

4. *Product evaluation.* The focus is on outcomes of the activity both during and at the end of the project. Although many outcomes could be measured, major ones should relate to change data for handicapped or regular students.

Discrepancy Evaluation Model (DEM)

The DEM views evaluation in a more restrictive light than does the CIPP formulation. It makes a distinction between the program and the evaluation function, with evaluation determining the extent to which the standards have been met (Provus, 1971). Brinkerhoff (1979) has applied the DEM to special education programs and differentiated the scope of local evaluation activities from program operations, as shown in Figure 7.

Brinkerhoff proposed four major purposes of evaluation:

1. To clarify and communicate the expectations, or standards, for the program;

2. To document operation of the program, particularly those phases of operation requiring legal compliance;

3. To assess the impact of the program on its intended recipients; and

4. To provide information to revise and improve the program. (p. 356)

This model uses an input-process-output format to describe each component. It has been used rather extensively by the Office of Special Education and Rehabilitative Services in evaluating personnel preparation programs.

FIGURE 7
Program Operations/Evaluation Responsibilities

Program Operation ↓	Evaluation Responsibility ↓
Determine standards for operating procedures and goals	Explicate program standards
Organize staff and resources	Document resources actually allocated
Identify and select the treatment population	Document and verify characteristics of treatment population selected
Deliver the treatment program	Document program activities actually delivered
Effect changes in the treated population	Assess changes in the treated population

Source: Brinkerhoff (1979).

Peer Review Evaluation Model

Approaches long used by various accrediting associations throughout the country are included in the peer evaluation model. It provides criteria, but the major work is done by the schools themselves through a self-study approach. When this is completed, a visiting team of professional peers observes for a few days, studies data collected in the self-study, interviews staff members, and renders judgments about the quality of the program. The self-study aspect is often seen as the major strength of this technique, because a school and community that invest enough of themselves to undertake the evaluation will likely be willing to make and implement decisions for improvement.

Which of these evaluation models a special education administrator selects is a matter of choice, depending on the purpose of the effort. Another consideration should be the level (local, regional, state, or national) at which the evaluation is being conducted. Stufflebeam et al. (1971) pointed out that different techniques and purposes are appropriate for different administrative levels. Whereas every child may be included in a building-level evaluation, this would be inappropriate at the state or national level. Sampling becomes an important cost-efficiency consideration in large programs or at the state and national level. Data collected at the local level must be aggregated into a summary form at higher levels, and this can be a problem. The next sections outline some techniques used at various levels and for different purposes.

COMPLIANCE MONITORING

Ever since PL 94-142 was passed in 1975, most directors of special education have been occupied with revising their procedures so as to be in compliance. Evaluation usually takes the form of checks — lists prepared to determine if the agency has met all of the due process and other requirements contained in the federal and state legislation. Monitoring, then, requires a "yes" or "no" response to each item. To be in compliance, a district or intermediate unit must earn a "yes" for each question included. Few, if any, currently meet this standard.

A district, one must remember, can meet all due process requirements and still not have an effective program for a handicapped child. Compliance evaluation usually doesn't convey much, if anything, about children's progress and performance. The presumption is, and legitimately so, that the likelihood of effective programming is increased if all the process evaluation checkpoints indicate legal compliance. But to be in compliance, a district must have a clear standard to meet. And part of the current frustration with implementing PL 94-142 relates to setting standards for concepts like "appropriate education" and "least restrictive environment" (Brinkerhoff, 1979). These and other partially defined and controversial ideas are common in new programs that undertake to make sweeping changes.

The Office of Special Education and Rehabilitative Services is responsible for evaluating and monitoring compliance with PL 94-142. Four components are included in its monitoring procedures (*Progress Toward a Free Appropriate Public Education*, 1979).

1. *Review of each state's annual program plan.* This plan must be received and approved by the commissioner of education before any funds are awarded to the state.

2. *Program administrative review.* The Office conducts on-site observations in at least half the states and territories each year. Table 5 lists the 30 variables checked in the 1977-78 program review.

3. *Complaint management system.* The Office acts on allegations that handicapped children are not receiving a free, appropriate public education and tries to resolve conflicts between laws of the various states and PL 94-142.

4. *Waiver procedures.* If a state can document that all handicapped children have a free, appropriate public education available to them, a waiver can be requested. If the waiver is granted by the commissioner of education, part of the PL 94-142 funds can be used to supplant local and state effort. Otherwise, the law requires that at least 75 percent of the funds go directly to local school districts and be used to supplement and not supplant state or local funds. The Massachusetts Department of Education is the first state to have made such a request.

PROGRAM OUTCOME EVALUATION

Outcome evaluation techniques focus on what actually happened and the factors to which any changes can be attributed. These are difficult questions in education evaluation and particularly so in special education. The most obvious outcome or product variables to consider are those that measure changes in pupil growth — affective, behavioral, and cognitive — over time. As always, the two major concerns are in the reliability and validity of measurements used. This section reviews several approaches to outcome evaluation; some are based on actual pupil change and others are more concerned with subjective perceptions and consumer satisfaction.

TABLE 5
Program Administrative Review Variables

1. Submission of annual program plan	18. Child count
2. Right to education policy	19. Administration of funds by SEA
3. Full education opportunity goal	20. Administration of funds by LEA
4. Priorities	21. State advisory panel
5. Child identification, location, and evaluation	22. State agency eligibility to participate under PL 89-313
6. Individualized education program	23. Flexibility of children to receive benefits
7. Procedural safeguards	24. Children transferred to LEAs from state-operated programs
8. Confidentiality	25. Measurable project goals and objectives
9. Least restrictive environment	26. Evaluation of education achievement of participating children
10. Protection in evaluation procedures	27. Project monitoring and technical assistance by SEA
11. Comprehensive system of personnel development	28. Dissemination of project findings
12. Participation of private school children	29. Distribution of funds among eligible schools and children
13. Placement in private school	30. Use of funds to supplement and not supplant
14. SEA responsibility for all educational programs	
15. Program monitoring	
16. Program evaluation	
17. Reporting	

Source: *Progress Toward a Free Appropriate Public Education* (1979).

Longitudinal Approaches to Evaluation

In my opinion, longitudinal designs based on observing handicapped persons in natural settings should be given increased importance in evaluating special education programs. It often seems that one of the major functions of schools is to prepare its students merely to go to school some more. Elementary schools prepare students for junior high, junior highs for senior high, and senior high schools for college. The argument could be extended further to graduate and professional schools.

One frequent measurement of a high school's success is how well its graduates do in college. But for the majority of handicapped children, and perhaps even for many regular high school students, success in formal schooling beyond high school is an inappropriate criterion. A primary goal of most secondary school programs for the mildly handicapped is to produce a person who is independent and employable at graduation from high school. Thus, a major focus of evaluation data should be on the adjustment and functioning of the handicapped as adults in the world and not on their scores on achievement tests or college entrance exams.

Although schools today consider their responsibility for the handicapped complete when these students graduate from high school or reach 21 years of age, evaluations of program effects should be longitudinal and follow them in their life adjustments as adults. Admittedly, such studies are confounded by all sorts of intervening variables over which the school has no control. Attributing students' relative success or failure as adults solely to components of the school program is hazardous. But regardless of these difficulties, evaluating handicapped children and adults on a long-term basis makes more sense than the one-time cross-sectional approaches that are now used so often.

Longitudinal designs are used infrequently even though such approaches to studying child development appear to have high promise, according to Gallagher, Ramey, Haskins, and Finkelstein (1976). These authors discussed longitudinal inquiry as it relates to the understanding of child development and the impact of preschool intervention programs, but the same arguments hold for older handicapped children. Gallagher et al. reviewed 2,561 studies of child psychology and found that fewer than 5 percent could be classified as longitudinal. They concluded that "the longitudinal design is used infrequently by social scientists interested in behavior development. Moreover, even when it is used, the dependent measures reported tend to be of relatively constricted types, and almost never included the emergence of, changes in, or relationships between naturally occurring behaviors" (p. 170).

Gallagher and his associates proposed increased use of the longitudinal approach in the study of child development and suggested that increased attention be given to such things as the types of data to be collected. More attention must be paid to observing naturally occurring behaviors in the child's environment. Thus, evaluation of preschool programs might examine things like whether a child with preschool experience, as compared to a child without it, can follow instructions better in elementary school, is more task oriented, and gets along better with his or her classmates. These are the kinds of variables to evaluate, rather than whether the child showed a change in IQ.

Cronbach's presidential address to the American Psychological Association in 1974 should have a sobering effect on those engaging in evaluation activities (1975). In reviewing Aptitude x Treatment interactions as related to instruction, he pointed to inconsistent findings, weak generalizations, and unidentified interactions. Instead of trying to be certain that our treatment is correct, he said, we should use our heads and monitor progress, changing the treatment on the basis of our observations instead of continuing with a fixed program on the basis of a generalization from prior experience with other persons or in other locales.

The usual research approaches create problems in evaluating programs for handicapped children. For one thing, control groups will be increasingly difficult to come by, since federal law requires an appropriate program for all handicapped children. One type of "treatment program" might be compared with another, but even this invites difficulties because of practices such as the experimental use of random assignment of subjects. Parents' rights to help design and to approve programs for their children do not mesh well with the idea of a random determination as to whether a child will be assigned to program A or program B. The concept of individualized education programs actually runs counter to most persons' understanding of such two-group statistical treatment.

Because of the emphasis on individual programs in special education, whether actual or theoretical, using the child as his or her own control has possibilities. The usual approach includes the pretest, the program or treatment, and the posttest. The common pattern is to test the child at the beginning and at the end of the school year. The major drawback of using this approach with handicapped children is that the change is often quite small; many of these studies show no significant differences. An advantage of the longitudinal evaluation approach is its ability to collect data on children at specific intervals (say each year) and thus to have data points for a period of years. This expanded time frame makes it easier to detect and evaluate changes.

Longitudinal evaluation should seek to measure factors that are direct and unambiguous. For mildly handicapped adults, meaningful measurements could include wages, days worked during a year, length of time holding a job, degree of independent living, law violations, use of leisure time, and other verifiable accounts of adult adjustment. For the more severely handicapped or developmentally disabled, evaluation of adult adjustment might take the form of observing the person against or within the degree of program restriction (Mueller, 1979). As applied to vocational training, for example, the work activity center is the most restrictive. Less restrictive environments in the hierarchy include the sheltered workshop, the work station in industry, and finally competitive employment. A series of gradated experiences in living arrangements could also be assessed with institutionalization representing the most restrictive environment and independent living being the least restrictive. Emphasis would be placed on controlled observation in natural settings over an extended time.

Such an approach would be more likely to portray accurately the actual circumstance of a handicapped person and to provide more reliable information. Although longitudinal evaluation may still not answer the question "why," it should be able to give some data on the "what." Many of the present approaches using various types of tests don't offer very good answers even to the "what."

Single-Subject Approach to Evaluation

In many ways, the individualized education program (IEP) required by PL 94-142 naturally lends itself to a single-subject design of evaluation for handicapped children. With the exception of special educators trained at places like the universities of Kansas, Washington, or Oregon, most have little formal training in the multiple-baseline single-subject research methods. Our research or evaluation training has been directed largely toward group comparative analysis designs. Guralnick (1978) argued that the use of these standard designs is not appropriate for much of special education, at least not at this time, because the relevant variables in handicapped children have not really been identified, nor have the most effective teaching approaches. What ordinary group designs tend to do is "cover up" or "wash out" treatments that may be effective for some — but not all — of the children in the group.

A cornerstone of the present belief system in special education is that different handicapped children learn in different ways. I think this is more rhetoric than fact at present, since the usual group design employs a single "treatment" for the entire group. The advantage of the single-subject design is that it is applied to one child. Such designs also lend themelves more readily than do group designs to changes in procedures throughout the course of the experiment. The major promise of the single-subject design for evaluation of special education programs lies, then, in its flexibility and in its consonance with the individualized education concept.

A brief explanation of single-subject multiple-baseline designs as used in applied behavior analysis may help sharpen the issue. In an article in the *Journal of Learning Disabilities,* Keogh (1977) proposed that for the field to make substantial progress, more focus must be placed on real behavior in the classroom and in natural settings, and more descriptive data must be collected that can be used in decisionmaking. The single-subject design accommodates some of these factors, as follows (Baer, 1977; Guralnick, 1978):

1. Baseline data are collected on several behaviors of one child over time, until the data seem stable. At this point, some teaching strategy or behavior modification technique is introduced and applied to one of the behaviors on which the baseline data were collected.

2. Changes in behavior are systematically collected. When the change reaches criterion, the strategy is applied to the second behavior and the process is repeated.

3. To increase confidence, these changes should occur only when the treatment is being applied. The other behaviors should stay about the same until the treatment is applied to them.

4. If the approach used doesn't produce the desired change, these data are used to confirm the need to try something else and to make similar recordings of results.

5. To increase confidence in a procedure that works with one handicapped child, the procedure is applied to additional children to see if similar results are obtained. This will give information on the generalizability of the technique.

6. Another variant is to measure the same behavior across different individuals at the same time to see if consistent changes in behavior or performance are noted.

Walker and Hops (1976) extended techniques for securing baseline information by developing methods to obtain normative peer observation data. They noted that multiple criteria are usually set to evaluate change but that there is often no standard against which to set objectives. So, obtaining normative observation data on the handicapped child's peers at the same time such data are being collected on the target child provides one answer. Using behavior disordered children with inappropriate classroom behavior as the targets, observations are made of these children and of their peers at successive 6-second intervals. The results provide a record of the proportion of appropriate classroom behavior for the handicapped children as well as an average for the same behaviors for their regular classmates. Such an approach allows determination of whether the behavior of the handicapped children is or is not within the normal limits for regular children in the same setting. The procedure adds to methodology developed in applied behavior analysis by permitting comparison of behavior at different times and in different settings to see if it remains within normal limits.

One of the difficulties with collecting observation data in natural settings is the time it takes, both in recording the observations and in analyzing the data on individual children. To deal with this, Fitzgerald and others (1979) used an electronic-memory data collector to record data on emotionally disturbed children and their normal peers. This portable, desk-size unit is plugged directly into a computer system. Advantages include speed of recording, versatility in types of data that can be handled, reduction of observer fatigue, and rapid data analysis.

Goal Attainment Scaling (GAS)

Fitzgerald and I have reported on the possibilities of using GAS as a tool in evaluating programs for handicapped children. Adapting work originally done by Kiresuk and Sherman (1968) in the field of mental health, we applied the technique to individual handicapped children (Howe & Fitzgerald, 1977).

> Goal Attainment Scaling can be viewed as a logical evaluation approach for individualized programs using instructional objectives, prescriptive teaching, and behavior charting methods. It asks the teacher to predict the results for a specified future-time and then provides a simple way of scoring actual outcomes. The method concentrates on the major priorities thought important for each child, and can handle different priorities for different children. (p. 5)

Predictions for levels of performance are written to conform to the expected level of success and also for a less-than-expected level and a more-than-expected level. Actual achievement levels are then assigned numerical scores.

A degree of controversy continues to surround GAS. Requirements for the IEP came along at about the time we introduced GAS as an evaluation tool, and teachers viewed the IEP and GAS as two different sets of forms they would have to complete. Teachers are used to setting objectives or levels of attainment they expect their children to reach, but they seem reluctant to write predictions that are higher or lower than their expected outcomes. In addition, valid objections can be raised about the legitimacy of using the numerical scaling summaries, particularly if the scores of different children are being aggregated as a measurement for program evaluation.

Calsyn and Davidson (1978) criticized GAS as an evaluation technique on the basis of considerable variability in the content of the scales when different goal setters determine these scales. They felt that GAS lacked some necessary psychometric qualities, particularly in the area of validity. They recommended that since much more work needs to be done on GAS, it should not currently be used in isolation as the sole instrument in program evaluation.

On the other hand, Carr (1979) supported GAS as a useful tool for evaluating the progress of handicapped children. He argued that it provides for mutual determination of goals through team input, which increases the likelihood that the goals selected will be worthwhile. Relative weighting permits prioritizing of the various goals. Alternative methods of calculating gains are presented based on an improvement or progress score. Carr believed the scores could be aggregated and provide a measure of program evaluation.

CONSUMER SATISFACTION IN EVALUATION

Obviously, the primary recipient of special education services is the handicapped child, yet we behave as though most handicapped persons don't know what is best for them. Thus, the major consumers of special education are rarely asked to evaluate the programs in which they are enrolled. Perhaps this attitude is a carryover from the field of law, wherein children are considered incompetent to make legally binding decisions until the day they magically become adults because of chronological age. Although an analogous posture may be justifiable for the more severely handicapped, mildly handicapped adolescents could well have something useful to contribute to the evaluation of their programs.

Parents as Evaluators

If handicapped children are not to be evaluators of their own programs, at least their parents seemingly should be. A review of the literature, however, yields almost nothing related to organized parental evaluation of their children's programs. PL 94-142 indirectly addresses the issue as it relates to multidisciplinary staffings and to the writing and review of IEPs, in that parents are to provide input and to agree with decisions made. But the closest thing to real evaluation being done by parents is the annual review of their children's IEPs.

We behave as though parents are not competent to contribute to the evaluation of their children's programs. This phenomenon is not restricted to programs for the handicapped or even to education. Generally, the role of evaluation is ascribed to professionals or "experts" in our society. For example, the field of medicine does not encourage individual decisions by the patient. The view is that "the doctor knows best" — or "the school knows best." Of course, this is by definition one characteristic of the professional. In special education, the lack of involvement by parents may also relate to the fact that a disproportionate number do have lower levels of education themselves and come from lower socioeconomic backgrounds. Parents from lower social classes tend to view schools differently than do assertive parents from upper-middle-class backgrounds, who may better understand the nature and use of power and, accordingly, make their opinions known to school administrators and school boards.

The point of all this is that special education administrators might be well advised to incorporate parental participation as a formal element of the program evaluation system. To offer fair opportunity for all parents of handicapped children, the director must take the initiative. This is critical if parents who are poor and come from disadvantaged backgrounds are to be heard from.

Exit Interviews with Students and Parents

One checkpoint for program evaluation should be the departure of the handicapped student from the special education program. Graduating, receiving certification of program completion, dropping out, or being kicked out each represent a termination of one phase of the handicapped person's life. Evaluation data at this point might take the form of responses to a structured interview. For the majority, these consumer satisfaction data should be collected directly from the handicapped person. In some cases, the parents may have to provide the information. In any case, parents should be interviewed as well.

STAFF/TEACHER EVALUATION OF THE ORGANIZATION

Although the procedure described in the next few pages is not outcome-oriented in the usual sense of the term, it does focus on the management style of the organization as perceived by the staff. It could be characterized as a type of needs assessment. Its purposes are to identify specific or potential problem areas, to seek staff input regarding solution of problems, and to provide data to the special education management team as to how subordinates view the leadership style of the organization. This is intended to promote interest in participatory decisionmaking. The procedure provides for staff input about their perceptions of immediate supervisors as well as the director of special education. Hence, a measurement of employee satisfaction or staff morale is gained. Figure 8 summarizes the major steps in this type of program evaluation. The procedure has been used principally with area education agencies but has also been applied in school districts.

Several observations of this approach's results can be noted since its use was first reported (Howe & Fitzgerald, 1977). Staff members have tended to be extremely interested in providing input through the questionnaire and subsequent structured interviews. Response rates have averaged from 77 to 96 percent with a single mailing and with no follow-up reminders. Such a return rate is extremely high and considerably exceeds that of the average questionnaire approach, which generates returns of from 50 to 70 percent. Moreover, subsequent structured interviews have consistently validated the issues and problems generated by the questionnaire. This seems to be so well established that the focus of the structured interviews could be shifted to exploring strategies and suggestions for problem resolution.

An example of the topics addressed in a current evaluation is given in the appendix at the end of this chapter.

This particular evaluation is being conducted in an area education agency with 129 special education employees (125 responded to the questionnaire). The management staff decided they were interested in the responses of eight different subgroups including support personnel plus some staff in low-incidence programs run directly by the agency. Analysis is to be done for each group and overall. The groups are:

1. school psychologists and social workers;

2. speech and language clinicians;

3. special education consultants;

FIGURE 8
Major Activities in Staff Evaluation of a Special Education Organization

Step	Persons Involved	Activity
1	Central staff leadership/ management team and evaluator (N = 5 to 10)	Group discussion with evaluator to develop trust; consider risk-taking; outline procedures; agree to proceed (2 to 4 hours)
	↓　　↓	↓　　↓
2	Individual supervisors and their staff members	Discussion of concept; assess degree of interest; generate questions to be asked on questionnaire
	↓　　↓	↓　　↓
3	Central staff team and evaluator	Determine questions to be asked and complete questionnaire
	↓　　↓	↓　　↓
4	Special education staff, including secretaries (N = 75 to 150)	Complete questionnaire
	↓　　↓	↓　　↓
5	Evaluator	Analyzes data; uses SPSS format that generates means, standard deviations, and percentages by group and overall
	↓　　↓	↓　　↓

Figure 8 (continued)

Step	Persons Involved	Activity
6	Central staff team and evaluator	Review data; determine major problems; resolve disagreements among subgroups; construct structured interview form to validate these concerns
	↓ ↓	↓ ↓
7	Team of peers from other districts or area education agencies (N = 5 to 7)	
	Stratified random sample of respondents; may include superintendents and school board members	Structured interview of respondents to validate issues generated from questionnaire and to solicit suggestions and ideas for improvement (N ≈ 50)
	↓ ↓	↓ ↓
8	Evaluator/peer review team/central staff team	Exit interview to review tentative findings from structured interviews
	↓ ↓	↓ ↓
9	Evaluator	Reviews all data and writes a report *within one week*
	↓ ↓	↓ ↓
10	Central staff team and evaluator	Review report and discuss findings
	↓ ↓	↓ ↓

Figure 8 (continued)

Step	Persons Involved	Activity
11	Director of special education	Communicates findings to all staff members and outlines strategies and timelines to deal with problems identified
12	Central staff leadership/ management team and evaluator	Repeat entire process in about three years and compare responses as a way of assessing impact of changes instituted

4. special education program supervisors;

5. teachers of preschool handicapped;

6. teachers of moderately and severely mentally retarded;

7. teachers of hearing impaired;

8. occupational therapists, physical therapists, and work-experience instructors; and

9. secretaries.

This approach is intended as one strand in program evaluation. The subgroups in this example happen to be all special educators, but other evaluations have been done using different referent groups such as superintendents, principals, regular teachers, resource teachers, and parents of handicapped children. Trust and anonymity are important to maintain if the data are to be accurate and useful, and if the process is to proceed without undue defensiveness. Backlash is not likely to occur

FIGURE 9
Evaluation of a Special Education Program

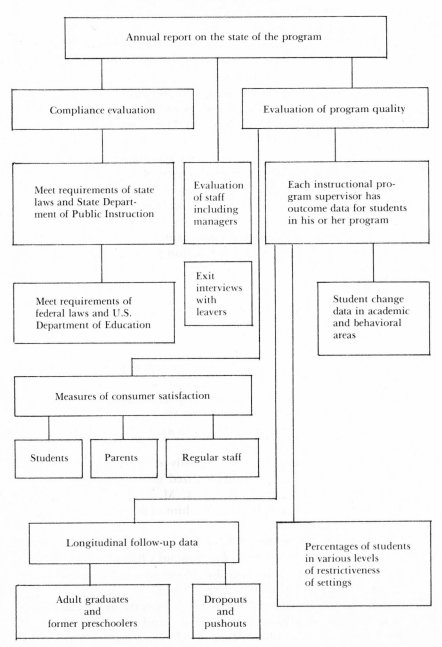

unless the central staff team approaches the evaluation in bad faith. Staff members generally welcome an opportunity to provide information and to participate in the management of the organization when their ideas are listened to and taken seriously.

This section has presented multiple sources and approaches to be considered when developing a more comprehensive system of program evaluation. Figure 9 is an outline of components that might be addressed in evaluating special education programs. Because of the complex of factors that interact to confound results of any evaluation system, a multiple-measures approach provides some checks and balances to reduce risk of error. Inferring causation is always difficult in education, but multiple measures over time should provide valuable clues about what does or does not contribute to the effectiveness of programs. Those who worry about the enormity of the task and the costs involved should remember that not every child need be involved in these evaluation procedures. That is what sampling theory is all about. Large school systems should employ stratified random sampling to obtain data from a representative group of the special education population.

REFERENCES

Baer, D. M. Perhaps it would be better not to know everything. *Journal of Applied Behavior Analysis*, 1977, *10*(1), 167-172.

Brinkerhoff, R. O. Evaluating full service special education programs. In E. L. Meyen, G. A. Vergason, & R. J. Whelan (Eds.), *Instructional planning for exceptional children*. Denver: Love Publishing Co., 1978.

Calsyn, R. J., & Davidson, W. S. Do we really want a program evaluation strategy based solely on individualized goals: A critique of goal attainment scaling. In T. D. Cook, M. L. Del Rosario, K. M. Hennign, M. M. Mark, & W. I. Tochim (Eds.), *Evaluation studies review annual*, 1978, *3*.

Carr, R. A. Goal attainment scaling as a useful tool for evaluating progress in special education. *Exceptional Children*, 1979, *46*(2).

Cronbach, L. J. Beyond the two disciplines of scientific psychology. *American Psychologist*, 1975, *30*(2), 116-127.

Fitzgerald, G. The use of objective observational data in the identification of emotionally disabled pupils. In *Identification of emotionally disabled pupils: Data and decision making*. Des Moines:

Iowa Department of Public Instruction and Midwest Regional Resource Center, 1979, pp. 73-113.

Gallagher, J. J., Ramey, C., Haskins, R., & Finkelstein, N. Use of longitudinal research in the study of child development. In T. D. Tjossem (Ed.), *Interview strategies for high risk infants and young children*. Baltimore: University Park Press, 1976.

Guralnick, M. J. The application of single-subject research designs to the field of learning disabilities. *Journal of Learning Disabilities*, 1978, *11*(7), 415-421.

Guttentag, M., & Saar, S. (Eds.). *Evaluation studies review annual.* Vol. 2. Beverly Hills, CA: Sage Publications, 1977.

Howe, C. E., & Fitzgerald, M. Evaluating special education programs. *Focus on Exceptional Children*, 1977, *8*(9), 1-11.

Keogh, B. Working together: A new direction. *Journal of Learning Disabilities*, 1977, *10*, 478-482.

Kiresuk, T., & Sherman, R. Goal attainment scaling: A general method for evaluating comprehensive mental health programs. *Community Mental Health Journal*, 1968, *4*(6), 443-453.

MacMillan, D. L., & Semmel, M. I. Evaluation of mainstreaming programs. *Focus on Exceptional Children*, 1977, *9*(4).

Mueller, A. *Philosophy of care and treatment.* Unpublished manuscript, University of Iowa, Division of Developmental Disabilities, 1979.

Progress toward a free appropriate public education. A report to Congress on the implementation of Public Law 94-142: The Education for All Handicapped Children Act. Washington, DC: U.S. Department of Education, January 1979. (HEW Publication No. OE 79-05003)

Provus, M. M. *Discrepancy evaluation.* Berkeley, CA: McCutchan Publishing, 1971.

Stufflebeam, D. L., Foley, W. J., Gephart, W. J., Guba, E. G., Hammond, R. L., Merriman, H. O., & Provus, M. M. *Educational evaluation and decision making.* Itasca, IL: F. E. Peacock Publishers, 1971.

Walker, H. M., & Hops, H. Use of normative peer data as a standard for evaluating classroom treatment effects. *Journal of Applied Behavior Analysis*, 1976, *9*(2), 159-168.

Whelan, R. J. Evaluation. In E. L. Meyen, G. A. Vergason, & R. J. Whelan (Eds.), *Instructional planning for exceptional children*. Denver: Love Publishing Co., 1978.

APPENDIX TO CHAPTER 7

Perceptions of Supervisors and Administrators
by AEA Support Staff Members

This form is an attempt to get feedback from various support services staff members in the area education agency (AEA). Current thinking suggests that staff evaluation procedures should include evaluation of bosses by the staff, as well as the more usual procedures of supervisors and administrators evaluating employees.

Below and on the next pages is a series of statements to which you may respond through a range of agreement to disagreement. Please blacken the appropriate box and return it in the enclosed envelope to The University of Iowa. Your responses will be anonymous.

	Disagree strongly	Disagree somewhat	Agree somewhat	Agree strongly	No basis on which to answer
A. The following 14 items relate specifically to your immediate supervisor:					
1. Listens to a staff member's concerns and alters procedures when it is demonstrated that it is in the best interest of the AEA.	☐	☐	☐	☐	☐
2. Follows through on commitments made with the staff.	☐	☐	☐	☐	☐
3. Is willing to schedule time to consider problems staff members may be having in fulfilling their job responsibilities.	☐	☐	☐	☐	☐
4. Provides feedback to you in addition to formally scheduled evaluations.	☐	☐	☐	☐	☐
5. Has an attitude toward supervision which is positive and democratic.	☐	☐	☐	☐	☐
6. Provides relevant and beneficial inservice programs and materials which lead to professional staff improvement.	☐	☐	☐	☐	☐
7. Will help you resolve those "tough" cases if you ask for help.	☐	☐	☐	☐	☐

	Disagree strongly	Disagree somewhat	Agree somewhat	Agree strongly	No basis on which to answer
8. If both agree on a course of action, will stand behind you even though controversy may develop and pressure is put on to compromise the situation.	☐	☐	☐	☐	☐
9. Communicates clearly in orienting new staff members and keeps the rest of the staff up to date on changes of AEA policy and procedures.	☐	☐	☐	☐	☐
10. Is supportive of some risk taking on your part as it relates to innovative approaches to programming or methods.	☐	☐	☐	☐	☐
11. Is sensitive to your needs as a person as well as a professional and will take time to listen to you.	☐	☐	☐	☐	☐
12. Demonstrates professional competence and knowledge of your field in working with the staff.	☐	☐	☐	☐	☐
13. Treats all fairly and without favoritism.	☐	☐	☐	☐	☐
14. Supports and helps you implement the new service delivery system.	☐	☐	☐	☐	☐

B. The next 12 questions relate to the positions of director and assistant director:

1. Demonstrates competency in providing leadership for the organization.

	Disagree strongly	Disagree somewhat	Agree somewhat	Agree strongly	No basis on which to answer
director	☐	☐	☐	☐	☐
assistant director	☐	☐	☐	☐	☐

2. Delegates appropriate amounts of responsibility and authority to supervisors and others.

	Disagree strongly	Disagree somewhat	Agree somewhat	Agree strongly	No basis on which to answer
director	☐	☐	☐	☐	☐
assistant director	☐	☐	☐	☐	☐

	Disagree strongly	Disagree somewhat	Agree somewhat	Agree strongly	No basis on which to answer
3. Shows a primary commitment and concern for quality of service and not just quantity.					
director	☐	☐	☐	☐	☐
assistant director	☐	☐	☐	☐	☐
4. Treats all AEA staff members fairly and shows little or no favoritism toward specific services or individuals.					
director	☐	☐	☐	☐	☐
assistant director	☐	☐	☐	☐	☐
5. Supports the provision of adequate secretarial help for the service you provide.					
director	☐	☐	☐	☐	☐
assistant director	☐	☐	☐	☐	☐
6. Is accessible if you need to see him or her.					
director	☐	☐	☐	☐	☐
assistant director	☐	☐	☐	☐	☐
7. Understands the service you provide and is supportive of it.					
director	☐	☐	☐	☐	☐
assistant director	☐	☐	☐	☐	☐
8. Disseminates necessary information regarding agency policies, plans, and programs to the staff.					
director	☐	☐	☐	☐	☐
assistant director	☐	☐	☐	☐	☐

	Disagree strongly	Disagree somewhat	Agree somewhat	Agree strongly	No basis on which to answer

9. Shows good judgment in maintaining integrity of programs and does not compromise quality except when absolutely necessary.

	Disagree strongly	Disagree somewhat	Agree somewhat	Agree strongly	No basis on which to answer
director	☐	☐	☐	☐	☐
assistant director	☐	☐	☐	☐	☐

10. The director and assistant director work well together as a team.

director	☐	☐	☐	☐	☐
assistant director	☐	☐	☐	☐	☐

11. Provides support to implement the new service delivery system through adequate allocation of resources and personnel.

director	☐	☐	☐	☐	☐
assistant director	☐	☐	☐	☐	☐

12. Listens to concerns about the new service delivery system and catalogs suggestions for use in refining/modifying the system.

director	☐	☐	☐	☐	☐
assistant director	☐	☐	☐	☐	☐

C. These last 9 items are intended to get at the overall perceptions you have of the AEA as an organization:

1. I would recommend to a professional colleague that he/she apply for a position in this AEA.

   ☐ ☐ ☐ ☐ ☐

2. This AEA is one of the best in the state compared to what I hear from my colleagues in other AEAs.

   ☐ ☐ ☐ ☐ ☐

3. There is a high "esprit de corps" among the staff and a feeling of all pulling together for the good of the organization.

   ☐ ☐ ☐ ☐ ☐

	Disagree strongly	Disagree somewhat	Agree somewhat	Agree strongly	No basis on which to answer
4. This AEA appreciates my services and treats me in a professional way.	☐	☐	☐	☐	☐
5. The local education agencies appreciate my services and treat me as a professional.	☐	☐	☐	☐	☐
6. I'm satisfied with my role here and plan to continue my employment in the AEA.	☐	☐	☐	☐	☐
7. This AEA provides a setting that will foster professional growth on my part.	☐	☐	☐	☐	☐
8. I like my job well enough and am committed to the point that I give my maximum to help this AEA succeed.	☐	☐	☐	☐	☐
9. Using this opinionnaire as an example, this AEA is open and will respond and make changs if such should be indicated by the results.	☐	☐	☐	☐	☐

D. Add any other statements you think should have been included:

1.

2.

3.

Comments (positive or negative) you may wish to make:

THANK YOU FOR PARTICIPATING

PLEASE RETURN IN ENCLOSED ENVELOPE BY:
_____

Administration and Special Education in the 1980s

Special education administration, after going along on a fairly even keel for a couple of decades, began to undergo substantial changes with the passage of PL 94-142 in 1975. For the most part, practicing directors don't like these changes. Some of the shifts in role and function are already taking place, and others lurk on the horizon. Whereas in the past directors perceived their role as ardent promoters of new programs and services for handicapped children, they now see themselves as compliance monitors, having to defend the appropriateness of their school district's service delivery system for the handicapped (Lamb & Burello, 1979).

OPPORTUNITIES FOR ADMINISTRATIVE POSITIONS

The Director of Special Education

During the next 10 years absolute numbers of persons employed as heads of special education programs will decrease. Several factors are involved: a stable or declining overall school enrollment during the 1980s, continuing school reorganization leading to a reduction in the total number of school districts, increased use of the intermediate education unit, pressure from teacher organizations to reduce the size of staffs in central administration, and increased emphasis on integrating mildly handicapped students under the general administration purview. Directors will more likely be full-time and responsible for larger staffs. The post of director of special education in small school districts (i.e., those with fewer than 5,000 students) will disappear. If small school districts do employ someone, they will hire a coordinator who may be part-time in special education.

Second-Level Administrative Positions in Special Education

Although the number of directors may decrease, the numbers of assistant directors, supervisors, coordinators, consultants, and team leaders will increase. This is happening already, as larger units are being established to make available a comprehensive set of services to all handicapped children. Most of the opportunities will present themselves in some type of consortium of school districts, with organizational titles such as intermediate education unit, regional education service agency, cooperative, and district joint agreement. In more populous areas, the county school system may be the basic unit.

Similar opportunities will arise in state departments of education and in the Office of Special Education and Rehabilitative Services, as these agencies deal with compliance monitoring and distribution of earmarked funds. Many of these positions, however, may not show up on the payroll of state and federal agencies because legislators are trying to curtail the size of bureaucracies. Agencies will try to get around this through the private contracting approach with outside organizations and individuals, using "program" money for "project" awards to complete a specific task. Another approach is the well-known technique of employing the outside consultant.

Women in Special Education Administration

Increasing numbers of women will compete successfully for administrative positions in the field. During the past decade the United States has been consistently moving toward more consideration of qualified women for leadership positions. Yet, Hennig and Jardim (1977) reported that although women made up 39 percent of the labor force, fewer than 5 percent were in managerial positions paying more than $10,000 per year. Legally, women have equal opportunity, but that does not mean they have been able to compete successfully with men for managerial positions. Hennig and Jardim traced the reasons for this and suggested things that women and senior corporate executives must learn in order for women to be able to compete on an equal basis with men.

Special education should be no exception. Many women held positions as directors of special education in major cities during the 1950s, but as they retired most were replaced by men. Vance (1973) found that of all students awarded fellowships to study special education administration between 1965 and 1971, 11 percent (22 of 208) were women. In the Kohl and Marro (1971) study, 28 percent of those holding special education administrative positions were women. Their analysis by age and sex caused them to conclude that the proportion of women to men was decreasing. Vance's (1973) data on those in training or in the field in the early 1970s added support to this view. Although more recent data apparently are not available, I believe the situation is beginning to change. Several special education administrative training programs with which I am familiar are made up of almost 50 percent women. It is too early to know if these women will obtain top leadership roles in special education administration, but my prediction is they will. Certification standards are moving toward more specific requirements of experience in teaching handicapped children; thus, the eligible pool will be predominantly female, because the majority of special education teachers are women.

CERTIFICATION OF SPECIAL EDUCATION ADMINISTRATORS

Certification is controlled by state departments of education, although teacher organizations have been trying to wrest this control from them for years. Certification should not be equated with competence in practice but, rather, should be viewed as a "gatekeeper" function that sets a minimum standard for obtaining a credential needed to enter the field. Many states have "approved program status" arrangements with teacher training institutions. Persons completing the requirements of the college or university and recommended by the institution are awarded credentials by the state. Again, all this means is that the institution certifies that the candidate has met the minimum requirements. Certificates can be revoked by the state, although this is done infrequently. The point is that having certification standards for administrators of special education doesn't necessarily result in quality leadership, except at a minimal level.

Most requirements for certification continue to be based on input variables such as degrees earned, majors, years of teaching or related experience, and course sequences completed. As we know is the case in general education, many of these variables have low correlations with subsequent teaching success. Until we know differently, it is probably safest to assume that this is also true in administration. One reason for these low correlations is a measurement artifact of restricted range of differences, both because of the common requirements for admission and because grades in graduate classes in education are confined to As and Bs. On the other hand, success in student teaching does seem to be related to later teaching success. For administrators, success in an internship may be an important prediction variable. In fact, students in special education administration training programs between 1965 and 1971 viewed the internship as one of the most important components of the program (Vance, 1973). Logically, successful past experience in a lower-level administrative position is an even better predictor than an internship.

The status of certification of special education leadership personnel has been reviewed by Kern and Mayer (1970), Ebersdorfer (1973), Vance (1973), and Forgnone and Collings (1975). As of 1975, the majority of states appeared not to have a certification for special education directors. Many, though, had certification for some other title, such as supervisor or director of pupil personnel services. Ebersdorfer (1973) reported that one-third of the states had no specific certification requirements for administrators of special education. Vance's (1973) nationwide follow-up survey of administrators in training between 1965 and 1971 found that only 58 percent held special education administrators' certificates for the state where they worked. Forty percent held general administration credentials, either in lieu of special education or in addition to it.

The most recent information is provided in a descriptive study by Whitworth and Hatley (1979) of the 50 states' certification requirements for the special education leadership position. They found great variation in requirements, definitions, and job descriptions among the states. Sixty percent (30 states) now require some type of certification of special education leadership personnel, as contrasted with 12 states in 1970. Fifteen states call them supervisors, and the other 15 use the terms special education administrator, special approval in general administration, or something similar. Although Whitworth and Hatley did not address the issue, some of those 20 states with no special endorsement most likely require some type of general administrative credential.

Of the 30 states with some type of special administrative credentialing, Whitworth and Hatley reported that nearly all required both prior certification as a special education teacher and teaching exerience, but this is misleading in that several states are known to include the phrase *related experience*. In the past, related experience has been interpreted to mean almost anything, but principally refers to non-teaching support personnel. The effect has been that the largest single source of special education administrators has been the field of school psychology (Kohl & Marro, 1971). Vance's (1973) follow-up data showed this situation changing for persons in training during the late 1960s and early 1970s. Of all persons holding USOE/BEH fellowships during that period, 67 percent had prior experience as special education teachers and only 20 percent had been school psychologists. This is not to say that others without teaching experience were not being trained or certified during that period, but only that they did not hold BEH fellowships.

150

The argument in special education about the importance of having actual classroom teaching experience before becoming an administrator goes on endlessly. To me, the important issue is whether one views special education as primarily involved in instructional programs or in identification and differential diagnosis. If one believes that instruction is what special education is all about, as I do, one is more likely to opt for administrators who are trained and experienced in education. It does seem to make a difference to special education teachers to know that their leader was, at least once, out in the "salt mines" with them. School psychologists, audiologists and other support personnel argue, on the other hand, for the specialist model, which contends that no one can know everything and that one does not have to have done something in order to supervise or direct others.

It might be more productive to look at the degree to which general administration competencies are being built into training programs for special education administrators. The University Council for Educational Administration (UCEA) provided impetus to this effort through the General-Special Education Administration Consortium Project. This was funded for three years in the early 1970s by BEH and attempted to improve communication between departments of educational administration and special education administration. Efforts were made to increase cross-training for students in both groups. Disappointingly, the outcomes have indicated that while persons training to become special education administrators took increasing amounts of coursework in general administration, general administrators rarely included competencies in special education. In a few exceptions, such as the University of Texas, the University of Wisconsin, and Indiana University, professors of special education administration are on the faculties of the departments of educational administration (Burello & Sage, 1979).

To expect that education administration programs will obligingly add a "core" of special education courses to the training for principals and general administrators would be naive. Every special interest group, of which special education is only one, wants to add its special content to general training programs. It would be more sensible to suggest including modules of special education content within generic education administration courses such as law, finance, managing individualized instruction systems, and personnel management. Yet it is doubtful whether any state will require substantial special education coursework in the preparation of general administrators. In a recent survey of the 50 states and the District of Columbia regarding special education requirements for regular teachers, Smith and Schindler (1980) found that most states have no such requirement and do not contemplate adding one.

151

Regular education in 25 states plus the District of Columbia includes no special education requirement, 11 are considering it, and just 15 states require some training at the preservice level, which usually amounts to something like an introductory course on exceptional children. Only Oklahoma requires more than one course.

On the other hand, evidence reveals that more competence in general administration is being required of leaders in special education (Whitworth & Hatley, 1979). Most of those states having special education administrative or supervision credentials require at least some coursework in general administration. Several university training programs, including Iowa's, require completion of the entire sequence in general administration, and graduates are certified as school administrators. Perhaps if directors really want to influence how special education is integrated with the total school system, their long-term objective ought to be to become assistant superintendents of instruction — that is, to get out of special education. Training and certification as general administrators at least opens the door for that possibility and gives them an opportunity to compete for a wider variety of positions.

FUNCTIONS AND COMPETENCIES OF THE
SPECIAL EDUCATION DIRECTOR

Several studies have been done on the functions, duties, and activities of the special education director. Some attempted to describe the role of the director and others sought to compare it with the function of the general administrator. Sage (1968), in comparing functions of directors with those of elementary principals, reported that the major difference was the greater involvement of directors with improving educational opportunities by securing services for the handicapped. Using Urwick's model to study seven types of administrative activities, Newman (1970) found that directors were doing everything they believed their role dictated, with the exception of evaluating programs for the handicapped and publishing materials for parents and the public. She concluded that, in 1970, the following 10 tasks were the major ones in administration of special education programs:

1. planning and providing for adequate classes and services;

2. coordinating services available within the school and community;

3. developing a system of communicating among schools, parents, and community;

4. helping to secure staff members in special education;

5. serving as the instructional leaders;

6. being responsible for local and state accounting of funds;

7. helping in financial planning and use of funds;

8. conducting research and evaluation of the program;

9. conveying new research findings to the staff; and

10. evaluating special education personnel.

Respondents in the Kohl and Marro (1971) study thought they spent too much time on clerical duties and administrative detail and should be putting more effort into supervision and coordination of instruction, curriculum development, direct services to exceptional children, self-improvement, and working with the community.

Weatherman and Harpaz (1975) studied special education directors in Minnesota, using position analysis techniques. They concluded that the following eight competencies are needed to perform the role of director of special education in that state:

1. developing procedures and establishing policies for the program;

2. evaluating programs and planning for program improvement/change;

3. organizing pupil services;

4. recruiting, supervising, and evaluating the special education staff;

5. interacting with general administrators in the operation of special education programs in the schools;

6. managing office work as it relates to communicating with parents and the public, publishing newsletters, and maintaining records;

7.   developing public relations with the community to promote the welfare of the handicapped; and

8.   helping plan and execute budgets, auditing fiscal reports, and monitoring reimbursement from state and federal sources.

One other recent study that examined competencies needed in special education was that of Harris and King (1974, 1976). Their approach was unique in that it focused on instructional supervisors in special education whose major role was to effect planned change as required by state legislatures or the least restrictive environment concept. The supervisor thus was seen as an instructional change agent. Through this federally funded special education supervisor training project, Harris and King identified about 24 competencies considered to be critical. Many were similar to those reported by others (Kohl & Marro, 1971; Newman, 1970; Sage, 1968; Vance, 1973; Weatherman & Harpaz, 1975), but there were also several unique competencies focusing on instruction. Included were such functions as designing instructional units, developing and adapting curricula, and organizing and evaluating instructional alternatives. Although the criteria admittedly were intended for an instruction supervisor rather than a director of special education, this increased emphasis on the tasks of instruction as major, perhaps essential, skills needed by special education leadership personnel is heartening.

Naturally, many of the competencies needed by administrators of special education in the future will remain about the same as those reported above. But passage of PL 94-142 at the federal level, and similar mandated legislation in the various states, may well alter the role significantly during the 1980s. The following are proposed as major competencies likely to be needed by directors of special education in this decade. (Shifts in function or focus have been emphasized.)

1.   *In-service training of significant adults*
     - Place emphasis on sharing information and techniques with principals so they manage their own programs, particularly for the mildly handicapped
     - Help organize meaningful learning activities for regular teachers
     - Attempt to accomplish change through persuasion of others

2.   *Developing and evaluating the effectiveness of instructional alternatives*
     - "Showcase" promising options for instruction

- Commit increased resources to evaluation on an ongoing basis and utilize the results
- Increase the use of longitudinal approaches to evaluating product outcomes

3. *Recruiting, selecting, retaining, and dismissing staff members*
   - Develop high morale among staff members in an adversary climate (collective bargaining agreements, union contracts)
   - Plan for staff reduction (a new skill needed)
   - Train and use paraprofessionals and adult volunteers

4. *Interpreting programs to schools and the community*
   - Defend the appropriateness of operating programs
   - Monitor legal processes in use and interpret them to schools
   - Relinquish to others the role of advocate
   - Open up accessibility to the handicapped of alternative living situations and occupations in the community

5. *Managing money*
   - Find new sources of funds for discretionary use
   - Secure grants as a source for experimental programs
   - Monitor use of federal and state categorical funds
   - Develop records and accountability systems

WHY WOULD ANYONE WANT TO BE AN ADMINISTRATOR?

Teachers' conversations in a school lounge create the impression that no one wants to be an administrator. Yet, when a managerial opening comes up, many applicants always vie for the position. What motivates a person to seek administration of special education as a career? Is it greed, ambition, idealism, encouragement from mentors, the desire to get out of the classroom, wanting to be in control so things can be done differently, freedom from being place-bound, the opportunity to "soar with the eagles," or what?

Maccoby (1976) has written that in the corporate structure, a person he characterized as "the gamesman" is now taking over leadership positions in technically advanced companies. These managers are motivated by the challenge of organizing a winning team. They are competitive but can be cooperative. They are change oriented and fascinated by technique and new methods. They like to take calculated risks, and they see "a developing project, human relations, and their own career in terms of options and possibilities, as if they were a game" (p. 100).

Maccoby was concerned that management, at least in the advanced-technology companies he studied, is selecting people who are highly competent intellectually in leading and managing groups but who have underdeveloped traits of compassion, generosity, and idealism. He argued for a form of more humane management, "of the heart" as well as "of the head." Maccoby speculated that the gamesman exists not only in industry but in most other organizations in the United States, and he concluded that "the engineers and managers we interviewed are no more competitive and a lot more cooperative with one another than most professors. If corporate managers engaged in the nitpicking and down-putting common in universities, little would be created and produced" (p. 209).

Whether school administrators in general, and special education administrators in particular, would fit the mold of the gamesman is a matter of conjecture. The popular conception of special educators is that "the heart" is at the core of their career choice and behavior. This assumption that special educators are all devoted, martyrs, or masochists has been overdone. Tolerance for a wider range of behavior is important, of course. But when people become administrators of total special education programs, their needed skills most likely approximate those Maccoby outlined for being successful in corporations.

One problem special educators face is what Berliner (1971) referred to as "apologizing for being an administrator." This tendency apparently comes from the value system of mental health workers, in which highest status is accorded to providing therapy or any other direct service activity. The apologies can be heard in remarks about "needing a higher salary" and "missing working directly with clients or patients." Whether the administrator really feels this way is another question. Berliner concluded that "if the administrator perceives his work as of peripheral significance (nontherapy) and himself as sitting astride an unwieldy pile of bodies, this perception will sabotage his efforts to be effective" (p. 563).

What *are* the rewards in being a special education administrator? First, the position offers the opportunity to manage money and people in ways that can result in a superior-quality program for handicapped children. This is not only a socially laudable goal but a source of pride to the director as well. If, in order to accomplish excellence, some of the behavior of the gamesman comes into play, so be it.

Second, the authority of the position provides some latitude for experimenting with new ideas and different ways of programming for handicapped children. Although there are always constraints, the director has some freedom to set the direction of the organization and to commit it to continued investigation of new models and approaches. Maintaining existing programs of the status quo need not rule the organization.

Third, a degree of status is connected with being the leader of an organization, and the director should openly admit this. To create a positive working climate in an organization where staff members and the community feel good about what is happening in the program is gratifying. If all goes well, directors probably receive more credit than they deserve, and if things go badly, they usually get more criticism than is warranted.

Last, the challenge of leadership in a good-sized special education program can be intellectually stimulating. Working with a group of bright, competent associates is exciting. Immersion in a series of complex, interrelated issues can be mind-expanding. It may or may not be more satisfying than teaching school for 40 years, but at least it is different!

REFERENCES

Berliner, A. K. Some pitfalls in administrative behavior. *Social Casework,* November 1971, pp. 562-566.

Burello, L. C., & Sage, D. D. *Leadership and change in special education.* Englewood Cliffs, NJ: Prentice-Hall, 1979.

Ebersdorfer, J. A. *A comparative analysis of state certification requirements for special education administrative and supervisor personnel.* Unpublished doctoral dissertation, Indiana University, 1973.

Forgnone, C., & Collings, G. D. State certification-endorsement in special education administration. *Journal of Special Education,* 1975, *9.*

Harris, B. M., & King, J. D., Co-directors. *Professional supervisory competencies* (Special education supervisor training project funded by the Bureau of Education for the Handicapped). Austin: University of Texas, 1974.

Harris, B. M., & King, J. D. *Training manual for a competency-guided individualized program for special education supervisors* (Special education supervisory training project funded by the Bureau of Education for the Handicapped). Austin: University of Texas, 1976.

Hennig, M., & Jardim, A. *The managerial woman.* New York: Simon & Schuster, 1977.

Kern, W. H., & Mayer, J. F. Certification of directors of special education programs: The results of a national survey. *Contemporary Education*, 1970, *42*, 126-128.

Kohl, J. W., & Marro, T. D. *A normative study of the administrative position in special education* (USOE) Project No. 482266, Grant No. (OEG) 0-70-2467(607). University Park, PA: Center for Cooperative Research with Schools, Pennsylvania State University, 1971.

Lamb, J., & Burello, L. C. The role of council for administrators of special education. *Exceptional Children*, 1979, *46*(1).

Maccoby, M. *The gamesman: The new corporate leaders.* New York: Simon & Schuster, 1976.

Newman, K. S. Administrative tasks in special education. *Exceptional Children*, 1970, *37*(7), 521-524.

Sage, D. D. Functional emphasis in special education administration. *Exceptional Children*, 1968, *35*(1).

Smith, J. E., Jr., & Schindler, W. J. Certification requirements of general educators concerning exceptional pupils. *Exceptional Children*, 1980, *46*(5), 394-396.

Vance, V. L. *A follow-up study of students of special education administration who received USOE/BEH training grants.* Doctoral dissertation, University of Iowa, 1973. (University Microfilms No. 74-7441)

Weatherman, R., & Harpaz, I. *A study of special education directors in Minnesota.* Unpublished report, University of Minnesota, 1975.

Whitworth, J. E., & Hatley, R. V. Certification and special education leadership personnel: An analysis of state standards. *Journal of Special Education*, 1979, *13*(3), 297-305.

II

Selected Readings

The readings in Part II, drawn from widely different journal sources, have been selected with an-eye toward augmenting the content of the eight chapters in Part I. Several are from journals that are probably not widely read by administrators.

The first three articles by Safer et al., Reynolds, and Herda, are largely "wisdom writings" that focus on forecasting future needs in special education. Because a major role of any manager is that of planning for the future, these articles should be of particular interest to the special education administrator.

The remaining articles are ones I have found useful as supplemental readings for graduate classes in special education administration. They range from a humorous account of how to keep others from giving you their problems to a discussion of how performance appraisal systems in industry should address the "human component" when evaluating managers.

Anticipating tomorrow's and next year's problems is a skill thought to be important for a successful administrator. Such planning can, to some extent at least, reduce the amount of last-minute crisis management that frustrates us all from time to time. The authors of this article have summarized the opinions of experts in five areas that could affect the future of the handicapped. The material included is all the more interesting because the experts are not the typical ones from education, but rather represent fields such as values, economics, social institutions, technology, and medicine.

Exploration 1993:
The Effects of Future Trends
on Services to the Handicapped

Nancy Safer, Jane Burnette, and Barbara Hobbs

The past decade has been characterized by rapid changes in patterns of service to the handicapped. Groups are now being served who were never served before, in ways they were never served, and handicapped persons are participating increasingly in all aspects of society. These changes have resulted from pressures, conditions, and forces within and outside of fields providing services to the handicapped. With change occurring rapidly and on many fronts, we too often find ourselves in a reactive position, trying simply to keep up with events rather than systematically planning for change. This sometimes has resulted in hasty "make-do" policies and service arrangements. A more controlled posture toward change requires both lead time and some perspective as to the future. Thus, for practitioners and policymakers, anticipating change is becoming more and more important.

From *Focus on Exceptional Children,* May 1979, *11*(3), 1-24 © Love Publishing Co.

Anticipatory policy decisons require that certain assumptions, implicit or explicit, be made about conditions in the future. Failure to consider future conditions indicates an implicit assumption either that future years will hold no change or that current trends will continue. The rapid rate of change in the last 50 years, particularly in services and rights for the handicapped, suggests that these assumptions would be short-sighted indeed.

Policymakers' need for information concerning future decisions or practices in various fields has focused increasing attention on forecasting methodologies and the study of the future (Cornish, 1977). Though it is impossible to make highly accurate and specific predictions about the future, it is possible to identify patterns, potential trends, and alternate futures. With this information, policymakers are in a better position to make decisions that will maximize the probability that desirable events or conditions will occur and minimize the probability that undesirable alternatives will occur.

Currently, a number of forecasting methodologies are available, and several of these have been used to forecast trends in services for the handicapped. For example, Shipper and Kenowitz (1975) used a Delphi procedure to ask special education administrators to forecast developments in the delivery of services to handicapped children. Schiefelbusch and Hoyt (1978) developed a scenario of special education in the year 1984. These efforts, and other previous efforts to forecast trends in the provision of services to the handicapped, although highly interesting, have been limited in that they have not systematically considered the context in which these services would be provided or how that context would affect the provision of services.

Changes in social institutions such as education or social services rarely occur in isolation. Thus, in considering the future in a particular area such as services for the handicapped, we must explore trends and changes in fields that potentially affect that area, and project the implications of such changes for services to the handicapped.

Five fields that have had historical impact on services to the handicapped are *values, economics, social institutions, technology,* and *medicine.* For example, in the last decade, shifts in values emphasizing civil and human rights have promoted the acceptance of handicapped persons in all areas of society. Greater acceptance of the handicapped has been facilitated by economic growth which has allowed more funds to be reserved for services to the handicapped without actually taking funds away from previously established programs. The shift in values has affected our social institutions, taking such forms as the movement to

162

educate many handicapped students in regular classes rather than in segregated special education classes and to maintain handicapped persons in community-based placements rather than in residential institutions. Technological developments have enabled handicapped persons to participate more fully in society by providing devices (such as printing machines for braille) that make the performance of occupational and daily living tasks easier for handicapped persons. Medical advances have played a great role in reducing the incidence of handicapping conditions — for example, through development of polio and rubella vaccines and in the amelioration of disabling conditions through treatment.

As part of its continuing effort to anticipate and facilitate changes in provision of services to the handicapped, the Bureau of Education for the Handicapped (BEH) sponsored a project to explore potential future changes in the areas of values, economics, social institutions, technology, and medicine. The project, entitled "Exploration 1993: The Effects of Future Trends on Services for the Handicapped," initially was conceptualized as a two-stage activity. The first stage was to look broadly across the five areas and provide an overview of potential trends in each area, as well as to examine the possible effects of these trends on services to the handicapped. If some trends of particular interest and potential impact were identified during this first stage, they could be explored in greater depth using more sophisticated future methodologies during the second stage.

As part of the first stage, the Newtek Corporation of Reston, Virginia, commissioned experts in the five areas to consider and delineate future trends in those areas, particularly trends that might impact upon services to the handicapped. These experts were selected on the basis of recommendations concerning their broad expertise in their respective fields and their experience in delineating and forecasting trends. They were: Willis W. Harman, Director of the Center of Social Policy, Stanford Research Institute, and author of *An Incomplete Guide to the Future*, in the area of values; Robert D. Hamrin, author of *Rethinking Economics; The Reality of the 1980s*, and formerly with the Joint Economic Committee, U.S. Congress, in the area of economics, Stephen L. Klineberg, chairman of the Department of Sociology, Rice University, and co-author of *The Present of Things Future: Explorations of Time in Human Experience*, in the area of social institutions; Joseph Coates, author of many articles, including "The Future of the Handicapped: Structural Factors Influencing the Employment of the Physically Handicapped," from the Office of Technology Assessment, U.S. Congress, in the area of technology; and Hugo W. Moser, Director of the John F. Kennedy Institute, Professor of Neurology and Pediatrics at Johns

Hopkins University, and author of numerous articles including "Biochemical Aspects of Mental Retardation," in the area of medicine.

A panel[1] of individuals representing various aspects of services to the handicapped were asked by BEH to consider the trends projected in the five areas, as delineated by the five experts, and to discuss the impact those trends could have on the provision of services to the handicapped.

The five sections that follow give some of the ideas, reactions, and projections resulting from this interchange. Each section first presents the trends delineated by the respective experts, followed by implications of those trends for the handicapped as discussed by the panel. Table 1 summarizes the trends and implications for each of the five sections. In some instances there were differences as to the interpretation of certain events or patterns of events and the likelihood or implications of trends projected from those patterns.

Alternative trends and their potential impacts can serve as a point of departure for thinking about the future. The Bureau of Education for the Handicapped is carefully considering the impact that particular trends discussed in this article could have on BEH policies and programs. These trends, if realized, also would affect state and local special education programs, university training programs, the parents of handicapped students, and handicapped persons themselves. Thus, the final section of this article considers some of the impacts that alternative trends could have on various aspects and levels of special education services —with the hope that this will provide stimulus for thoughtful consideration of the future among special educators, parents, and students.

VALUES

Mr. Harman pointed out that our values affect who we define as handicapped, what services we think they are entitled to, and who is responsible for providing services. For example, our definitions of

---

[1] Panel members included: Betsy Anderson, Massachusetts Federation for Children with Special Needs; Bruce Balow, Department of Education, University of Minnesota; Jane Burnette, Newtek Corporation; Kenneth Cross, Department of Special Education, University of Buffalo; Jerry Gross, LaGrange Area Department of Special Education; Joseph Heinmiller, Youthwork, Inc.; Stanley Herr, Harvard Law School; Martin Kaufman, Bureau of Education for the Handicapped; Edwin Martin, Bureau of Education for the Handicapped; William Mimms, Newtek Corporation; Carson Nolan, American Printing House for the Blind; Nancy Safer, Bureau of Education for the Handicapped; Raphael Simches, Bureau of Education for the Handicapped; Allen Sullivan, Dallas Public Schools, Department of Special Education; and Michael Ward, Council for Exceptional Children.

handicaps such as learning disabilities and emotional problems are somewhat loose and could be narrowed or extended according to shifting values. Although language and cultural handicaps presently are limited to ethnic groups, this category could be extended. Currently, our values support the view that the handicapped are entitled to those services that will allow them to participate fully in society. This view could change, however, if circumstances cause us to shift our values. Thus, changes in values are of obvious concern in regard to the handicapped.

Occasionally in human history values have undergone transformations of such magnitude that the effect has been a restructuring of the social order. Mr. Harman suggested that such encompassing transformations take place slowly, over several centuries. The most recent example is the transformation from the religious values of medieval society to the values and beliefs of industrial society. The change started centuries ago with the secularization of values and the growing belief that persons could improve the material environment through their own efforts. These changes were the precursors of the industrial revolution, with its emphasis on economic and technological progress.

Our present society still reflects the values of the industrial revolution — characterized by an emphasis on expanding technological and scientific expertise to facilitate economic growth. Economic productivity is the primary basis for employment and, as such, it is a focal point in the individual's relationship with society and a major source of self-esteem. The criterion for judging the quality of education is its effectiveness in preparing the student for employment; knowledge is valued for its ability to generate manipulative technology. Ever since the industrial revolution, our primary goals have centered on material growth and our belief system has reflected these goals.

The economic and technological growth of our society has brought an abundance of goods and services that have improved the quality of life; yet, inevitably, negative side effects have resulted from this emphasis on material growth. Environmental damage has adversely affected the quality of air, water and land; natural resources are being depleted; and society has tended to exclude persons who are unable to contribute to material growth. Reactions against such negative effects may indicate that our value system is changing.

In fact, Mr. Harman suggested that we may be going through a major transformational period, equal in magnitude to the transformation from the middle ages to the industrial age. The following trends discussed by Mr. Harman may be the harbingers of a new system of values.

Trends

1. *Society's standards may be changing, with less emphasis being placed on economic rationality in which social contributions are measured in economic terms, and greater emphasis being placed on the quality of life.*

   Concern for maintaining a habitable environment. An effort is being made to protect wildlife, conserve energy and natural resources, reduce pollution, and control population growth. Technological growth without regard to the consequences has been challenged by those who recognize the need to assess the long-range impact of new technologies on the environment.

   Self-actualization. There is a growing emphasis on self-actualization, with individuals being valued for more than their economic productivity. Widespread interest is being shown in self-exploration and mind expansion and control through experiences such as individual and group psychotherapy, transcendental meditation and est.

   Focus on the equality of all groups. The past two decades have seen an extension of equality and rights to numerous minority groups. Although the initial impetus for this change often has been court decisions, such decisions could be made and implemented only when supported by the belief system of the society.

   Decentralization. Increasing concern has focused on obtaining more manageable government and social institutions through decentralization and through forming stronger personal ties within smaller communities. Thus, demands are increasing to limit the impact of federal government by strengthening programs and decision making at the community level.

2. *The knowledge system shows signs of being expanded and refocused to include not only objective but also subjective, spiritual, and creative knowledge.*

   Research in subjective areas. More scientists are investigating subjective phenomena including the unconscious, creative imagination, pscyhosomatic illness, and psychic experiences. At one time, persons undertaking research in these areas were viewed with suspicion, but such research is becoming more and more respectable and is being carried out under the auspices of well known and highly regarded institutions.

   Wholeness and connectedness of persons. There is a movement toward viewing the person as a whole being rather than as a collection of parts. Evidence of this is seen in the holistic health movement, which recognizes that the mind and the body function together and that the individual's attitude is an important part of his or her illness and healing. There is also increasing concern about the effects of labeling and classifying, which tend to identify individuals by certain characteristics that are used as a basis to differentiate and separate these persons from the rest of society. In short, there is a greater awareness of the oneness and connectedness of human beings.

Public participation in scientific and technological issues. The general public is less dependent upon and less in awe of the expert than was once the case. Consumers have made it clear that they intend to be involved in decisions related to issues like nuclear safety, hazardous substances, and recombinant DNA. Parents believe they should be included in the educational decision-making process. Thus, issues that formerly were scientific or pedagogical issues are often viewed now as political issues, open to public participation.

An Alternative View

Some panel members felt that many of the trends outlined above were aberrations rather than harbingers of a new value system and would not grow significantly in the future. Instead, they believed that the current belief system would continue into the future, with an even heightened emphasis on the rugged individual and on measuring the individual in economic terms. These participants felt that the increase in self-exploration could be viewed as a preoccupation with the self and a decline of concern for others; they expressed views that the potential economic slowdown (discussed later), combined with self-preoccupation, could result in increased competitiveness and conflict among individuals, less interest in extending rights or equality to groups outside the mainstream (because of fear arising from their economic competitiveness), and continued evaluation of others in terms of actual or potential economic productivity.

Thus, some disagreement was voiced at the panel meeting as to whether or not we are currently in a period of changing values. This is not surprising. Mr. Harman pointed out that during a transition period, there are movements and countermovements, and that as parts of society are changing, other parts are reacting against those changes. Which of the specific trends or movements endure will be determined only by time. Of greater importance is the existence or nonexistence of an overall pattern of changing values and beliefs and whether this pattern will or will not be a continuing thrust.

Implications for the Handicapped

Changes in our overall belief and value system in a direction away from an economic rationality and toward an expanded knowledge system could have a number of implications for handicapped individuals. An emphasis on the self-actualization of individuals rather than on their economic productivity could reinforce the current national policy of educating every handicapped person to his or her maximum potential through appropriate educational systems. Such an emphasis on self-actualization, combined with an expansion of the knowledge system to include the subjective and creative, could mean that educational programs for the handicapped would place less emphasis on vocational (economically productive) training than in the past, and more emphasis on subjects aimed at enriching the life of the individual, such as art and music.

A value system that would judge individuals on a basis other than economic productivity also could increase the likelihood of handicapped individuals who cannot work being accepted on an equal footing with nonhandicapped individuals. Similarly, societal concern with the equality and rights of groups such as the handicapped who have been discriminated against in the past could cement handicapped persons' access to and full participation in the mainstream of society.

The trend toward decentralization already has affected the handicapped through the normalization movement — that is, the transferring of handicapped persons from large state institutions to community-based facilities. Concern with obtaining more manageable government and social institutions would reinforce the movement toward deinstitutionalization, and the concern with forming stronger community ties could result in less alienation and more normal social relationships for handicapped persons returning to or remaining in communities. Potential problems resulting from decentralization center on less coordination of services and a lack of availability of low-incidence services in smaller communities and more widespread locations.

An expansion of the knowledge system beyond the objective could result in increased attention to the whole individual in planning treatments for the handicapped. Rehabilitative and educational services would attend to the attitudes and spirit of the individual, along with his or her physical and cognitive characteristics. A new orientation would be required for service deliverers, one which would focus on providing holistic services to the handicapped, with an increased emphasis on feelings and attitudes. In addition, the movement away from labeling the handicapped would be expected to continue, as categories and classification schemes would be viewed as too narrowly defining the individual in terms of only one of his or her many characteristics and attributes. Thus, categorical funding systems and programs could be met with increasing resistance.

A feeling of the connectedness of all persons could affect attitudes concerning the separateness and isolation of the handicapped — both the attitudes of the handicapped themselves and the attitudes of others. Not only would a feeling of connectedness increase the acceptance of handicapped persons within the community, but it would also affect the educational and rehabilitation services they receive. Instead of these services being one-sided, with the therapist or the educator trying to change the attributes of the handicapped person, the two people would become interactive, with changes, particularly attitudinal changes, occurring in both parties.

Finally, greater consumer questioning of the experts and "lay" involvement in decisions previously made by experts suggest that the current trend of increasing involvement of handicapped persons and their families in planning, implementing, and monitoring the appropriateness of programs could be strengthened in the future.

On the other hand, a continuation of the current belief system based on economic rationality, material productivity, and objective knowledge could, if combined with an economic slowdown, lead to increased conflict and competitiveness, with individuals being excessively preoccupied with their own self-interests. This alternative future could have a negative impact on the handicapped. A highly competitive society would seem less likely to extend rights to the handicapped, to support affirmative action programs, or to take steps that might increase the competitive advantage of the handicapped economically.

Similarly, an emphasis on economic productivity in a time of scarce resources could result in programs for the handicapped being evaluated strictly in terms of their ability to produce individuals who would be fully productive economically. This could result in a sharp cutback of programs for handicapped individuals who could be helped to reach their fullest potential but who would be unlikely to be economically independent. Within surviving programs, an economically oriented belief system suggests that programs would become more narrowly focused on vocationally related skills with even less attention given to developing other aspects of the individual.

Either a transformation in the value system or increased competitiveness resulting from an economic slowdown clearly will affect the lives of handicapped persons profoundly. The specific effects, however, could be quite different depending on whether or not a transformation occurs.

169

Thus, trends and movements in upcoming years must be scrutinized not only in terms of their specific implications and effects but also as pieces of a potential pattern indicating a transformation of the value system.

ECONOMICS

Following World War II and through the 1960s, this nation experienced high rates of economic growth. The extension of rights, support, and help to disadvantaged, minority, or other groups outside society's mainstream owes a great deal to that economic abundance. Periods of great economic growth allow a generosity to excluded groups and improvement of their lot in the form of social services, education, and employment opportunities, without taking away from those who are already well fixed. Thus, any changes in the overall economic picture can have important implications for groups seeking to become better assimilated into the social and economic mainstream.[2] Three economic trends discussed by Mr. Harman at the panel meeting seem to have important implications for the handicapped. These are a shift to an information/service economy, changes in employment patterns, and a slowdown in the economic growth rate.

Trends

1. *The shift to an information/service economy is expected to continue.*

The United States economy gradually has been shifting from an industrial to an information/service economy. In the early 1950s for the first time, more than 50 percent of the population was employed in industries that do not produce goods (e.g., transportation, banking, utilities, education, health, communications, and entertainment). It is projected that by 1985, 80 percent of the work force will be employed in information/service jobs and only 20 percent will be employed in producing all of our agricultural and manufactured goods.

Although this trend has been underway for some time, its impact on the economy will be felt increasingly as advances are made in electronic technology. Already computers are dispensing money in banks, recording

---

[2] The relationship between economic growth and the extension of rights and services to excluded groups was discussed by Mr. Klineberg at the panel meeting.

prices in supermarkets, and monitoring patients in hospitals. Further advances along these lines may transform our whole way of life and certainly will affect employment and economic growth.

2. *Employment patterns will change.*

New jobs will be created in the information/service sector of the economy as people continue to want more services and especially as advances are made in electronic technology. Many information jobs opening up as a result of growth in electronic technology will require high-level skills, particularly stressing facility in manipulating symbols. Other jobs will require lower level skills, such as entering data into and retrieving data from computers, but will allow the upgrading of some clerical and technical workers to positions involving computer operations. The general trend away from working directly with industrial machines to working with computers should reduce the physical demands on factory workers.

Other factors that will affect employment are demographic changes and underemployment.

Demographic changes. As a result of the lower birth rate after the mid-1960s than during the post World War II baby boom years, there will be a dramatic slowdown in the number of new workers entering the work force in the late 1980s. The slower rate of growth, however, is expected to be offset somewhat by an increase in the number of women entering the work force (from 46 percent of all women in 1975 to a projected 51 percent in 1990) and by a decrease in the rate of unemployment. As fewer young workers are entering the work force, the post World War II baby boom generation will be reaching middle age. Thus, the average age of the work force will increase. Fewer young workers will be available to take entry level jobs and more middle-aged workers will be competing for career advances.

Underemployment. The problem of underemployment is expected to increase in the 1980s. Already there are more college graduates than jobs requiring higher order skills. The Bureau of Labor Statistics has estimated that by 1980 there will be an annual excess of 140,000 college graduates. Because of this excess, the educational level required to obtain jobs is increasing. In the 1980s, even more than now, a person will likely need a college degree to obtain a job that does not require college-level skills. College graduates are likely to be dissatisfied with jobs that do not use their higher level skills, and persons who have the skills to do the work but do not have a college degree may have difficulty finding a job at all. One possible outcome of this situation is that workers may seek changes in the structure of work that would enable them to use their abilities more productively.

3. *The economic growth rate is expected to slow down.*

The steady economic growth rate that characterized the period from 1946 to 1966 has slowed, and this trend will likely continue into the 1980s. The following factors are expected to reduce the growth rate.

Concern for the availability of natural resources. This country is using natural resources at a rapid rate, and although no serious scarcity is expected in the 1980s, fear of future shortages will put constraints on the use of resources. Prices most certainly will increase, as will dependency on foreign sources.

Low level of business investment. The proportion of the Gross National Product going to business investments has been low in recent years. Futhermore, businesses have been required to invest capital that they otherwise might have used to increase productivity to meet environmental standards imposed by the government. If the level of business investment remains at recent low levels, capital expenditures could be insufficient to meet production demands, causing supply bottlenecks and sporadic shortages.

Technological maturity. The rate of technological invention has slowed in such traditionally productive industries as steel, household appliances, clothing, and automobiles. Since inventions in these industries have accounted for much of our growth in the past, this slowdown is expected to affect our overall growth rate negatively.

Worker dissatisfaction. Unless creative solutions are found to be the problem of underemployment, many workers are apt to be dissatisfied with their work and, thus, less productive than they would be if they found their work satisfying.

Slower growth rate of the work force. The demographic changes described earlier suggest a potential shortage of new workers entering the work force in the 1980s.

Together, the above five factors are expected to result in a slow rate of economic growth in the 1980s. One factor that is expected to increase growth and, therefore, to offset these negative factors to a certain extent is an increase in labor productivity. Although worker dissatisfaction could negatively affect labor productivity unless solutions are found to the problems of underemployment, two factors are expected to increase productivity. First, slower growth of the labor force is expected to result in an increase in the capital stock per worker, or the capital/labor ratio. Although it has not been established, it is generally believed that the more capital equipment or facilities allocated for the use of a worker, the more productive the worker will be. Second, demographic changes resulting in a greater percentage of mature workers in the labor force are expected to increase productivity.

While the predicted increase in productivity is expected to alleviate an economic slowdown somewhat, there are several factors whose effects on the economy are still unknown. First, resource substitution could lessen the effects of the short supply of some natural resources, but the development of substitution technology is expensive and can take many years. Second, changes needed to meet government-imposed environmental standards will be made by the 1980s for the most part and, thus, more capital will be available for investments to increase productivity.

Third, the slowdown in the rate of invention in the traditionally productive industries may be offset somewhat by the rise of the electronics industry and associated technological innovation in that area. In addition, use of computers in the manufacturing process could increase productivity dramatically, at the same time greatly reducing manufacturing costs. However, because the initial conversion to computer-assisted manufacturing (CAM) is expensive, and accompanied by resistance on the part of labor, it is still unknown how much computer-assisted manufacturing will affect the economy of the 1980s.

Fourth, productivity in the service sector of the economy may be heightened, both through use of better management techniques and through use of new technologies. Fast-food services such as McDonald's are examples of how improved management techniques are being used to increase the reliability and efficiency of services; the automatic car wash and automatic coin receptacles at toll booths demonstrate the use of technology. Again, however, it is unknown how much change will be instituted and, thus, it is impossible to predict the impact of such change.

Finally, the effect of increasing affluence on the economy is unknown. Once people reach a certain level of affluence, their interest tends to shift from material goods and income security to comfort, leisure, safety, and intrinsic rewards in their jobs, such as being involved in interesting work and having a sense of accomplishment. Such a shift, already underway, is expected to affect the pattern of economic growth in the 1980s, but the extent of the change remains to be seen.

Implications for the Handicapped

The economic trends described here could significantly affect the lives of handicapped individuals and the services provided them. The projected decline in the rate of economic growth will mean a decreased number of federal, state, and local dollars available for new or existing services and programs. Because implementation of concepts such as "appropriate education," "normalization," and "full participation of the handicapped in society" often requires new services and programs, these movements may be curtailed as a result of decreased levels of funding. Also, programs and services for the handicapped may be forced into competition with those of other groups such as the disadvantaged or ethnic minority groups. Thus, the movement to obtain equality for handicapped individuals, though compatible with the changing values and beliefs of the society, could be stalemated by changing economic conditions. This, in turn, could result in more litigation and political pressure on behalf of the handicapped.

Decreased levels of federal funds could be used as a compelling argument for "block funding," or distribution of federal education funds to the states in a lump sum without earmarking them for specific programs. Under such conditions, programs for the handicapped would be in competition with all other educational programs for federal funds, and historical precedent suggests that they would not receive their fair share of funds. Futhermore, when programs have received adequate funding, the comparatively high cost of services for the handicapped has been perceived by other groups at times as more than a fair share, leading to hostility and backlash.

If levels of federal funding for programs and services for the handicapped were to remain constant or be cut back, state and local agencies would likely be much less willing to submit to increased federal regulation and monitoring of programs in order to qualify for decreasing dollars. Critical initiatives in extending equal rights to the handicapped, such as PL 94-142 or Section 504 of the Vocational Rehabilitation Act of 1973, have come from the federal government and have been supported in large part because of financial incentives (federal dollars to cover a percentage of excess costs) or sanctions (the withholding of HEW funds). Decreased levels of federal funds could make the incentives seem less attractive and the sanctions less damaging, and thus could seriously slow this movement.

On the other hand, decreasing funds for the handicapped may force existing programs and services to become more efficient by reducing redundancy and increasing coordination of service agencies. To date, efforts to coordinate services offered to the handicapped by various agencies have met with resistance and "turfmanship." Decreased dollars could provide the impetus for cooperation among agencies, somewhat mitigating the impact of slower economic growth.

In terms of employment, the projected trends could have a positive impact upon the handicapped. The increasing percentage of information jobs, with their emphasis on manipulation of symbols rather than physical operations, strength, or stamina, should mean that physically handicapped individuals will be eligible and easily able to fill an increasing range of jobs in the labor market. Furthermore, the projected slowdown in the number of workers entering the work force in the 1980s should make employers more willing to adapt facilities and jobs to meet the special needs of handicapped workers. Therefore, the employment picture for the physically and sensorially handicapped in particular should be greatly improved.

Although many information jobs involving direct manipulation of symbols may be beyond the capabilities of the mentally handicapped, other information jobs will be relatively routine and clerical in nature. Too, with the increasing application of management techniques that standardize procedures within the services industry, more service jobs may become relatively routinized and thus more easily carried out by the mentally handicapped.

As more jobs fall into the information and service categories, so will the need grow for vocational and educational programs for the handicapped emphasizing different types of skills. Curricula will need to include skills with electronic devices and computers and will need to give greater attention to mathematics, engineering, computer programming, data processing, and the information sciences. Similarly, as the range of service jobs expands, vocational programs will need to be updated constantly to include requisite skills.

Overall, employment opportunities for the handicapped should continue to improve. It was suggested, however, that an effect of the disparity between the number of workers attaining higher levels of education and the number of jobs requiring those levels of education was to raise the education requirements of lower level jobs even though the tasks themselves might not require a high educational level. This phenomenon may close some jobs to some handicapped individuals that they otherwise would be perfectly capable of carrying out.

SOCIAL INSTITUTIONS

The values, economic conditions, and technology of a society inevitably are reflected in its social institutions. As changing values and beliefs interact with economic and technological developments, correlative changes can be anticipated in various social institutions. Mr.

Klineberg pointed out as an example that prior to the industrial revolution when 80 percent of the nation lived on farms, the family was the economic and productive unit, the center for socialization, and the basis for identity of individuals. Men and women had clear-cut divisions of role and responsibility. Families were large, and divorce rates were kept low by structural bonds of mutual dependency. With industrialization, urbanization, and the passage of child labor laws, children no longer were economic assets, and over a period of years the average size of families has progressively declined. Reduced family size, the invention of work-saving devices, and improvements in health resulting in greater longevity have made it more difficult for women to turn childbearing and homemaking into the lifelong, meaningful occupation they once represented. Women's need to find meaning in new areas, combined with economic conditions, has inevitably resulted in a growing number of women entering the work force. As a result, not only has the structure of the family changed, but pressures are increasing for change in the conditions of work.

Mr. Klineberg cited evidence similar to that discussed in the values and economics sections, that economic conditions, as well as many of society's beliefs and values, are changing. People are becoming more and more aware that continuous growth in resource utilization or world population cannot be sustained without seriously straining the environment and threatening the quality of life. At the same time, in response to large bureaucracies and centralized government, many individuals are seeking new modes of freedom in more manageable social units wherein they can attain a sense of personal control over as many areas of their lives as possible. One example of this is the growing focus not just on jobs, but on *meaningful* work roles. Unfortunately, society is having a hard time in meeting the demand for meaningful work, for reasons such as slower economic growth, higher educational levels of the population, and the entry of more women into the work force. At the panel meeting, Mr. Klineberg discussed changes that are occurring in the structure of families, work roles, communities, social services, and education.

Trends

1. *The nature of families is changing rapidly and will continue to change.*

    Smaller families. The average size of the family decreased from 3.67 members in 1960 to 3.37 members in 1977; from 1960 to 1977 the percentage of families with three or more children decreased from 20.5 percent to 14.7 percent whereas the percentage of families with only one child increased from 18.4 percent to 19.6 percent.[3] One result of couples having fewer children may be that each child will become the recipient of greater levels of parental attention and resources.

A greater variety of family types. The nuclear family — a working husband, a wife at home, and several children — no longer is the predominant family pattern. The number of two-career families has increased. In fact, in 1975 only 34 percent of husband/wife families were families in which the husband was the sole breadwinner. In addition, single-parent families are becoming more prevalent because of a rising divorce rate.[4] In 1960, 9.3 percent of children under eighteen years of age lived in single-parent families; in 1975 the percentage had increased to 17.1.[5] Finally, an increasing percentage of couples choose to remain childless.

Shifts in the roles of men and women. As women share increasingly in the financial support of the family unit, men are likely to share increasingly in the responsibilities of homemaking and nurturing.

Demand for services. Greater numbers of women in the work force will mean that service delivery patterns that assume someone is home during the day, or when schools are dismissed at 3:00 p.m., are increasingly inappropriate. A demand may arise for new services or for changes in current service delivery systems to accommodate these factors.

2. *The next 15 years will demonstrate a press to expand the number of meaningful jobs and to make work roles and lifetime work cycles more flexible.*

More flexible work schedules. As more women enter the work force, as single-parent families become more common, as men begin sharing in homemaking and nurturance, and as people place a greater emphasis on personal development, they will likely demand more flexible work schedules. This change may include more widespread use of flexible work hours, expanded opportunities for part-time work, new interest in unpaid leaves of absence, and in other ways of broadening individual choices and integrating work with other responsibilities.

---

[3] From U.S. Bureau of Census. *Statistical Abstract of the United States: 1978.* (99th edition). Washington, DC, 1978.

[4] The number of divorces in the U.S. has increased from 393,000 in 1960 to 1,122,000 in 1978 (from the National Center of Health Statistics).

[5] From U.S. Department of Commerce. *Social Indicators 1976.* Washington, DC, 1977.

177

Lifelong learning. Schooling may become a lifelong activity. More rapid expansion of the knowledge base will create a need for continual re-education and updating of skills. Individuals will need to be able to move back and forth between work and school with greater ease. Sabbatical leaves and radical career or job changes may become much more common.

Worker democracy. A more highly educated work force may press for a greater say in how work is done. Workers may demand a role in decision making in order to make jobs more meaningful and to gain a greater sense of control over that portion of their lives.

3. *Smaller communities may be considered desirable places to live once again.*

The desire for a sense of greater personal control and for more manageable social units also may affect the communities in which people choose to live. Since 1970 a remarkable reversal has taken place in the 200-year-old pattern of urbanization. Until the beginning of this decade, the population in American cities and suburbs was growing rapidly and the population in rural counties was declining. Between 1970 and 1976, the total U.S. population grew by 5.6 percent; the population in metropolitan areas grew by 4.7 percent, and the population in non-metropolitan areas grew by 8.0 percent.[6] This may indicate that cities have surpassed the limits of manageable size in terms of the amenities they can offer, and that people are seeking work and social settings more "human" in scale. Small towns and rural areas may experience a revitalization because their smaller scale — enhanced by cultural linkage to the outside world through sophisticated, interactive communication systems — will make them more attractive places in which to live.

4. *The cost of social services may increase.*

To date, many social service agencies have relied on a small professional staff supplemented by community volunteers to provide high-quality/low-budget services to clients. Most often, community volunteers have been non-working women who could devote a day or more a week to the social service agency. As more women enter or return to the work force, a decline in volunteerism can be expected. This will cause problems in the delivery of social services. New paid professional

---

[6] Testimony entitled, "Internal Migration in the United States since 1970," presented to the House Select Committee on Population, February 8, 1978, by Calvin Beale, Department of Agriculture Economic Research Service.

roles may have to be established, and the cost of social services can be expected to increase. This could be mitigated somewhat by a movement toward more flexible work schedules that might permit greater range of individuals — working and non-working men and women — to devote time to human services.

5. *The decline in birth rate will continue to result in declining school enrollments.*

Fewer students resulting from a declining birth rate, combined with technological advances in teaching devices (computer-assisted instruction), could permit educators to pay more attention to individual differences among children and to develop individualized educational programs for all children. On the other hand, deteriorating economic conditions may lead to a growing reaction against monies spent for public needs and welfare. Passage of Proposition 13 in California may be indicative of such a mood. Thus, in the face of declining enrollments, people may choose to maintain the same homogeneous, large-group approach to education and to cut public spending by closing schools and laying off teachers.

Implications for the Handicapped

Trends in the social institutions will have specific effects on the provision of services to the handicapped. As the number of single-parent or two-career families increases, the demand for extended day programs, particularly for severely handicapped students, may become greater. In the past, severely handicapped children who remained at home have required extensive parental care and attention. As family structures change, families may seek assistance in providing this care through extended day programs or summer school programs. Parents also have less time to participate in activities designed to assure an appropriate education for their handicapped children. With fewer children and more attention focused on each one, though, parents are unlikely to be willing to settle for less than a quality education for their children. Thus, it is likely that there will be a growing demand for paid child advocates who can assume parts of the parental role and responsibilities in activities including due process procedures.

More flexible work schedules should allow jobs to be more easily accommodated to special needs of handicapped individuals. If work cycles and education cycles become more interspersed, and if the concepts of life-long learning and mid-life career changes become more common, educational programs will have to be developed and extended to meet the needs of handicapped adults. New curricula and new types of personnel will be needed for such an effort. Declining numbers of school-age children may facilitate this movement by creating a surplus of school facilities and personnel that could be used for programs for handicapped adults.

Traditionally, rural areas have had inherent problems in providing and coordinating services for the handicapped. If the population is increasingly dispersed, service delivery may become even more difficult. The efforts of various service agencies in rural areas *must* be coordinated to assure comprehensive services. Interactive telecommunications capabilities, as they are developed, may alleviate this problem somewhat by allowing sophisticated linkage systems to connect service providers in rural areas with diagnostic or consultative personnel in metropolitan areas. For example, by using interactive television, a distant diagnostic prescriptive teacher could assist a regular class teacher in a rural area in making curricular adaptations for a handicapped student.

Service agencies for the handicapped, like other service agencies, have relied heavily on volunteer help. The next few years will show an increasing need to fund, recruit, and train a wide variety of auxiliary personnel to supplement a diminishing corp of volunteers, and also to develop certification standards and career ladders for these new kinds of personnel. On the other hand, some service agencies may be able to change or extend their hours of operation, to adapt to single-parent or two-career families and to utilize volunteers who may have full-time careers but also would like to devote some time to human services. This change could alleviate the upcoming personnel shortage somewhat.

Finally, if school systems take advantage of declining enrollments to provide all students with individualized educational programs, more handicapped students could likely receive major portions of their educational programs in regular settings — because classes would be smaller, regular education teachers would be more accustomed to dealing with individual differences among children, and technological advances in teaching devices would facilitate individualized instruction. If, however, communities decide to cut school budgets in the face of declining enrollments and tightening economic conditions, these conditions that would facilitate integration of handicapped students probably would not occur; instead, a decline in the support system offered to teachers and increasing resistance among regular educators to the integration of handicapped students would likely result.

TECHNOLOGY

Technology pervades our lives. This has been seen in the preceding discussions of values, economics, and social institutions. Technological advances have allowed only a small percentage of the labor force to produce all of our food and material goods. Because as a society our basic needs are well met, for the most part, we have begun to look for new ways to improve the quality of our lives.

One technological innovation that has opened up limitless possibilities for further changes to our way of life is the computer. The recent development of microcircuitry has made it possible for computer circuitry that used to require a large amount of space to now fit into a space smaller than a dime. The smallness of these new computers allows them to be used in innumerable previously inaccessible places, and it also increases their speed. The new mini-computers, further, are more reliable and considerably cheaper than the previous computers. In fact, technology has progressed so rapidly that computers with the same capabilities as those used by American scientists in 1959 are presently available to the general public for $700.

Computers and microelectronics can take over or greatly improve many of the routine tasks at home, school and work, giving us further freedom to explore and enhance other facets of our lives. For example, at home, computers can keep track of family financial and personal records and can regulate appliance usage; at school, they can teach skills such as spelling and addition, match students with appropriate programs, and keep track of the progress of individual students; at work, computers already are handling all kinds of data processing functions for large companies and will be increasingly available to smaller companies in the future.

Because of the computer, many tasks that previously required physical labor can now be accomplished by pushing a button. And in the future, even button pushing may become unnecessary. As computers are made more sensitive, any body movement — wave of the hand, a stomp of the foot, a wink, a vocal command — will be able to activate a computer or other electronic device. In addition to taking over many routine tasks, computers will extend our physical abilities and our abilities to communicate. At the panel discussion, Mr. Coates described some of the technological devices available to increase our physical abilities and to facilitate communication. He also discussed problems that interfere with technological advances.

181

Trends

1. *Technology that will expand our physical abilities and our abilities to communicate will continue to be developed.*

Physical abilities. Many technological devices to increase our physical abilities already exist. Improvements to these devices and development of new devices are expected in the 1980s. Some of these devices and their functions are:

— The *voice chopper,* which compresses tape recorded speech without distortion so a person can obtain information through listening almost as fast as through reading;

— *Radar devices* that can be worn on the body, to increase a person's ability to perceive the environment;

— *Biofeedback devices* that convert physiological responses to a sound or light signal, used in combination with operant conditioning to give persons control over their physiological responses; with these devices, persons have learned, for example, to lower their blood pressure, rid themselves of migraine headaches, and increase their circulation;

— The *hardyman exoskeleton,* developed as part of the space program, which can increase a person's strength tenfold;

— *Electronic devices* such as the pacemaker, implanted in the body to assist in carrying out natural functions.

Ability to communicate. Satellite hookups and interactive television are beginning to broaden the capabilities of our telecommunications systems. People from various areas of the country or of the world now can hold group discussions over the telephone. By connecting the telephone with television, visual contact becomes available during telephone conversations; by connecting it with a keyboard (Cyberphone), typed messages can be transmitted.

Computer linkages allow even more sophisticated interactions. Wider application of this capability is expected in the 1980s. Systems will begin to bring services available in urban centers to rural areas, link persons with specialized knowledge to those with a need for their knowledge, and bring persons in contact with others who have similar interests, making possible more effective coalitions.

2. *Effective new products that are feasible may not be developed.*

Although technological potential is almost limitless, many new products that would better our lives either will not be available or will not be as effective as they could be. Some of the reasons for this are discussed below.

Information. Although technological expertise abounds, we have no systematic way of making that expertise generally available. Often, a need exists and a technological capability or product exists to meet that need, but those with the need are unaware of the technology, and vice versa. Even supposing a broad mutual awareness, persons aware of a need may have difficulty describing the problem in enough detail for technological experts to devise a practical solution.

A communication problem also exists from field to field among the professions. The body of knowledge is so fragmented by specialty area that developments in one area often are unknown in another. Thus, vital connections that would allow technological advances may be overlooked.

Economics. Some technological advances are prevented by economic conditions. If a company is making a profit from an existing product, little incentive exists to improve the product by applying more current technology. Also, new products may not be developed because the market is unproven or because the product's use is limited to a small group of persons. Furthermore, many innovations are conceptualized by individuals who do not have the resources available to test, evaluate, or market their inventions, and therefore are unable to carry out their concepts. Even when new products are developed, they often are too expensive to be of use to many of the persons they were designed to help.

Standards and certification. No source similar to the Underwriters Laboratory is available to set standards for all new products, so the public has no satisfactory means of knowing if a product is reliable or that it incorporates the best technology available. Additionally, there is no outside incentive for companies with existing products to keep up with technological advances, other than competition from other companies.

One solution to each of these problems would be for the government to become involved in disseminating information and setting standards. It even could provide a guaranteed market for products that would benefit only a small group of users. Unfortunately, according to Mr. Coates, the government, like all bureaucracies, is a fragmented and conservative organization that is afraid of change, has a narrow rather than broad focus, has no structure for rewarding a job well done, and is more likely to play it safe than to take the risks needed to find creative, large-scale solutions to existing problems.

Implications for the Handicapped

Many forces in our society have combined to change our attitude toward the handicapped from one of exclusion to one of inclusion. Handicapped children are being educated in regular classes in schools, and handicapped adults are becoming part of the work force. Technological advances have reinforced this trend toward inclusion of the handicapped.

The movement toward a telecommunications-rich society, less dependent on mobility and more on the ability to operate intellectual machinery, is opening vast job opportunities for the handicapped. Technology is a great democratizer, a great equalizer. Buttons do not care about race, religion, national origin, ex, or handicapping conditions.

Technological devices can be used to increase handicapped persons' abilities to participate more fully in the activities of society. The voice chopper can allow blind persons to hear almost as fast as others can read; the Cyberphone can allow deaf persons to communicate by phone; radar devices can increase the mobility of blind persons; and hardyman armor can increase the strength of persons who are physically weak. Sensitive electronic devices implanted in the body could be used to increase the muscular control and coordination of those whose physical difficulties interfere with their ability to function. These are just a few examples of how technology can be used to aid handicapped persons.

As noted, although many of these devices are available, the technology exists to improve what is available and to develop new devices designed for specific problems. Because the handicapped are a relatively small group with diverse needs, and because their problems are not standard nor easily standardizable, many devices that could be useful to them are not being developed. Development of such devices would require collaboraton among persons from various fields. The problems and costs of such collaboration, along with the difficulty in standardizing equipment for the handicapped, make it unprofitable for businesses to develop devices for the handicapped.

Many of the devices that are developed are done so by individuals who have the ingenuity to find solutions to personal problems but who lack the inclination or the resources to make those devices generally available. This situation may improve somewhat in the future if developments in computer-assisted manufacturing allow small-lot manufacturing to be more feasible economically. As was pointed out in the economics section, though, it is not yet clear whether the capital investments necessary to introduce computerization into manufacturing industries will be made.

Another factor that could improve the situation is the increased number of politically active aged persons in America. These persons are likely to have certain needs similar to those of the handicapped. As a combined group, the handicapped and the aged would increase the market for new devices and, therefore, increase the incentive for businesses to develop such devices.

The Bureau of Education for the Handicapped and other government agencies have funded the development of a number of devices for the handicapped but, as Mr. Coates pointed out during the panel discussion, much more could be done. Government agencies could bring together, on a long-term basis, technologists, handicapped persons, and persons involved in providing services to the handicapped, to explore specific problems of the handicapped and technological solutions to those problems. Over a period of time, these persons could develop a satisfactory and productive way of communicating with one another. Government agencies also could provide more support for the development and certification of a number of technological devices that would benefit the handicapped, could subsidize the marketing of these devices so they would be available at reasonable cost, and could lobby for funding of these activities. Too, government agencies could serve an important function by disseminating information about products to potential users.

As handicapped persons become more and more politicized, better ways almost certainly will be found to apply technological advances to products for the handicapped. In the past, handicapped persons have been isolated, with few means to make their needs known. but handicapped persons are beginning to move out of isolation. Telecommunications systems can assist in this movement. People with similar problems who are scattered across the country could have the means to communicate with each other, discuss their mutual needs, and collaborate in getting those needs met. Persons with specialized knowledge could be made available to handicapped persons even in remote rural areas. Information and resources could be brought into the homes of handicapped persons who are unable to go out. Finally, increased communications could facilitate the sharing of information vital to development and distribution of needed technological devices.

MEDICINE

In the past, medical progress has done much to reduce the incidence and severity of handicapped conditions. For example, control of rubella has reduced the number of deaf and blind persons; development of the

185

polio vaccine has reduced the incidence of orthopedic handicaps; and treatment of Wilson's disease actually has reversed mental deficiency in individuals who improperly metabolize copper. Severe handicapping conditions probably have more than 4,000 separate causes. The major causes change with medical advances.

New breakthroughs in fields including biochemistry, neurophysiology, and genetics are expected to further reduce the incidence of physical and severe mental handicapping conditions. In addition, medical technology has been aided by electronic/information technology in the production of promising devices and techniques for use in diagnosis, treatment, and prevention of handicapping conditions. Interaction between these fields has produced computerized x-ray type diagnostic devices and ultrasound applied to diagnosis, as well as computerized laboratory analysis and record-keeping techniques that increase accuracy and shorten time requirements, potentially reducing costs. At the panel meeting, Mr. Moser discussed medical advances in diagnostic techniques, neonatal care, and public health, which are expected to contribute to the reduction of handicaps.

Trends

1. *Dissemination of new diagnostic techniques is expected to contribute to the reduction of many conditions.*

The great need for new diagnostic techniques is indicated by the high percentage of cases in which the cause of severe mental retardation is unknown (40 percent). Widespread use of new diagnostic tools and techniques promises to make a drastic cut in such statistics. For example, it has been estimated that widespread use of the CAT scanner, a computerized device that produces in three dimensions the type of image that traditional x-rays produce in two dimensions, could determine the cause of retardation in as many as 10 percent of the cases in which cause is currently unknown. Other diagnostic procedures that are expected to make major contributions to the reduction of handicapping conditions are amniocentesis and genetic screening programs.

Amniocentesis. The process of amniocentesis allows examination of fetal cells and amniotic fluid before a child is born, enabling the earliest possible diagnosis and treatment for a variety of conditions. Amniotic fluid is extracted from the womb, and fetal cells contained in the fluid are centrifuged and microscopically examined. Nearly 200 different disorders are detectable through amniocentesis; those with highest incidence are

Down's syndrome and meningomyelocele (incomplete closure of the spine). Although amniocentesis is considered a relatively safe procedure (complications occur about once in 5,000 cases), it is recommended only in instances of clear risk of a pathological condition. Computer analysis is not yet used for chromosomal studies of the fetal cells, but it is technologically possible and holds promise for reducing the expense and laboratory time required by amniocentesis.

Ethical problems arise, however, when early diagnostic techniques identify a condition that cannot be treated, such as Down's syndrome. Some genetics centers will not perform amniocentesis unless the parents indicate that they would interrupt pregnancy if results are positive. Some people also believe that if parents choose to continue the pregnancy with the foreknowledge that the child has Down's syndrome, the parents should take financial responsibility for meeting the special needs of the child. Mr. Moser expressed repugnance toward this position. Others think that foreknowledge of the child's condition is worthwhile if the parents choose to continue pregnancy, since it will at least allow time to prepare for the child and begin learning ways of caring for the special needs associated with the handicapping condition.

Genetic screening. Reduction of metabolic disorders has been facilitated greatly by newborn screening programs such as those used to detect phenylketonuria (PKU). PKU is characterized by an inability to metabolize phenylalanine, a nutritional substance contained in many foods. Babies found to have PKU are put on a special diet until age four to six, and then they may go on a normal diet. If the children are not given the special diet, excess phenylalanine in their blood will cause retardation. Screening techniques for diseases like PKU are becoming simpler to use and less expensive, exemplified by the Guthrie technique, which allows tests for as many as 10 disorders to be performed on a single spot of infant's blood sent to the laboratory on a postcard.

2. *Improved neonatal care is expected to continue reducing the incidence of handicapping conditions through better facilities and earlier treatment.*

Armed with the knowledge provided by new diagnostic techniques, the physician is much better prepared to deal with special needs of the newborn infant. It is anticipated that prematurity not complicated by or caused by other health problems will be manageable and that many major lifelong complications will be preventable. Because many forms of cerebral palsy are related to prematurity and difficulties at the time of birth, the incidence of cerebral palsy is anticipated to be materially reduced. Recent reductions in one form of cerebral palsy (cerebral diplegia) support this expectation.

Regional perinatal care centers have established excellent records in reducing the incidence of cerebral palsy and in saving premature babies. As more such centers are established and new technology is disseminated throughout the country, we can expect a drop in problems associated with cerebral palsy and prematurity.

Some concern has been expressed that babies who are saved from death caused by prematurity may be left with handicapping conditions. Recent studies suggest that this is not the case — babies of average weight for their gestational age usually survive prematurity in good health, but babies of small weight for their gestation age, whose small size indicated that they had some health problem *in utero,* are more likely to be left with some disabling condition. Thus, medical treatment can make up for time lost in the womb but cannot yet cure many pathological conditions that begin *in utero.*

3. *The field of public health is expected to contribute to the reduction of handicapping conditions through immunization programs, screening for environmentally related conditions, better record keeping and tracking of potential victims of disease, and dissemination of medical techniques and technology.*

Infectious diseases. Infectious diseases account for about twice as many cases of mental retardation as do genetic causes or inborn error of metabolism. Various forms of measles (rubella and rubeola), the major handicapping infectious diseases, can be prevented through immunization programs. Rubeola possibly can be entirely eradicated, since it has no animal carrier and immunity is permanent.

Although immunization for many diseases is often free and required by municipal law, many families still neglect to have all their members immunized — possibly because of the logistics involved in obtaining the health care or because of ineffective publicity campaigns. Some such campaigns present immunization as a bureaucratic requirement rather than stress it as a necessary health protection measure. For a variety of reasons, the problem of reaching every citizen who needs immunization is a significant one.

Environmental hazards. Environmental hazards are the cause of a variety of debilitating conditions. Discovering and controlling harmful substances and preventing their disabling effects are major public health tasks. Lead poisoning, for example, accounts for about two percent of the cases of retardation. Screening for lead poisoning can identify and minimize damage in some cases, but the screening is subject to the same problems as immunization programs in reaching citizenry — too many cases go undetected and untreated.

Record keeping. The importance of record keeping is exemplified by a major public health task facing us: control of maternal PKU. This problem has arisen because a relatively large number of women who were treated successfully in childhood for PKU are now approaching the childbearing age. Screening programs that began in the 1950s and 1960s prevented these women from developing PKU retardation, but a recent discovery has been that unless they return to the special diet during pregnancy, their children may be born retarded as a result of the excessive phenylalanine in the mother's blood. Although the child does not have the disease, the mother's excessive phenylalanine will cause the child's retardation. Thus, unless a follow-up to the screening that took place in the 1950s and 1960s is undertaken, the cases of retardation saved by screening will be replaced by cases caused by maternal PKU.

Since computer use greatly facilitates performance of such screening and tracking tasks, the record-keeping function of public health services is expected to be aided increasingly by more efficient computer linkage systems. Thus, in addition to aiding statistical and etiological research, computer technology can increase the capability of the public health system to track potential victims.

Such tracking, as well as the storage of massive data concerning individuals by a centralized (government) source, is complicated by privacy issues including those of individual rights. The seeming incompatibility of keeping such data and at the same time ensuring the individual's privacy may be resolved by new developments in technology that would allow storage of an individual's entire medical history on his or her own portable "floppy disc" (an information storage device similar to a flexible phonograph record). In this way, the individual could have control over who would have access to the information, yet still allow it to be entered (with or without identification) into statistical data bases at his or her discretion.[7] Although such a system is technically possible, its feasibility for widespread use will depend upon the general availability of computers in medical facilities.

Dissemination of medical technology. As part of its charge to ensure the availability of basic health care, the public health system performs *de facto* dissemination of medical technology. The success of many of the techniques discussed in regard to reducing handicapping conditions (e.g., neonatal screening programs) will depend upon their availability through the public health system.

---

[7] Mr. Coates discussed this idea at the panel meeting.

Such dissemination of technology, though, usually occurs sporadically, often characterized by clear geographical centers of excellence. In the example of neonatal screening, programs have been successful in some states, while other states have lagged behind. The variety of conditions and problems affecting application of new techniques in various areas led some panel members to question how rapidly public health program improvements actually would occur.

IMPLICATIONS FOR THE FIELD OF SPECIAL EDUCATION

The trends just discussed could impact upon the field of special education in a variety of ways. This section considers some of these implications.

1. *Changes in the Target Population*

Currently, special education programs and projects focus primarily on handicapped infants and children through age twenty-one, encompassing all forms and degrees of handicap. Information presented in this article suggests that changes are possible in the target population for special education programs that would greatly affect those programs.

Educational programs for handicapped adults. The trend toward adult education and lifelong learning is expected to become stronger, particularly if augmented by trends toward midlife career changes, sabbatical leaves, updating of obsolete job skills, and desires for self-actualization. This trend is likely to create a push for educational programs for handicapped adults, both to encourage personal fulfillment and to teach career-related knowledge and skills.

Fewer handicapped students. The decline in the birth rate and in school enrollments will mean fewer handicapped students. Futhermore, technological advances may continually reduce the number of students with handicapping conditions who need special education or related services. New prosthetic devices may allow increasing numbers of students with physical or sensorial impairments to function in regular education programs. Advanced information and telecommunication systems might make some skills, such as reading ability, less critical in terms of participation in regular education programs and in society at large. Therefore, for a growing number of students having handicapping conditions, the provision of prosthetic devices or some special materials may constitute the extent of services needed. Also, medical advances may continue to reduce the size of the severely handicapped population. This

190

could be particuarly true for certain types of handicapping conditions including Down's syndrome, cerebral palsy, and deaf/blind conditions.

2. *Changes in the Concept of Educational Programs*

With increasing numbers of single-parent and two-career families, the concept of school as a place children go six hours a day, nine months a year for academic instruction is likely to be challenged. Faced with the need for high-quality child-care arrangements, parents will likely demand extended day-care programs and programs that operate year-round. These extended programs probably will differ from the traditional academically oriented school programs by emphasizing more recreational, social, artistic, and musical activities. Such programs are as likely to be demanded by parents of nonhandicapped students as by parents of handicapped students.

Additionally, increased concern about treating people as whole entities, combined with budget cuts necessitating careful coordination of services, may mean that new kinds of educational organizations integrating a variety of social, educational, and medical services would emerge. The concept of educational programs as teachers instructing groups of children under the supervision of an educational administrator, then, could change drastically.

3. *Needs for New Curricula, Technological Devices, and Service Delivery Models*

Curricula. Some of the potential future developments would create a need for different types of curricular materials. An increasing focus on the whole person and self-actualization could stimulate an interest in music, the arts, and other nonacademic, nonvocational subjects that often have been deemphasized in programs for the handicapped. This type of interest would create a need for curricular materials in these areas.

The shift to an information/services society will require curricula that emphasize occupational and living skills needed by handicapped individuals to function in that society — curricula that emphasize electronic devices and computer operation. Furthermore, the rapid growth of knowledge in this area will necessitate continual updating of these curricula. Finally, if programs are extended to include the handicapped adult, curricula appropriate to this population will need to be generated.

Technological devices. Technological progress will continue to make possible a whole range of prosthetic and instructional devices that will allow handicapped students to increasingly function in and benefit from less restrictive educational programs. Thus, there will be a continuing demand to develop or adapt and certify such devices. To do this efficiently will require an on-going dialogue and a way of communicating with technologists in fields such as electronics or telecommunications so that they will be able to understand the individual problems and needs of the handicapped and can offer specific technological solutions to those problems.

Service delivery models. Several of the trends discussed earlier would necessitate new service delivery models. For example, an extension of programs to include handicapped adults would likely create a demand for service delivery models for this population. Traditionally, delivery of services in sparsely populated areas has been problematic, so decentralization and a greater dispersion of the general population would make even more critical the identification of effective service delivery models for low-population areas. Furthermore, given the rate of change in telecommunications, the models explored should make use of sophisticated telecommunication systems to the maximum extent possible. Finally, the potential structural and curricular changes within schools would require service delivery models using new educational techniques and different patterns of staff utilization.

4. *Needs for New Educational Media and Materials, Devices, and Distribution Networks*

Media and materials for use in regular classes. If more handicapped students are enabled to participate in regular education programs because of new prosthetic devices or changes in regular education programs to make them more individualized, the demand for educational media and materials for these students most likely would increase, particularly for materials that interface with the regular education program.

Telecommunications linkage systems. Advances in telecommunications will enable sophisticated, interactive systems that could link handicapped individuals or service providers with educational services, resources, and information banks at sometimes distant points. As more handicapped students participate in regular programs, and if the greater population dispersion continues as forecast, the importance of such systems would grow. Development and coordination of such linkage systems could be an important function of special education agencies.

Development and marketing of devices. To the extent that technological knowledge is applied to problems of the handicapped and new prosthetic devices are developed, the demand will increase for government agencies such as BEH to market, distribute, and subsidize those devices as well as to disseminate information. This could raise a number of issues concerning the appropriate government role in technological development and marketing.

5. *Need for Different Types of Personnel and Personnel Training*

Child advocates. An increase in single-parent or two-career families may create a greater demand for trained child advocates who could share some of the parents' responsibilities in home/school interactions. Qualifications and training programs would have to be conceived for this advocate designation.

Support personnel. A decline in volunteerism and reduced levels of funding for special education could create a need for more support personnel such as teacher aides, clerical aides, and assistant physical or occupational therapists. Training programs and career ladders would be important in filling these personnel needs. Also, if technological advances are to allow more handicapped students to be educated in regular education programs, the need will arise for more diagnostic/prescriptive teachers, instructional planners, master teachers, and inservice teacher trainers.

Personnel familiar with media and materials. Technological advances that would allow more handicapped students to be educated in regular education programs also would require regular and special education personnel to be more familiar with educational media and materials. Training programs would need to be revised to add media and materials competencies. A need for increasing numbers of special education media and materials specialists also might occur.

Personnel to work with adults. If special education programs and services are to be extended to include adult handicapped persons, great need will develop to prepare personnel to work with this population.

Coordinators. As interagency arrangements become more necessary for providing comprehensive services to handicapped students, coordination of services will become critical. Personnel will be needed who are familiar with the range of services provided by various agencies who can coordinate and facilitate the melding of services from various agencies into comprehensive programs for particular students. Though this task logically could fall within the roles of various existing types of personnel such as guidance counselors or social workers, these persons still would need to be afforded the skills and resources to carry it out.

Personnel to serve severely handicapped students. Over a period of years, advances in medicine could decrease the number of personnel needed to serve declining numbers of severely handicapped students. The impact of this development would not be felt for a number of years, particularly in view of existing personnel shortages to serve this population.

Personnel renewal programs. The rapid rate of legislative,legal, technological, and educational developments concerning services to the handicapped may be inspiring a need for retraining or renewal of both regular and special education personnel. Future years may bring a great deal of interest in programs that would update the skills of certified personnel.

6. *Changes and Problems in Programs to Assist States and Local Districts in Assuring Every Handicapped Child a Free, Appropriate Public Education.*

Difficulty in obtaining compliance. Slowed economic growth likely will affect the amount of money available for services to the handicapped at local, state, and federal levels. Local and state education agencies may respond to reduced funds by changing regulations in ways that affect the quality of services or the number of students served (e.g., increasing permissible class sizes, allowing nonteaching personnel to provide certain services, allowing greater flexibility in procedures and programs, changing the definitions regarding handicapping conditions, omitting certain expensive services from individualized education programs). At the same time, reduced levels of federal and state funding may decrease the potency of sanctions (withholding of PL 94-142 and 89-313 funds or of state funds) for failure to comply with the standards set forth in federal legislation. Thus, to forge a partnership among federal, state, and local agencies in assuring handicapped children a free, appropriate public education conceivably may become more difficult.

Need for new monitoring procedures. Federal and state monitoring could become more difficult as a result of the possible greater flexibility among state regulations, greater numbers of handicapped students served in regular programs, and/or expansion of the concept of education to include other types of programs during a lengthened school day and year, or to include other services such as medical or social. A greater breadth of services, with fewer state guidelines to serve as reference points, would cause problems for state and federal monitoring personnel in determining from annual program plans, end-of-year reports, or administrative reviews whether or not all handicapped children in a given state were receiving appropriate educational programs and services. New monitoring procedures may have to be developed, and staff members may have to conduct administrative reviews to become familiar with a range of new programming and service options.

7. *Need for Vigilance and Advocacy to Assure that Progress toward Implementing National Goals for the Education of Handicapped Students is Maintained*

Slower economic growth coupled with fewer dollars for programs for the handicapped could result in a push to "ease up on" or change provisions of federal and state laws and regulations that assure free, appropriate education programs to all handicapped students and equal opportunities to all handicapped persons. If the gains made in recent years by and on behalf of handicapped persons are not to be jeopardized, special education agencies and personnel must join with other organizations and individuals to advocate the maintenance and implementation of national policies related to the handicapped.

8. *Need for Interagency Coordination*

The implementation of legislation promoting comprehensive services for the handicapped has highlighted the need for coordination and cooperation among agencies serving handicapped persons. In recent years, activities to promote interagency agreements and coordination have been initiated. Information in the previous sections suggests that such activities may become even more important in the future.

Federal, state, and local agencies. A greater degree of population dispersion combined with decreased levels of funding of services for the handicapped would necessitate careful coordination among agencies if comprehensive services are to be provided. It would be critical to develop interagency relationships at the national level and to explore mechanisms that would assure that these relationships would move down and be implemented at state and local levels.

Vocational rehabilitation services. An increasing demand for educational programs and services for the handicapped adult would require careful coordination with agencies dealing with vocational rehabilitation of handicapped persons. The push for services likely will be broader than demand for vocational training, focusing on self-actualization as well as job skills, and the potential for overlapping programs could be great, making planning and coordination among agencies paramount.

Medical and social services and education agencies. Increasing recognition of the need for medical screening, follow-up, and immunizations in preventing handicaps, along with the provision of certain medical services to handicapped students, could focus attention on the school as a good interface point for service delivery. Similarly, the schools may increasingly become an interface point for delivery of certain social services. Then, there would be a strong need to encourage cooperation among medical and social services and education agencies — and to anticipate the possible evolution of new types of multipurpose organizations.

Agencies serving other populations. Many of the prosthetic devices for the handicapped that are or shortly will be technologically feasible will be expensive to develop, certify, manufacture, and market. Many of these devices, though particularly important for the education of handicapped students in terms of permitting better access to programs, will be beneficial to a broader population (handicapped adults, disabled veterans, the aged). It may become increasingly important for agencies serving this broader population to work together in developing joint mechanisms for assuring the development, testing, and marketing of important prosthetic devices.

CONCLUSION

Exploration 1993 provides a picture of certain developments that could transpire in five professional areas that impact upon the provision of services to handicapped persons. These developments have been suggested by experts in the five areas who have looked at trends and events in the present and used them as a basis for projecting the future. Many of the projected trends clearly could have significant effects on the handicapped and on the field of special education and provision of services to the handicapped. At the same time, differences sometimes were voiced among the experts or between the experts and panel members as to the likelihood or implications of particular events or trends. Thus, in many instances the projected trends may seem too speculative to guide policymaking in the present or near future.

What this picture can do is give focus to a previously undifferentiated but open future and highlight some potentially important alternative trends. Some of these trends we may wish simply to track, periodically updating their potential implications for policy. Other trends may be of such importance as to warrant further analyses on delimited trend areas, using more sophisticated and powerful future methodologies.

196

At a minimum, information from the project shows that we would be short-sighted in making future policies regarding programs and services for handicapped students with an assumption that present trends will continue far into the future.

TABLE 1
Relationship of Trends and Implications

Trends If these trends occur . . .	Implications* We would expect . . .
VALUES**	
1. Individuals no longer judged on the basis of economic productivity	Reinforcement of national policy of educating every handicapped person to maximum potential (2,3)
2. Greater emphasis on self-actualization	Less emphasis on vocational training in educational programs for the handicapped, and greater emphasis on subjects such as art and music (2,7)
3. Continued focus on the equality of all groups	
4. Decentralization	Increased acceptance of handicapped persons who cannot work (1,2)
5. Stronger community ties	
6. More manageable government and social institutions	Reinforcement of handicapped persons' full participation in society's mainstream (2,3,4)
7. Expansion of knowledge system to include spiritual, subjective, and creative knowledge	More handicapped persons living in the community rather than in institutions (3,4,5,6)
8. Increased feeling of wholeness and connectedness of all persons	More normal social relationships for handicapped persons; less alienation (4,5,8)
9. Public participation in scientific and technological issues	Increased attention to the whole individual, including attitudes and spirit, in service delivery (2,7,8)
	Increased resistance to labeling and categorical funding systems (8)
	Increased interactive approach in service delivery (8)
	Increased involvement of handicapped persons and their families in planning, implementing, and monitoring programs and treatments (9)

*Numbers in parentheses following each implication designate the trend(s) from which that implication was inferred.
**Some panel members believed that these trends would not occur, that instead an even greater emphasis would be placed on economic productivity, competitiveness, and individual material success.

TABLE 1 (Continued)

Trends If these trends occur . . .	Implications* We would expect . . .
ECONOMICS	
10. Continued shift to an information/ service economy	Decreased government program funding (16)
11. More information/service jobs, including more jobs involving computer operations	Forced competition for dollars between programs for handicapped and other programs at all levels of government (16)
12. Physical demands on factory workers reduced by increasing use of computers	Increased litigation and political pressure on behalf of the handicapped (16)
13. Fewer persons overall entering work force in the 1980s; however, increasing numbers of women entering work force	Increased pressure for federal "block funding" (16) Reduction in the power of federal laws that are enforced by funding incentives and sanctions (16)
14. Decreased unemployment	Need for an increase in efficiency and coordination among service agencies (16)
15. Growing underemployment resulting from increasingly higher educational levels required for jobs	Increased employment opportunities for the handicapped (10,11,12,13,14)
16. Slowed economic growth	Increased number of routine jobs potentially available for the mentally handicapped (17)
17. Application of management techniques and new technologies increasing productivity and reducing costs in the service industries	Curricular changes in educational programs to increase emphasis on information skills (10,11) Unavailability of some jobs to handicapped persons because of spiraling educational requirements (15)
SOCIAL INSTITUTIONS	
18. Greater variety of family types	Greater demand for extended day school programs (18,20,21)
19. Smaller families	Growing demand for paid child advocates (18,19,20,21)
20. More single-parent and two-career families	Easier accommodation of work schedules to meet special needs of handicapped persons (23)
21. Changes in traditional husband/wife roles	
22. Changes in service delivery patterns and demands for new services	Increasing need to develop and extend educational opportunities for handicapped adults (24)

TABLE 1 (Continued)

Trends If these trends occur . . .	Implications* We would expect . . .
23. More flexible work schedules	Need to develop curricula and to train personnel for the instruction of handicapped adults (24)
24. Lifelong learning	
25. Return to smaller communities	Use of surplus educational facilities for adult instruction (24,27)
26. Increased costs for social services/ decline in volunteers	Need for better coordination and communication among service agencies, particularly in rural areas (25,26)
27. Continued decline in birth rate and school enrollment	
	Need to fund, recruit, and train a wide variety of auxiliary personnel to supplement a diminishing corps of volunteers (26)
	Possible opportunity for increased individualization of educational programs, allowing more handicapped students to receive more of their education in regular classes, or decline in support for regular teachers and increased resistance to integration of handicapped students because of school budget cuts (27)

TECHNOLOGY

28. Continued expansion of human physical abilities through the use of technology	Greater opportunity for handicapped persons to participate in mainstream of society, including school and work force (28,29)
29. Better communications through use of technology	Increased sharing of information vital to the development and dissemination of new assistive devices (29)
30. Continued problems in disseminating information	
31. Continued economic problems in supporting the research and development of new products	Continued need for government to disseminate information, coordinate and support research and development, establish standards and quality control (30,31,32)
32. Continued problems with standards and certification of new products	Continued increase in politicization of the handicapped (29,30,31,32)
	Greater opportunity for handicapped persons to obtain information and resources and to communicate with others having similar problems (29)

TABLE 1 (Continued)

Trends If these trends occur . . .	Implications* We would expect . . .
MEDICINE	
33. Continued dissemination of new diagnostic techniques and medical technology	Decrease in the incidence of cerebral palsy (33,34)
34. Improved neonatal care	Fewer handicaps ascribed to premature birth (33,34)
35. Increased control of disease through immunization, screening, and better record keeping	Reduction in genetic disorders through amniocentesis and abortion; continued need to develop treatment for genetic disorders (33)
36. Continued problems in reaching all citizens with health care service	Reduction in acquired handicapping conditions (35)
	Continued need to develop better methods of reaching citizenry for immunization and screening (36)

REFERENCES

Cornish, E. S. *A study of the future.* Washington, DC: World Future Society, 1977.

Schiefelbusch, R. L., & Hoyt, R. K., Jr. Three years past 1984. In M. C. Reynolds (Ed.), *Futures of education for exceptional students: Energizing structures.* Minneapolis: National Support System Project, University of Minnesota, 1978.

Shipper, W. V., & Kenowitz, L. A. *Special education futures: A forecast of events affecting the education of exceptional children, 1975-2000.* Washington, DC: National Association of Special Education, 1975.

Although Maynard Reynolds highlights needs for change in pre-service education in this article, nearly all of his points apply with equal force to staff now working in the schools. He makes an interesting point about the need to deinstitutionalize special education staff as well as students. Administrators should find his ideas useful as they struggle with ways to make in-service training more meaningful.

Basic Issues
in Restructuring Teacher Education

Maynard C. Reynolds

To meet the broad and many-faceted changes occurring in the nation's schools in response to PL 94-142, corresponding changes in teacher education are both necessary and inevitable. Judicial pronouncements and the provisions of the law are leading to the adoption of the following new policies.

1. Deinstitutionalization of many seriously handicapped children. In many states, enrollments in special schools and hospitals for retarded, deaf, blind, and emotionally disturbed children have been halved or more.

2. Rapid return of many mildly and moderately handicapped students from special day classes and schools to regular classrooms.

From *Journal of Teacher Education*, November-December 1978, *29*(6), 25-29. Reprinted by permission.

3. Decreasing direct service of special education teachers and emphasizing indirect service, such as consultative and support functions.

4. Virtual elimination of all forms of school demissions (school excuses, exclusions, suspensions, and expulsions), except when due process requirements are met.

5. Redeployment of school psychologists, social workers, and other personnel to serve exceptional students in decentralized settings.

6. Formal involvement of parents of exceptional students in assessment, placement, and planning activities. Due process must be observed in all educational decisions, and special safeguards for parents' rights are detailed in the law.

7. Participation of regular classroom teachers in determining and writing Individualized Educational Plans (IEPs) for exceptional students.

8. Determination of educational goals and programs for exceptional students, based on specific individual learning need rather than gross categories of exceptionality.

These and other policies that focus on handicapped students may be openers for changes that could affect all students. How can one justify working through details of educational plans with the parents of one child and not with those of another, or observing due process in educational decisions in one case and not in another? Fundamental changes are being made in the governance of schools as well as in the rules of most school personnel. College programs must change to meet new school policies and to prepare school personnel for new roles.

As compared with most educational innovations, two distinct features mark the current changes: (a) They are backed by strong legal imperatives, both legislative and judicial. (b) Events and needs already are ahead of the necessary changes in training programs.

This paper gives attention first to changes in the regular classroom teacher role and in the roles of other school staff members, and then to issues and problems that must be resolved by teacher educators.

ROLE CHANGES

A major renegotiation of relations between special and regular education is occurring. Children are crossing old boundaries between special and regular education more often and more easily. Teachers are collaborating more frequently, but much training and retraining are needed.

One view of the renegotiation is the schema of a special education cascade (Fig. 1), an elongated triangle in which the base represents regular school classes as the ultimate mainstream of education — the basic resource for handicapped students. Many students — perhaps even most students with mild and moderate handicaps — are and always have been enrolled in regular classes conducted by regular teachers alone.

Higher levels on the cascade correspond to more specialized and isolated administrative structures for the education of handicapped students. Children placed near the top are separated almost completely from what might be termed the normal home-school-community environment.

Over the past two decades, special education has moved from the "two box" arrangement — children placed in either special or regular classes — toward the more complex cascade structure in Figure 1. A general attitude expressed in the cascade is that handicapped children should be placed no higher than necessary, that their educational progress should be monitored regularly, and that they should be returned toward the regular class as rapidly as feasible. That is one way of expressing the principle of mainstreaming or placement in the least restrictive environment. Alternative placement opportunities will be maintained, but the child will be pressed toward placement in the mainstream whenever possible and reasonable.

Roles of Specialists

PL 94-142 requires a new dimension in the cascade: new and more expansive roles for specialists such as special education teachers, school psychologists, and audiologists. Many specialists are being assigned to roles as resource persons for entire schools. As such, they work closely with regular teachers. Arrows in Figure 1 depict their move toward the mainstream; note the stress on moving personnel as well as children toward the mainstream whenever feasible.

Specialists tend to create environments that only specialists can manage. We know that handicapped children who remain too long and

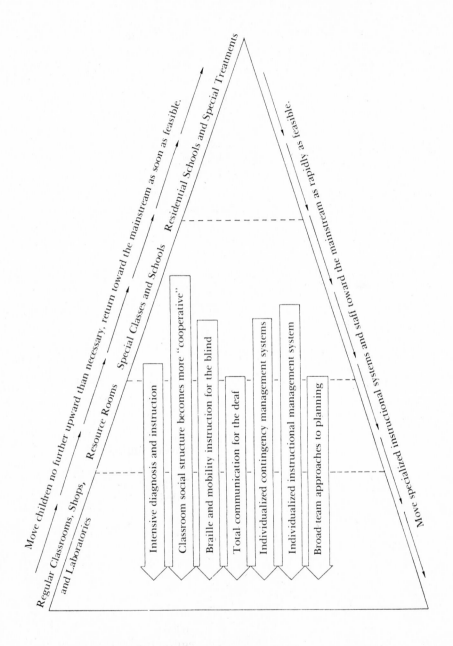

Figure 1. The changing special education cascade: fewer specialized places, more diverse regular places.

exclusively in specialized environments often are prepared poorly for a return to normal school, home, and community life. Specialists left in isolated environments may lose skills, and mislead themselves and others about significant survival skills that handicapped students need.

The brief notations within the arrows in Figure 1 give a few examples of the many changes being made. For example, blind students do not need to be taught mobility, orientation, and braille only in isolated, specialized environments. Such instruction usually can be offered advantageously and in a supportive way while blind students are enrolled in regular school programs.

Specialists' roles in the cascade require many new functions, such as:

1. Competencies in consultative functions. Most specialists now working in the schools have little or no knowledge of the basic literature about and skills of consultation.

2. Ability to diagnose classroom and family situations, as well as student performance. Specialists need strong orientation to ecological models of problem analysis and treatment.

3. Training skills needed to instruct other workers. In a decentralized system, specialists help other workers to perform some functions that earlier may have been their exclusive domain.

Roles of Regular Teachers

The roles of regular classroom teachers are changing and expanding to complement specialists' role changes.

Regular teachers need preparation in the proper and efficient use of consultants. A brief outline of the skills needed by classroom teachers is given in Table 1.

Regular classroom teachers need orientation to the requirements of exceptional students in mainstream environments. Most current literature and college courses overstress the specialists' roles and do not provide good orientation for regular teachers. However, Freeman (1977) has described several programs wherein regular classroom teachers have become close working partners of speech-language pathologists to serve children with speech problems. Reynolds and Birch (1977) have written a textbook specifically to meet the needs of regular teachers and principals.

Regular classroom teachers need to know how to make educational assessments and diagnoses and how to specify goals/objectives in clear

TABLE 1:

CONSULTATION GUIDELINES FOR TEACHERS*

1. Remember that you "own" the problem; you are in charge of the pupil's education or the classroom procedures that are under consideration.

2. Be sure that there is early agreement with the consultant on the nature of the "problem" and how decisions about plans for solution will be made. Draw up an oral or written contract early in the relationship on goals, methods, and responsibilities.

3. Be sure that it is clear that you (the teacher) are the client — that all communication flows to you. The consultant is there to help you structure your work, not somebody else's. This relationship does not preclude some direct assessment of children and observations in the classroom by the consultant, if agreed upon as part of the contract.

4. Avoid status problems. Consultants and clients are co-equals.

5. Avoid entering personal subjective materials (letting attention shift to personal needs and problems); instead, keep content of the relationship centered on the child and the instructional situation.

6. Seek alternative suggestions from the consultant rather than a single, or set plan.

7. Try to use each consultation as a learning experience to increase effective communication and listening skills, build trust among professionals, and maximize instructional effectiveness.

8. Evaluate each consultation objectively, and share conclusions with the consultant.

---

*Reynolds & Birch, 1977.

terms. Most teachers probably learn about educational diagnosis through psychometric concepts that stress norm-referenced testing. Individualized education requires that they understand domain-referenced assessments, task analysis, and how to write meaningful educational objectives.

Regular classroom teachers need more preparation to work with parents. Most teachers approach parents of handicapped children with apprehension, and parents display considerable anxiety in conferring with teachers.

When pupils have various degrees of diversity, regular teachers need skills to command classroom social situations. Impressive evidence indicates that cooperative group activities enhance the achievement of all students — bright, average, or slow — in traditional skill subjects as well as in social skills (Johnson & Johnson, 1975).

Regular classroom teachers need preparation to comply with PL 94-142's due process procedures. Also, they need to understand their rights to due process, including the right to appeal for changes in educational plans, to which they cannot agree, for children in their charge.

PROBLEMS AND ISSUES

In this section, problems and issues confronting teacher education faculty are discussed. Many have been identified and addressed, with varying degrees of success, by the colleges and universities holding Deans' Grants from the Bureau of Education for the Handicapped, U.S. Office of Education (Grosenick & Reynolds, 1978).

Faculty Orientation and Commitment

The legal force of PL 94-142 is directed to school districts and their employees. Teacher educators have not been enjoined directly in any legal sense in these developments, although the regulations in the amendments to Section 504 of the Federal Rehabilitation Act that affect college environments are having effects. Teacher educators have not displayed broad interest in and concern about PL 94-142, and colleges of education have tended to lag behind the public schools in upholding the rights of handicapped students.

In launching programs on college campuses, careful attention must be given to the levels of awareness among teacher education faculty. In terms of Hall's (1976) "Concerns Based Adoption Model" of innovations in teacher education, most education faculty probably are at the lowest two of the seven hierarchical levels of concern. Usually, basic information on the new legal imperatives and policies relating to the educational treatment of handicapped students is provided. But some faculty members will avoid such information on grounds that they are occupied with their subject areas, and that "the special education department takes care of the handicapped." Some will regard mainstreaming as a power play in which one department wants to instruct others about its latest fad. Consequently, resistance is common.

207

Progress in winning broad faculty support and development seems to come best when deans or other central officers of teacher education programs provide leadership, and when the total teacher education faculty is involved in the changes instituted. An examination of required school personnel role changes shows that these persons need more than lessons on exceptional children by special educators. Many of the required changes will be initiated better in units such as foundations of education, law school faculties, family life departments, and others. It has proven helpful for faculty members to participate in projects on specific subjects conducted by colleagues in those fields.

Superficiality

Several conditions are causing superficial responses to the PL 94-142 mandate. Legal rights take effect immediately; that is, all necessary program changes are expected to be delivered at once, which, of course, is patently absurd. Never has it been more clear that change is a process, not an event, and that the schools face the work of a decade, not an evening.

Another cause for superficiality grows from the heavy procedural load attendant upon compliance. The danger of one facet of the new procedural demands is described in another context:

> About half of my special education friends these days seem to be out giving lessons to the masses on individualized educational programs (IEPs). Without even trying I have been shown at least six sets of transparencies, listened to endless audio cassettes on the requirements of Public Law 94-142, and I have been guided through several versions of "sure fire" forms to satisfy all the new regulations.
>
> What I see and hear seems well designed to keep teachers out of jail — to comply with the law, that is — but usually I sense little vision of how people might come together creatively to design environments for better learning and living by handicapped students (Reynolds, 1978, p. 60).

Much inservice teacher education on PL 94-142 is devoted to the superficialities of "filling out the forms" and like matters. Teacher educators need to examine the situation for its fundamental requirements and, as quickly as possible, direct their activities beyond mere surface requirements. They have a responsibility for providing leadership to identify the pivotal ideas and skills needed to implement PL 94-142, and to help organize training activities that penetrate to the fundamentals.

Restructuring the Teacher Education Faculty

Departmental boundaries within teacher education units on a single campus often are impermeable. Special education departments, for example, may have more frequent interactions with comparable units in other states or in the U.S. Office of Education than with local departments in other fields, such as elementary education or vocational education.

The renegotiation process between special and regular education on the campus is producing a variety of new administrative structures. In some cases, existing departments are proceeding unilaterally to install new teacher-training components relating to exceptional or "special needs" students. But little or no collaboration with special education faculty or others may be involved. A more common early pattern, however, is to change the credit requirements for various teacher education curriculum to include all or nearly all studies required for both "regular" and "special education" teaching.

Still more comprehensive restructuring is probably inevitable for the reformation of training programs of such specialities as school psychology, audiology, and social work, and the specialized teaching areas (resource teachers, teachers of the deaf, etc.). The sources of relevant knowledge and skill for such specialists are spread more broadly in college environments than usually are reflected in training programs, but pressure for reformation is mounting.

Faculties in education may try to resist the structural changes inherent in the social policies on handicapped students. But, if changes are not made in the colleges, public schools probably will develop new programs and roles independently of colleges of education. Colleges then may be forced to make less desirable changes in their structures and activities.

Continuing Education in the Context of Basic Changes

Teachers and other school personnel need continuing education regarding PL 94-142, but college faculties cannot conduct all necessary teacher training by direct business-as-usual methods. By indirect methods, such as training and supporting selected adjunct instructors who can work in community settings, colleges can help meet the burgeoning needs.

However, other challenges exist. Inservice training probably should be conducted for working groups of teachers in individual schools. Such instruction though, confronts the political problems of schools, such as class sizes, administrative commitments to support changes, programs and priorities of local teachers' unions and associations, and questions about career changes that many teachers must face.

On the other hand, college faculties can ignore these difficult continuing education efforts. Some people may wish that. Because most money for continuing education under PL 94-142 appears to be going to local educational agencies, it will be easy to maintain the status quo among college faculties. But this situation is not in the public interest of colleges or college faculties.

CONCLUSION

When all factors and conditions are added, the need for more competent teachers becomes apparent. PL 94-142 calls for teachers who have powerful teaching skills, who are committed to education for all children, who are resourceful enough to accommodate children with special needs, who are sufficiently competent and confident to use expert consultation to further their understanding of handicapped children, and who can avoid shunting the children onto others.

Present teacher preparation programs lack the time and resources necessary to prepare such teachers. Perhaps PL 94-142 can and should provide the stimuli and energies to carry teacher education across traditional boundaries, and to help confront serious questions such as a minimum of five years for initial teacher preparation.

REFERENCES

Freeman, G. G. *Speech and language services and the classroom teacher.* Reston, VA: Council for Exceptional Children, 1977.

Grosenick, J. K., & Reynolds, M.C. (Eds.). *Teacher education: Renegotiating roles for mainstreaming.* Reston, VA: Council for Exceptional Children, 1978.

Hall, G. E. The study of individual teacher and professor concerns about innovations. *Journal of Teacher Education,* 1976, *27*(1), 22-23.

Johnson, D. W., & Johnson, R. T. *Learning together and alone.* Englewood Cliffs, NJ: Prentice-Hall, 1975.

Reynolds, M. C., & Birch, J. W. *Teaching exceptional children in all America's schools.* Reston, VA: Council for Exceptional Children, 1977.

Reynolds, M. C. Staying out of jail. *Teaching Exceptional Children,* Spring 1978, *10*(3), 60-62.

This far-reaching and thoughtful article goes beyond the ordinary discussions of the impact of PL 94-142. Contending that education is a "declining industry" if considered on the basis of student enrollment, the author argues that we must nevertheless expand our horizons and think of the individualized education program as applying to nonhandicapped as well as handicapped learners. This is indeed a tall order in an era of declining funds for the public schools. Future administrators are portrayed as needing different skills in leadership and more authority at the building level. Dr. Herda adds that they must acknowledge that school management is no longer apolitical (if it ever was).

Aspects of General Education Governance and PL 94-142 Implementation

Ellen A. Herda

Implementing the intent of PL 94-142 calls for insightful leadership and governance on an integrated and expanded basis involving the total school system. In many instances, current social demands on and subsequent shifts in general educational governance undergird the mainstays of public laws. Implementation of PL 94-142 and Section 504 of the Rehabilitation Act of 1973 can have — and in many Local Education Agencies (LEAs) is having — positive and supportive impact on general education administrators facing social, political, and educational demands.

Administrators' activities in today's schools encompass more than the neutral tasks often associated with administration. Governance — which perhaps better describes a major portion of these activities than does "administration" — involves carrying out policy decisions. In

From *Focus on Exceptional Children*, January 1980, *12*(5), 1-12. © Love Publishing Co.

several areas of implementation, PL 94-142 provides an impetus for and coincides with such activities. Even though many school systems have made strides, implementation remains a highly complex, problematic process. Currently, far more questions, concerns, and unresolved issues exist than alternative courses of implementation based on assertive, confident actions.

In short, the general education administrator is responsible for implementing a mandate that yields a multitude of interpretations and ambiguities while governing a "declining industry" in a country facing social, economic, and political unrest. This feat is to be accomplished in collaboration with special (or exceptional) education administrators, many of whom are holding onto long-time "turfs" and established empires and at the same time struggling to come to terms with the new "faces" of exceptional education.

The leadership training needed to understand this complex situation and to execute the legal mandates places heavy demands on administrative in-service education. But in-service programs cannot be responsive without addressing the context in which general educational governance takes place.

In the integration of exceptional and general education, exceptional education personnel have a two-fold charge. They first have to be aware that the shifting of major cornerstones in general education has had a profound impact on schools and their governance. The monopolistic control of education by a social and economic middle class has been challenged, and the result has been the development of new sets of priorities, policies, powers, and forms of governance. Second, special educators must develop some common understandings about the nature of education given the implementation of PL 94-142. These understandings have to emerge along with an awareness of current demands on general educational governance.

The movement within special education is part of a total picture of the last 25 years that reflects ongoing critical examination of America's educational institutions and leadership. Schools must operate in a radically different context today than they did a few decades ago. Watson (1977) identified the most significant aspects of this new context as

> . . . the demythologizing of education — putting to rest the fiction that education is apolitical — the unprecedented involvement in education by the courts and the federal government, the balkanization of school personnel, and the mobilization of client (student and community) interest power (p. 73).

Perhaps no federal involvements in the school reflect the underlying timbre of emerging national trends as much as do the problems and

212

potential benefits of PL 94-142 implementation. The legal mandates on federal, state, and local levels are in response to demands for social and political forms of equity in the name of the "least restrictive environment" in education. This concept has widespread implications for both exceptional and general education. Implementing PL 94-142 in most cases demands a close examination of general education conditions by both general and exceptional educators.

Implementing legal mandates cannot take place apart from the general education classroom, students, teachers, administrators, and community. Gilhool (1976) has indicated that ". . . if the directions taken by the special education (court) cases are to be fully realized, general education, into which special students shall be integrated, must itself take on characteristics of individualization" (p. 13). But educators are currently in no position to provide individualized education to each student. To do so, as Lortie (1976) pointed out, would require a complete overhauling of current schooling practices. It would be naive to expect any major changes to "occur rapidly or easily as the outcome of legal pressure" (p. 18).

Somewhere on a continuum with individualization at one end and cellular group process learning at the other will come negotiated forms of education that meet students' needs more appropriately than they are being met today. The expectations placed upon administrators to provide some guidelines through this process demand an examination of the nature of the challenges and force individuals to draw upon forms of governance and leadership, at all levels of education, that can accommodate societal fragmentation, disunity among educators, and the decline of institutional authority. An increasingly popular position among many educators is that legislation in the name of exceptional education can provide some bases for those guidelines.

Educational administrators in local education agencies hold major responsibilty for implementing PL 94-142 and Section 504. But the majority of administrators in the field, including both exceptional and general education administrators, did not receive pre-service training designed to meet such responsibility. In fact, the affluent era during which most current administrators received their training relied on a self-containing bureaucratic and hierarchical model of administration that placed heavy emphasis upon maintenance functions.

Credentialing is changing at the state level, and several institutions of higher education are revising administrative pre-service education curricula and integrating exceptional and general administrative training. Several years, however, will elapse before there are enough administrators in the field to carry out (or, by that time, carry on) implementation. For this reason, administrators in local education agencies must assume responsibility for professional growth and development through in-service education.

The professional growth and development of exceptional and general education personnel are integral to implementation of PL 94-142 and Section 504. Staff development experiences will not automatically ensure handicapped individuals appropriate educational rights and opportunities, although these experiences are important steps toward achieving integration and coordination of efforts among general and exceptional educators. In turn, these efforts cannot operate in a separatist fashion apart from the total school system nor in isolation from an awareness of the larger socio-political context of educational governance — for it is in this larger context that implementation of PL 94-142 actually takes place.

To aid in achieving the intent of that law, Section 121a, 380 of PL 94-142 requires that all personnel engaged in education of the handicapped receive appropriate training. The Bureau of Education for the Handicapped (BEH) has placed high priority on in-service education and has funded numerous staff development projects. A BEH-funded project,[1] Special and General Education Leadership, provided several education agencies with funds specifically targeted for administrative staff development. Based upon information obtained from needs assessment instruments and information gained by informal means, administrative in-service education programs were developed in each education agency participating in the project. Planning and implementation of the administrative staff development programs in each of the participating agencies reflected the specific context and needs of the agency. The national-level effort, however, did indicate several global issues and concerns that arise in implementing PL 94-142.

The remainder of this article focuses on the following three issues and concludes with a discussion of some implications for administrative in-service staff development:

1) A total system approach toward implementation of PL 94-142;

---

[1] The Special and General Education Leadership Project (1976-1979) was sponsored by the University Council for Educational Administration and funded by the Bureau of Education for the Handicapped. The participating education agencies and local coordinators included Dade County Schools, Miami, Florida — Wylamerle Marshall; Mesa Public Schools, Mesa, Arizona — Carolyn Raymond; Metropolitan School System, Nashville, Tennessee — Phyllis Shutt; Milwaukee Public Schools — William Malloy; North Carolina State Department — Lowell Harris and Fred Baars; and Tacoma Schools — Henry Bertness. Staff development efforts and the interchanges and exchanges between education agencies and institutions of higher education involving professors of both exceptional and general educational administration were major components of the project.

2) Integrated and expanded forms of administration; and

3) Governance policy, and implementation at the building level.

A TOTAL SYSTEM APPROACH
TOWARD PL 94-142 IMPLEMENTATION

In efforts to implement PL 94-142 and Section 504, administrators of both general and exceptional education face several challenges including the re-examination of administrative and organizational structures, curriculum and pupil personnel services, and administrator and teacher staff development programs. Traditionally, general and exceptional education administrative and teaching responsibilities were carried out in separatist fashion. Where dual administrative systems between general and exceptional education still exist, PL 94-142 implementation necessitates an eventual breaking down, to some degree, of that dualistic system. One must recognize that not just exceptional educators are responsible for implementing PL 94-142 and Section 504 but that implementation rests upon the responsible acts of *all* educators.

General education administrators have difficulty acting on the belief that they are suddenly able (and required) to respond to exceptional education concerns. This may be better understood in remembering that for years special education students relied on personnel with specific training and were taught in facilities separate from the general education student population. In other words, special education turf was "protected" from general education by specialized training and isolated housing. This turf was not always held in awe by general educators. In fact, acknowledging the type of classrooms often assigned to special education personnel and students, special education could be thought of as general education's stepchild. At the same time, though, it was thought of as *specialized* education — if for no other reason than that special education language and vocabulary differed from that of general educators.

Today, it is assumed at times that if rooms containing handicapped students are located within regular school facilities, the least restrictive environment concept has been achieved. This may be a step up from teaching students in church basements, but for many children it does not fulfill the intent of the law.

A number of problems currently facing school administrators are further aggravated by a separatist approach toward exceptional and

215

general education. Areas of concern that must be approached on a system-wide basis include desegregation, minimum competency standards, and unionism (Malloy, 1979). Some special education classes, such as for the mentally retarded and emotionally disturbed, contain an over-representation of minority groups. Many of these children really belong in general education classes. Questions arise about the legality and morality of applying the same minimum competency standards to handicapped and nonhandicapped students. And unions, for example, are encouraging teachers to refer "problem" students to special education classes to lighten the burden on the regular classroom teacher. These problems have no simple solutions and are highly emotional subjects for teachers, administrators, and parents.

The total school system approach can provide a good avenue for action concerning these problems — as opposed to the dualist approach, which perpetuates the attempts of exceptional and general education administrators to solve such problems independently. The total system approach does not necessarily mean the complete unification of exceptional and general education programs. Rather, it refers to collaboration between and among exceptional and general educators to generate alternative solutions to problems that are better solved together than separately. This requires that administrators first identify the problems and then assume responsibility to work on alternative solutions on a participatory and collective basis, recognizing when and what kinds of changes in general and exceptional education are needed. It also demands trust and respect among the various operating divisions within a school system, which derive from open and working communication lines among superintendent, assistant superintendent, and their administrative teams.

For a variety of reasons (e.g., new mandates, union encouragement, inappropriate curriculum and instruction programs, program experimentation), movement of students among various learning situations is inherent. This involves students' going to and from exceptional and general education classes, as well as intermediate settings including resource rooms and general and/or exceptional classes on a part-time basis. This fluidity is integral to carrying out the intent of PL 94-142, but it represents one of the most complex problems related to implementation, touching virtually all of the components and personnel within a school system. Referrals, evaluations, conferences, and re-referrals, re-evaluations, and more conferences take up enormous amounts of personnel time and involve voluminous amounts of paperwork. The whole process often bogs down and perpetuates the backlog of students needing evaluation as well as the noncompliance status of many LEAs.

Student backlog is often identified only in terms of the numbers of students needing evaluation. These data may give an indication of the problem but do not begin to provide the kind of information needed to propose guidelines for reducing the numbers of these students. Further examination reflects the nature of the problem as it affects both general and exceptional education personnel and students on the following issues: the use of grades as indicators for needed exceptional education services; overburdened diagnosticians at certain times of the school year; inappropriate referrals; and in-service education content.

During spring quarter the number of referrals in a school system often increases drastically as teachers realize that certain students are "failing" or receiving low grades. This pattern can indicate that grades are being used for identification of students needing exceptional education services, rather than identification relying on classroom observation, intermittent teacher assessment of students' learning, and so forth. Emphasis on grades earned instead of intervention and preventive measures can also indicate the inappropriate use of or lack of classroom teacher skills.

Since many of these referrals come at the end of the school year, diagnostic personnel and evaluation teams are subject to unrealistic expectations. If a State Education Agency (SEA) had mandated a timeline to follow in evaluating referrals, the chance of meeting that timeline is slim. And it automatically ensures that the LEA will be out of compliance.

Building-level referrals by teachers using inaccurate measures result in many inappropriate referrals and thus contribute to excess paperwork and wasted person-hours. A system-wide perspective on problems of student identification procedures, student referral processes, and diagnostic services is essential for initial remediation steps and subsequent preventive steps.

The system-wide, or total system, approach entails "ownership" of these responsibilities by both exceptional and general education. SEAs can enhance this type of ownership by defining compliance as it relates to a total system instead of just the Division of Exceptional or Special Education in an LEA. Compliance should be defined in terms of initial identification procedures by general and exceptional education personnel and ongoing diagnostic and evaluation processes. Anything less places unrealistic expectations on the Division of Exceptional Education. Compliance, commonly thought of as the responsibility of the Director of Exceptional Education, involves both exceptional and general education personnel. Also, compliance has system-wide implications for the least restrictive environment for all students. More appropriate and accurate referrals on the part of regular classroom teachers, for example, would be a reflection of higher quality teacher preparation (via pre-service or in-service education).

The planning, development, implementation, and impact of teacher in-service education can foster a total system approach. The implications for such in-service education are many. The tradition of patchwork-type workshops and one-shot in-service meetings, coupled with an inadequate amount of research on in-service education, offers scant basis to rely upon, especially considering the magnitude of the task at hand. In recent years, though, the federal government has funded programs to aid SEAs and LEAs with their in-service needs; and the current flurry of in-service activities throughout the nation indicates some available monies along with an awareness of the need for staff development programs.

Current emphasis on developmental in-service models rather than deficit models reflects a reliance on the strengths of education personnel and attempts at further development of those strengths. But this process needs to be complemented with appropriate content that will make a difference to teachers, administrators, and students at the building level. Deciding specific content (based on the needs of the particular LEA) is the responsibility of both exceptional and general education personnel.

In times of scarcity of resources, mistakes show up more easily. In-service educators now have less time and fewer resources with which to work than during any recent period in educational history. And demands to make available quality in-service education are intimately connected with legal mandates. The above discussion demonstrates this connection — by indicating the need for classroom teachers to become skilled in appropriate and accurate assessment and evaluation of students. Meeting this need does not entail educating all teachers to use highly specialized evaluation tools; rather, it places an emphasis on observation skills and analyses of individual students' actions and attitudes on intervention and preventive forms of teaching, and on appropriate use of support personnel and services.

Packets distributed during in-service meetings often contain massive amounts of required reading for teachers (and in some cases administrators) with role playing and simulation activities attached to provide a "feel" for what the IEP and the Safeguard Procedures (due process) involve. This kind of information and activity helps the recipients understand some aspects of implementation, but in-service education must go beyond information-giving and role-playing levels. It should be based on careful assessment, both formal and informal, of the needs of a particular education agency and also on a conceptualization of what education might be like given implementation of PL 94-142. The various facets of implementation also must be considered in view of the larger context of education and society.

To illustrate this larger context: in-service teacher education that would include attention to assessment, intervention, and prevention is highly appropriate to Child-Find and preventive care movements in other service agencies, many of which are now combining their efforts with exceptional children divisions in local and state education agencies. One indication that these have not been primary emphases in either pre-service or in-service education is the necessarily heavy emphasis on remedial education.

By focusing on assessment, intervention, and prevention of educational problems, the IEP concept can be part of an overall approach toward education instead of an aspect of exceptional education services alone. This would provide some basis for ownership of the idea behind the IEP process. Assessment would result in placing a particular child on a continuum of handicapping and nonhandicapping conditions; and the individual learning program for the child based on that assessment would indicate the nature of his or her program. The IEP, or some variation of it, then would be an important element of an appropriate education for all children.

Within this framework, the IEP process is not taught to teachers as something extra attached to handicapped students, but as part of an approach toward providing the least restrictive environment to all students. The kinds of resources and activities devoted to developing a child's individual learning program, IEP or otherwise, and the follow-through, would be relative to the complexity of the student's learning procedures and his or her place on an educational continuum of emotional, social, and physical conditions. The emphasis would be on the development of individual students and less on moving students through grades. By following a developmental rather than a deficit process, instruction and learning for educators and students alike eventually can go beyond remediation and assume a preventive stance toward socio-economic problems.

When problems initially appear to be related to a certain division in an education agency but upon closer examination turn out to reflect needed changes on a system-wide basis, resolutions require joint ownership of responsibility and support among and between exceptional and general education personnel. The above discussion points out the need for administrators and personnel in various divisions within an LEA (curriculum and instruction, health services, etc.) to work closely together. In working out potential and alternative solutions, administrators have to rely upon leadership styles that respond to the nature of the demands. Problems can no longer be treated as if the bureaucratic and hierarchical system, by virtue of its design, designates what is a problem and how it is resolved.

INTEGRATED AND EXPANDED FORMS OF ADMINISTRATION

In an attempt to provide the least restrictive environment for handicapped individuals, general and exceptional education personnel face certain problems (as mentioned above) that cannot be easily separated. These problems would appear to be approachable through collaborative and participatory recourse over a period of time. Implementation of PL 94-142 not only promotes the integration of exceptional and general education, but also places schools in partnership with other sectors of society (e.g., vocational rehabilitation centers, Child-Find agencies) and in specific partnerships with community members (e.g., parents of handicapped children). Integrated and expanded forms of administrations are not unique to education but are also viable options in business, unions, and government. They have a sound and broad basis in practice.

Various captions are used to express integrated and expanded forms of leadership in education. The team concept abounds at all levels in a school system — Management Teams, Administrative Resource Teams, Multidisciplinary Teams, School-based Resource Teams, and other such teams. The art of participatory team leadership calls for the leader to stand back and let others share the role while he or she still assumes major responsibility to justify the actions of the team, if necessary, to advocates of various interest groups, clients (teachers, students, parents, etc.), school boards, and other teams. The leader has to establish a code that appeals to the members and meets needs for participation, individualism, and equity. Members of teams who assume some leadership functions and requisite responsibility make the task of leadership easier. The combination of increased competition, demands for cost reduction and new programs, changes in government regulations, and continuing increases in client militancy requires a higher quality of leadership than ever before.

Assembling a team can be accomplished in a relatively short period, but a certain amount of time is needed to establish principles that allow for trust, cooperation, and negotiation to become integral parts of a working team. Michael Maccoby (1979), Director of the Harvard Project on Technology, Work and Character, suggested that during this era of social and character changes in America, "the primary tasks of leaders are to understand both motives and resistance to change, and to establish operating principles that build trust, facilitate cooperation, and explain the significance of the individual's role in the common purpose" (p. 20). The significance of individuals in a team or an organization cannot be overestimated.

Public education agencies are traditionally thought of as service organizations. The emphasis is on the client. While this is an important tenet to hold, working conditions of teachers, administrators, support staff, paraprofessionals, volunteers, etc. are taking on more significance in light of a "declining industry" that is offering fewer opportunities for advancement. Advancement up a career ladder is no longer automatic. A decline in student population and public sector retrenchment are reasons for this switch in the nature of mobility. Patterns of lateral and upward mobility are increasingly becoming qualitative concerns. As Gappert (1979) pointed out:

> Job satisfaction is likely to be a major issue as the work force becomes "tenured up" and opportunities for even lateral mobility are reduced. It should also be noted that, in the 1980's, the Bulge Generation will be maturing into their late 30's and the associated life style changes can be significant" (p. 2-3).

The focus for the near future will be on improving one's performance of, and satisfaction in, a current position. This focus is on individuals rather than on groups. Negotiation of individuals' rights and responsibilities in an organization will include reference to less restricting conditions for personal development rather than to those conditions found in more traditional bureaucratic and hierarchical modes of organization.

New attitudes exist today on the part of workers in most organizations, stemming from the movement for individual rights, demand for equity, and interest in self-development and self-determination. Many workers, or "subordinates," will no longer accept directives merely because they come from a "superior." The state of willingness of individuals to participate fully in their own positions or as team members is a serious issue for educational, corporate, and business leaders alike. In schools, as in most places of work, unwilling or unhappy employees can pose serious problems to the administrator who is responsible for changes mandated by laws.

These changing values, evidenced currently by the numerous advocacy groups, play an important role in determining attitudes at work. "Unless leaders understand [these shifts in values]," wrote Maccoby (1979), "they may bring out the worst rather than the best in the [nation's] emerging social character" (p. 19). In his research with leaders who are

221

developing new modes of organizations in education, business, industry, and unions, Maccoby reported two personal characteristics these leaders have in common — characteristics that may be essential for a new "model" of leadership to bring out the best in individuals working in organizations. These leaders:

1. have developed or are developing a philosophy of management which is rooted in a concern for their workers and resentment of wasted human potential. This rooted conviction, in contrast to a rigid ideology, provides a basis for pragmatic experimentation and satisfaction in step-by-step gains. Although most of these leaders share the gamesman's respect for strategy and tactics, they do not share the need for perpetual adventure and drama.

2. are students of the organizations they lead and are willing and able to "problematize" both the mission (definition of the product or service) and the control systems. They take time from the tiring managerial tasks of responding to crises to question whether the mission serves society and individuals. They are not willing to gain power or money by appealing to the worst in people. They are engaged by the task of analyzing and reconstructing the organization (p. 22).

Maccoby concluded that time spent in participatory decision making is well spent if decisions are made and if the commitment to results is based upon analyses of problems and willingness to give up control and power.

The notion of participatory management, leadership, and decision making is conceptually vague. With the present emphasis on the team or participatory approach toward administration, one must exercise care so that the words "team" and "participatory" do not become merely catchwords — popular usages masking disagreement over substance with apparent agreement over form. A genuine commitment must be made to expanding the bases for decision making and problem identification. The results of expanding these bases, however, ramify themselves in a way that creates further situations requiring attention.

A case in point is the battle for the public's or the client's "right to know," which has resulted in information being available to people who did not previously process such information. But gaining access to information without concurrently gaining understanding of its potential uses can perpetuate the "information-rich, knowledge-poor" syndrome. For example, parents who now have more information than before also have to come to understand the implications of identification, evaluation, and educational placement of their child. In short, information is a necessary but insufficient condition for participation in an IEP development process or any other participatory type of activity. In the case of the patient, the challenges include a search for realistic and satisfactory balance between the role of the school and the role of the parent. These challenges extend to other forms of participation and have implications for policy issues as well.

These challenges will probably be met through negotiations that could lead to less restricting environments for team members, other staff members, students, parents, and anyone else who participates. In negotiations, the balance between individual rights and least restrictive environment is precarious, dependent upon shifting values, sources of information, and interpretations. But the concept of least restrictive environment is an important tool and can be applied to many situations in which negotiations are the main resource in making decisions. We must exercise care that this concept does not outlive its usefulness before we have moved beyond our present problems to new ones!

The concept of least restrictive environment, as pointed out, need not focus solely on exceptional children. Each child and adult is faced with continually learning to assume personal and social responsibility for sustaining a quality life in the face of the social and political limits to growth in Western society. The least restrictive environment is a right mandated by a law applying to handicaped individuals, but before the intent of this law can move beyond technical compliance issues, the concept of least restrictive environments has to be understood in terms of reaching beyond the mechanical elements of implementation. It must be understood as a *responsibility* assumed by individuals before it can be a *right* for anyone.

In the pressing need to survive in a society beset with ambiguities, complexities, and stresses, our efforts should focus on ways in which satisfaction can be gained by quality living and working rather than solely on competitive advance. Hirsch (1978) has suggested that the mismatch between current expectations and resources in our society is qualitative rather than quantitative. He cautioned that we must not "set up expectations that cannot be fulfilled, ever" (p. 9). This statement is not contradictory to the concept of least restrictive environments for exceptional individuals. It addresses the issue of recognizing the nature of individuals' environments and providing the least restrictive alternative for all persons. Handicapped individuals and, for example, professionals in non-mobile positions all have the right and responsibility to design quality lives for themselves.

Speaking to a more specific issue, which is at the same time related to a larger context, Skrag (1978) suggested that "special education administrators will provide leadership for needed curricular changes. In the years ahead, millions of Americans may move beyond materialistic values and choose an outwardly more specific and inwardly more rich life style" (p. 9). When these changes occur, they must be accompanied by organizational changes and must also coincide with an awareness that the least restrictive environment connotes realistic expectations in socially and politically equitable forms.

Facing the issues of appropriate forms of administration, individuals' rights and responsibilities, and the least restrictive environment for staff and students is an ongoing and unending task for administrators. This task will not be automatically undertaken systematically or rigorously. It requires a vehicle to provide the impetus for looking closely at the nature of changes and the consequences of such changes. A law as pervasive as PL 94-142 can serve as that vehicle. It reaches out to virtually every division in an education agency and expands into the community. It can be used to examine and change many aspects of schooling, governance, curricular content, staff development, and school and community settings. A law, however, can only motivate (strongly, at times) people to follow legislative guidelines. In the end, providing individuals with least restrictive environments for work and learning relies on individual commitment to quality administration, teaching, and lifelong learning, and on discovery of ingenious ways to finance appropriate programs and services.

Implementing PL 94-142 to provide each handicapped child a free and appropriate education entails massive changes in our educational system. If our present education system had already provided least restrictive environments for the nonhandicapped and now it were only a matter of appropriately identifying the handicapped who belong in the mainstream of education, the task would still be arduous and difficult enough. But educators are faced with the larger task of finding human, material, and financial resources to create least restrictive environments for handicapped and, in many cases, nonhandicapped students as well. Who gives up what in order to accomplish this task will rely on long-term negotiations among educators, members of the community, the courts, and federal and state governments. Within this context, negotiating and interpreting policy are well-entrenched activities at all levels of schooling.

GOVERNANCE, POLICY, AND IMPLEMENTATION AT THE BUILDING LEVEL

Schools were for some time (and in many cases still are) considered to be institutions in which effective management is based on apolitical activities. The governance structure was traditionally built upon separation of politics and administration. Neutral competence and avoidance of conflict were held at a premium. Several conditions have made this position no longer (if it ever was) credible within an education agency. The change has been perpetuated by various factors including increasing court intervention and governmental control demanding changes that often carry highly emotional and political overtones; an increasingly vocal constituency and supportive client group; and a fragmentation of educators through unionism and special interest groups. The school district, including building-level entities within a district, can no longer operate under the assumption that decision making can be separated simply into administrative decisions and policy decisions.

For many of their everyday decisions, principals and teachers need several kinds of information, along with an understanding of potential political and legal consequences of those decisions. This is particularly true of issues related to due process procedures. The distinction between politics and administration is far less clear today than during the era when schools were believed to operate autonomously, independent of the larger socio-political context. Now, the scope of potential and real conflict clearly extends beyond the building-level administrator.

Because of the variety of social and political changes (such as citizen dissatisfaction at the local level, which in turn created national-level attention, pluralism, the proliferation of narrow interest advocacy groups, increased state-level funding, collective bargaining, and a loss of local monetary discretion), the administrator has to rely on different forms of governance than the hierarchical and bureaucratic structures of past recent decades. The overall political and social unrest today threatens the claims to expertise and the power bases at all levels, and at the same time places additional demands upon administrators' participatory and coordinative skills.

Laws and the implications of their impact have rapidly moved to the foreground in governance concerns today. Awareness of this larger picture is not to be reserved for only the top management of local education agencies. Schooling and its governance have for some time been the business of far more people than solely the superintendents. Local-level building administrators, division directors, teachers, and community members (in addition to board members) are becoming important players in the process of schooling governance.

The governance process at all levels is highly complex and demands more responsibility and assertive, yet participatory, administrative styles. Principals, in their attempts to follow mandates and administer programs, rely on policy actions. And policy is becoming less oriented

225

toward what should be done and more directed at everyday problems in building-level units. Local building-level policy is subject to standards and values that are constantly shifting, depending upon the group giving input and the particular situation. Principals' actions in following a policy are part of a political process that includes expanding and interpreting the policy. As Everhart (1979) has suggested, policy has to be able to fit a variety of circumstances. Further, if policy does fit a variety of circumstances, decisive leadership is necessary at all levels of an education agency. But administrators, particularly at the building level, often are caught in a frustrating position between emerging participatory governance demands and fragmentation of total school programs.

The principal's role, of course, is of primary importance in implementing innovations, but it is complicated by the fragmentation resulting from a multitude of simultaneously ongoing building-level programs like Title I, bilingual/bicultural, vocational development, exceptional education, and special services personnel programs. Many of these programs receive directives from personnel other than at the building level. This situation places the principal in a position that demands strong coordinative skills — offset by administrative formats of the various programs that often prohibit decision-making powers, participatory and otherwise, from resting with the principal. Roles can be played in appropriate fashion, but the strength of, and current demands for, participatory administrative styles is lessened by acute fragmentation among various building-level programs.

Traditionally, the principal had a significantly stronger power base in the more hierarchical and bureaucratic administrative framework of the past. Decisions made at the school level were often concerned purely with management activities, while policy decisions were made "downtown." This situation is changing somewhat because of "grassroots" involvement at the building level and also because of participatory activities mandated by laws. In any case, more power has to be extended to the principal if he or she is to be successful in participatory forms of governance. Personnel in individual buildings in a local education agency reflect needs that in turn require autonomy and a certain amount of independence in order to meet the demanded changes. Principals' obligations have shifted from being solely managerial to providing leadership in coordinating individuals from a myriad of sectors, along with their respective programs. Least restrictive environments can be created more easily if policy decisions are integral to everyday activities coordinated by an administrator who has autonomy and support from the central office to establish the most appropriate overall building-level program.

Exceptional education personnel can play a significant role in providing support and knowledge to building-level administrators in their attempts at participatory forms of governance. But advocates among general education administration are often thwarted in their efforts on this behalf by having to assume passive roles in developing least restrictive environments for handicapped students. Exceptional education personnel are assumed to have (and in fact do have) certain kinds of expertise, but the changes needed in a given school involve more than just exceptional education personnel. The knowledge and experiences of general educators are equally important in contributing toward the least restrictive environment for handicapped and nonhandicapped students. Appropriate governance structure and willingness to cooperate, along with the autonomy to decide upon appropriate actions, are requisite for PL 94-142 implementation at the building level.

IMPLICATIONS FOR IN-SERVICE EDUCATION

In-service for administrators is not appropriate without integrative efforts that include the members of teams for which they provide leadership. In-service focusing entirely on one group at a time, whether principals, vice principals, or guidance personnel, leaves important facets of in-service education unattended. Activities involving implementation do not divide themselves neatly among the various groups of educators. Categorization of in-service education according to different groups, though, can be appropriate in initial stages of the overall in-service education program. For example, general information and broadly based interpretations of the innovations sometimes merit presentation to groups composed of one division of personnel. And certain kinds of technical information and understandings are more directly related to principals, for example, than to other groups of personnel.

In-service programs, however, must also address mixed groups including general and exceptional administrators and teachers and support personnel. This composite more closely reflects the configuration of individuals facing implementation. Ultimately, in-service programs must respond to needs of the specific schools. These individual schools represent highly appropriate in-service sites for such in-service activities because they involve the people who carry on everyday affairs of schooling in a particular building. This approach requires a certain autonomy from the rest of the education agency in developing in-service education programs.

Central office staff, area and building-level administrators, class-room and support personnel, paraprofessionals, volunteers, parents, and the like should play major roles in discerning their own in-service requirements. Their being asked to help determine their own in-service education may prove to be far more motivating and positive than in-service given on the basis of credits received or money paid to the participants. As Hutson (1979) pointed out, "The research literature does not support the notion that extrinsic rewards such as extra salary credit, extra pay and so on, will induce teachers to work hard planning or participating in in-service programs if professional motivation is absent. The effective implementation of in-service requires, in a word, *human* support . . ." (p. 1).

Perhaps the most significant role education agencies can play in PL 94-142 implementation is to develop highly comprehensive in-service education programs based on their own unique context and problem identification. But pre-service education, for the most part, has not prepared educators for the current needs and demands. Most educators were trained in programs based on different assumptions than those needed for responding to the highly complex social and political contexts in which schools operate today. In-service education must continue the growth and development begun, or not addressed, in pre-service pro-grams — which in turn requires open communication between prac-ticing administrators and professors in exceptional and general educa-tion.

In providing in-service education for administrators, one must first conceptualize the kind of administrative education needed to address current demands for participatory leadership. But in-service education cannot be assumed to have positive results and impact without some concomitment changes in the organizational structures to help support the new kinds of information and knowledge gained through local education agency education programs. This may involve restructuring the organization by, for example, establishing working communication channels, changing staffing patterns, unifying disparate support service programs, and giving more decision-making powers to individuals at building-level units.

Good leadership is critical for the 1980s. Encouraging adaptability to major socio-educational changes is a different challenge than is devel-oping in-service education to train personnel who lack the necessary skills to do an effective job. In-service education must include not only explanations of new mandates and technical information but under-standings and interpretations of the nature of problems facing educators today. The exceptional education movement reflects these problems through concrete legislation mandating changes in the schooling process for exceptional children, but it is also an impetus for providing concrete, positive changes for *all* children.

Least restrictive environments for exceptional children will be possible when least restrictive conditions are part of the program for nonhandicapped students also. This goal entails more than the "band-aid" approach to in-service. It means looking at the wider picture and envisioning what education should be like in this broader view. It forces exceptional educators to arrive at some common understandings about exceptional education, along with the integrative aspects of exceptional and general education following implementation of PL 94-142. Views among exceptional educators are currently so disparate that it is difficult at times to determine in-service content that reaches beyond purely technical aspects. General educators too, have an important responsibility, to look at the implications of PL 94-142 for general education and develop responsive in-service education programs in collaboration with exceptional children.

In-service education programs should reflect the specific situations and contexts of individual education agencies, but some general implications for administrative in-service may be applicable to a variety of contexts. These are summarized as follows:

1. *Both technical and nontechnical information and knowledge are needed by administrators.* Administrators must thoroughly understand technical information in order to minimize the possibility of legal or compliance complications. Implementation also requires awareness of the kinds of problems that improved human relations skills can avert or "solve." Group process and interactional talents are as important as knowing the rules and regulations and are requisite for participatory leadership.

2. *Administrators should have the opportunity to "problematize" the mission and services presently existing in their education agency.* Ownership of a jointly identified problem is an important initial step to establishing alternative courses of action.

3. *Vertical and horizontal administrative in-service provides awareness of other administrators' problems and can set the stage for more effective communication channels.* Often, elementary school principals participate together, as do junior and senior high principals. A continuum of concerns and issues can help

229

provide a broader perspective on the nature of education concerns for all administrators if some of the in-service programs include a mixture of administrators from the different school levels. Central office administrators and directors should take part in in-service programs, too. Not only do they need the information and experiences of the in-service education programs, but principals, for example, must realize that the issues discussed at in-service meetings merit the attention and interest of top-level administrators. This, of course, places time demands on the central office administrative staff since the most effective in-service occurs in small group sessions.

4. *Administrative and non-administrative personnel should take part in in-service programs together.* Along with emphases on participatory governance and the team approach to problem identification and decision making, there must be opportunities for the team approach to be "practiced" on various levels throughout the school system. Different attitudes are required toward participatory activities than toward hierarchical and bureaucratic activities. The multidisciplinary approach emerging in education should be complemented with in-service education that is multidisciplinary.

5. *School site in-service relates to specific building-level concerns.* The school site offers the advantage of being highly job-related. Each school has some unique strengths and areas of concern that may be resolved more easily at the local building level.

6. *In-service programs should include joint efforts by school personnel and other service agencies.* The worlds of preventive medicine, work, law, science, and humanities are important corollaries to educators' efforts. Issues of ethics and values are part of the larger context in which administrators and other educators work; and these issues are often intimately tied to both education and these other worlds.

7. *In-service programs must address the self-education and quality living issues facing administrators.* Administrators are part of the larger society whose members are facing these issues. The work place is becoming an increasingly important issue for individuals in organizations. The concept and mission of "education" must be extended to students *and* staff.

8. *In-service education related to PL 94-142 implementation should reflect the expertise of both exceptional and general educators.* The implementation of PL 94-142 requires the best of both worlds of exceptional and general education.

9. *Pre-service and in-service education programs based on partnerships among local education agencies and universities can promote a growth and development continuum for educators.* Training administrators for a total system approach and participatory forms of leadership should begin in pre-service education. Demands on current school administrators are different from those facing administrators several years ago. Working communication networks among schools and universities can aid in appropriate preparation of personnel.

In-service education programs can set important directions for the future of education. Anticipating and contending with socio-political pressures on traditional forms of governance and society are part of the larger context that educators must address. Educators may never have the opportunity to become highly active in this larger context, but they obviously are becoming increasingly active when an education law as pervasive as PL 94-142 can be interpreted as reflecting social, political, and educational imperatives.

The impact of PL 94-142 upon general education governance extends to changes in the schooling for all students. Possibilities for these changes are innumerable. Deciding which courses of action are most appropriate includes negotiating in good will. It also requires envisioning education in the larger social context and making decisions based upon conceptualizations of the future. The future involves "problematizing" education, making choices, parlaying strengths and transforming present conditions to less restricting conditions.

REFERENCES

Everhart, R. B. Ethnography and educational policy: Love and marriage or strange bedfellows? *Anthropology & Educational Administration.* Tucson: Sandero de Juana, 1979.

Gappert, G. *Does educational administration need a revolution in training?* Policy development paper prepared for the May workshop on school administrator training, U.S. Office of Education, April, 1979.

Gilhool, T. K. Changing public policies: Roots and faces. *Mainstreaming: Origin and Implications*, Spring 1976, *2*(2). (Minnesota Education Series, University of Minnesota)

Hirsch, F. *Social limits to growth.* Cambridge, MA: Harvard University Press, 1978.

Hutson, H. PAR in in-service. *Practical Applications of Research*, June 1979, *1*(4).

Lortie, D. C. Discussion on Gilhool's remarks. *Mainstreaming: Origin and Implications*, Spring 1976, *2*(2). (Minnesota Education Series, University of Minnesota)

Maccoby, M. Leadership needs of the 1980's. *Current issues in higher education.* Washington, DC: American Association for Higher Education, 1979.

Malloy, W. W. *A total school system approach to the management of exceptional education programs.* Paper presented at Syracuse University Colloquy, April 19, 1979.

Skrag, J. A year of progress: What lies ahead? *Dimensions of the future and the challenges of change.* Report of the National Association of State Directors Annual Meeting, 1978, pp. 6-10.

Watson, B. C. Issues confronting educational administration, 1954-1974. In L. Cunningham, W. Hack, & R. Hystrand (Eds.), *Educational administration: The developing decades.* Berkeley, CA: McCutchan Publishing Corp., 1977.

Here is a delightful article from Canada, and one of the few that focuses on middle management responsibilities: After the planners have determined the mission, someone has to do the work. Written for the business world, almost everything included applies to education if such words as principal, coordinator, *and* consultant *are substituted for terms like* department overseer *and* foreman. *Although originally published in 1970, most of the issues this article describes sound much like what we have been hearing as our nation struggles to implement PL 94-142.*

From Paper Plans to Action

Royal Bank of Canada

Like a sheet of music, paper plans are ineffectual unless performed. The conductors who bring business plans into action and conduct their performance are the middle-management people, supervisors, foremen and department overseers.

The committee stage has been passed; the shuffling of papers has ended; the big picture has been drawn: now we get down to the bolts and nuts of production.

The man charged with bridging the gap between the laboratory or the draughting room and the shipping door still has planning to do, but of a different sort. He has a written description of what the finished product is to be; the outlay of money and time and energy has been computed: now he must take the podium and direct his department's performance with skill and sensitivity so as to interpret the planners' score successfully and with some felicity.

From *Royal Bank of Canada Monthly Newsletter*, October 1970, *51* (10), 1-4. Reprinted by permission.

PERSISTENT MIDDLE-MANAGEMENT PROBLEMS

The three persistent problems of middle-management are: the efficient application of technical skill; the systematic ordering of operations; and the organization of sustained co-operation, called teamwork. If these are out of balance no other virtues will compensate and the operation as a whole will not be successful.

This is the place where middle-management ability shows itself. One of the chief skills is understanding the plan to the point of accepting it as being workable. Some men may greet a plan with the hoary statement: "it is all very well in theory but it won't do in practice." That is false reasoning which gets one nowhere. If a thing will not work in practice then there is a mistake in the theory. Something has been overlooked and not allowed for. The plan had better go back for revision.

MODIFICATION MAY BE NECESSARY

There is a need to interpret the plans in accord with their purpose. Sometimes this requires modification of them, but with care. We do not know precisely how he carried out his orders, but obviously Noah did not do his job exactly in accordance with the plan given him. If the story of the Great Flood be taken literally, it is pointed out by Mark Twain in *Letters from the Earth*, he would have had to collect 146,000 kinds of birds and beasts and freshwater creatures, and more than two million species of insect in his 550-foot long ark. Obviously, as a middle-management man he used his head in achieving the purpose of preserving animal life upon the earth.

Methods which cannot be adopted and used "as is" can be adapted with surprising ease by adding a personal twist. But if a vital change has to be made in the plan for a major operation, then the whole plan must be re-examined from start to finish.

Field Marshal Montgomery stated this principle like this: The master plan must never be so rigid that the Commander-in-Chief cannot vary it to suit the changing tactical situation; but nobody else may be allowed to change it at will.

The start of activity on a plan is not the time to be timid, but to face up to difficulties and get all the help needed. This does not indicate distrust of one's self, but common sense. Churchill sent a memo to the Home Secretary about expediting a bit of business. He added: "inviting me to assist you in suppressing obstruction."

Plans are subject to change in detail, sometimes because a customer has changed his mind about the pattern or size; sometimes because of executive second thoughts; and sometimes because of difficulties met in execution. Part of nearly every plan has to be reedited in the light of events as action proceeds.

ABOVE ALL: GET ON WITH IT!

You may have been over the same drill a dozen times, but it does no harm to review it once in a while. If you learn that you have made progress and are headed in the right direction that is heartening. If, on the other hand, your review reveals that you have deviated from the straight path, or that your time schedule is lagging, such a discovery saves you from the mortification of ending up at the wrong place or at the wrong time.

You cannot begin a task effectively by coasting. Start with energy. Initial inertia is a law of all life. It takes more effort to get going than to keep going.

Fortune does not smile on those who, having prepared to do a job, hesitate. Dr. Donald A. Laird wrote in his book *The Technique of Getting Things Done:* "Don't look at a thing: start it. Don't put it off a day: start it. Don't pretend you must think it over: start it. Don't start halfheartedly: put everything you can muster into your start."

When taking up a task that is mainly a series of acts all of which you have previously handled well, you ought to strike your pace in a few seconds or minutes. If you spend five minutes in warming up to a job easily performed and thoroughly mastered, the chances are that there is something wrong with you, the job, or the environment.

Closely akin to procrastinating, or putting off, is dithering. Some people habitually putter around instead of getting down to work. They should copy and paste on the wall a saying of King Claudius in *Hamlet:* "that we would do we should do when we would."

There is no enjoyment in putting things off. We get no pleasure out of postponing our chores. The undone things nag at us. We risk losing our self-respect. Moreover, when an accumulation of things to be done descends inescapably upon us we encounter unending ills.

DIVIDE AND CONQUER

Theodore Roosevelt is remembered because he preached the strenuous life. But his own energetic handling of his many duties was not a matter of temperament and muscle only: he had a systematic organization of his working day.

There are two hints that may be useful in overcoming the common fault of procrastination. The first is: commit yourself. Having promised performance by a set date, you find yourself in honour bound to fulfill it. The second is: do not tackle an accumulation of work like a bulldozer. Break the pile down into small, accessible units, and grapple with them one by one. It has been said that the best way to peel a sack of potatoes is to start on the first one.

Having defined your goals you may or you may not need to write plans for your part of the job. Taking pains at this stage, checking even small details in the blue-print, helps toward efficient work. At least make a note of the things to be accomplished and indicate priorities.

Every part of every job lends itself to listing in two columns on a sheet of paper: steps in the job, and, opposite each step, the key points about which to be careful.

THE VALUE OF SUBJOB SCHEDULING

It is not necessary to write minute instructions for every job. Avoid needless work in the transition from plans to accomplishment. But if there is some part of the job that is specially intricate or carries particular danger of error, make a detailed description of that piece of work.

When a plan reaches the action stage there is likely to be a convulsive scene. It is necessary to assign proportions and priorities as far as possible. Unless progress is planned reasonably well, confusion is likely to occur.

The major schedule will be set in the master planning: completion by such-and-such a date. There remains the subsidiary scheduling so that all parts fit into the ultimate result. This divides the job into individual operations which some foremen call "subjobs."

When you provide yourself with a complete picture of the work to be done you will not feel under compulsion to press all subjobs with equal vigour. You can pick the parts that need to be hurried along. Some will run in parallel: others must follow one another.

THE IMPORTANCE OF SEQUENCE

Distribute the functions involved in the jobs according to time. Dating back from the target completion date, what must be done today, tomorrow? Sequence is vital. If the nature of the job does not dictate in what order operations are to be done, perform the most essential things first.

Write down the five or six essential segments of the job. Then number them in order of their importance. This will take about five minutes of your time. Now tackle the subjobs one by one.

What is the advantage? You are always sure that you are working on the most important things; your mind is not cluttered up with worry about whether you are doing the right things.

If the job has several subdivisions, keep a memo on every one. Memory is not a substitute for a memorandum.

Sometimes a chart is the proper sort of schedule. A chart shows everyone where the action is and what progress has been made.

Some managers and foremen use what they call the Critical Path Method. This shows by arrows how the project activities relate to one another, the time they must start, and the completion deadline for each. This reduces idle manpower to a minimum and reveals in advance where there are possible trouble spots.

CONTROL BY "DEDUCED RECKONING"

Elaborate control boards are used in some offices and factories to keep track of progress. Every individual can have his own very simple control system. All he may need are three spikes marked: "to be done, doing, done." He will move assignment sheets or memos from one to another so that he is not carrying in his head all that he has on his hands.

Airplane navigators used to have a system they called "deduced reckoning." This, which is still at the base of navigational science used on steamers, submarines and airliners, is described in a technical dictionary as "calculation of the position of the ship from the speed and time from its last known position." It means laying out your work and then keeping track of how fast you are going, in what direction, and of when you slow down, speed up, or change course.

Such a system contributes to orderliness. When you work in an efficient way, you solve more problems, make fewer experiments, incur fewer incorrect reactions, use less time and expend less energy.

Everyone, whether in factory or executive office, will study the efficiency of his environment and tools. Do they save time and steps and prevent fumbling? O. J. Greenway, Management Consultant of Honeywell, Inc., St. Petersburg, handling the production of inertial guidance systems for missiles and rockets, described the benefits neatly: "The quality of orderliness and cleanliness is an indication of the efficiency and cleanliness of operations." And 2,500 years earlier Confucious declared: "Order is Heaven's only law."

SEEK SIMPLICITY OF LAYOUT

The workshop arrangements are important in doing the job. A well-arranged office, desk, workbench or tool board contributes to efficiency. The best magic for the supervisor is to put useful tools where they can be easily and quickly found. Streamline your work with as few hindrances to its flow as possible. Photographs and bric-a-brac on a desk may add to its picturesqueness, but they are obstacles and distractions.

To do a job completely, seek simplicity of layout. The day of the massive roll-top desk has gone, but many an office is crowded with needless files full of records, books in inconvenient corners, and trays of letters, trade papers and documents either awaiting action or put there for storage. Some people, even those with important managerial jobs, seem to think that an office strewn with magazines and papers waiting to be read adds to the impression of business and importance they wish to give callers.

You stand at the point where planning and theory terminate in the cutting-edge of direct action. The executives have prepared a statement of what they want done, or the customers have ordered the goods they desire: these are the objectives. Now the thing to do is to outline the steps to be taken and to take the first step. Set up milestones to tell you how far you have progressed and how far you still have to go. Be alert to foresee bottle-necks and be ready to move around them.

From here on, you must interpret and direct. Business is not run on the old town meeting basis, with everyone having a say about what is to be done and how the project is to be carried out. As the First Murderer said to the Duke of Gloucester in *The Tragedy of King Richard III:* "We will not stand to prate, talkers are no good doers: be assur'd we come to use our hands, and not our tongues."

ASSURE INTEGRATION OF EFFORT

Brief everyone who is concerned in the project as far as is necessary to assure integration of effort. This is particularly necessary when several departments or sections are affected. As in a play, give the actors cues so that everyone knows when to come on stage and start doing his bit.

You will have assured yourself before this point is reached that you have all the factual information you need in order to do a professional job. It is not wise for the supervisor to have to go back for additional information after he has started the job. By that time the planners have other things on their minds.

You will have checked to see that the necessary equipment is available and in good condition and that the needed supplies are on hand or on the way. You cannot afford to sit back waiting for a dilatory supplier to act.

Share your work. You already know the strengths and weaknesses of your organization. Now you need to delegate to others, those who will do the work; and co-operate with people in other departments.

HANDLE CORRESPONDENCE BUT ONCE!

Having a pattern of orderliness helps you when difficulties arise. Life would be very dull if it presented no problems. But instead of waiting for them apprehensively try to prepare for them by advance thinking. Methodical anticipation is just as important as, and in many ways better than, the capability to handle crises.

When a job does not move toward completion as on greased skids, there is no advantage in panic and no benefit in melancholy mumblings. Dig through all the reasons for the slow-down until you pin down the one that counts.

When your work is interrupted or interfered with by outside influences, size up the situation and analyze it; act decisively to get back on the beam and get your job running smoothly again; learn by the incident and take steps to prevent a recurrence. Draw upon all available resources. use your own talent to the full, but do not be so high and mighty that you think you can do everything yourself.

When you have had a job in process for a reasonable length of time, take a look at it to learn if there is an easier or more efficient way of doing it. This perceptive look is what creates the remarkable insight a manager displays, a new look at things that produces improvements in layout, work ways and techniques that seem like wizardry to the unenlightened.

On the top planning level there is room for imagination, invention and the spirit of adventure; when the plan reaches the desk or the work-bench there is room for ingenuity and skill of the old-fashioned artisan sort. Get a fix on what is required, then go to work on the details that affect your part of the job.

Group the activities so that one follows the other with least disruption and effort. If you have a letter to write, dig up the necessary facts before dictating "Dear Sir." If you have a carpentry job to do, think it through from beginning to completion and collect what is needed on the site of the job. The best mechanic will be the one able to organize his jobs, know where to find necessary information, and know when to ask for guidance.

Perform the work in the most efficient and economical way possible. Set your speed to suit the job and the conditions under which you are working. An even pace, rather than a series of spurts, makes the best use of your energy so that you effect most with the least effort.

THE PROFESSIONAL TOUCH

Whether on the middle-management level or at the desk or workbench, develop professionalism. No matter what your job may be you can develop some form of art or achieve pride in craftsmanship. Resolve to put the stamp of your own spirit upon the work and to be above the mediocrity that satisfies a man who is not a real pro. Even in the Stone Age there were masters of their craft who were proud of the hatchet heads they chipped from flints.

A professional enjoys what he is working at. He knows its value and meaning and he experiences that perennial nobleness in work that gets things done. The word "efficiency" comes from the Latin "efficio," meaning "I do thoroughly, completely, triumphantly." The highest efficiency is attained when a given amount of energy is so wisely directed that a task is completed in the least possible space and after the lapse of the least possible time.

All the precepts in the systems manuals are worthless unless a man has the spirit to make them work. This is a law of life as old as the first caveman's fire. Emerson put it into a line: "Nothing great was ever achieved without enthusiasm."

Enthusiasm means having real interest, and everyone knows what having a real interest in an endeavour can accomplish. One's spirits rise when action starts, and there is an enlivening feeling of zest. Enthusiasm is interest plus energy, a wish to do something and the spirit to get on with it. It is doing things — not talking about them. As Theseus, King of Athens, said in one of Sophocles' plays: "Nor am I careful to adorn my life with words of praise, but with the light of deeds."

The satisfaction to be derived from completing a constructive enterprise is one of the most massive that life has to offer.

The tests are: (1) Does the piece of work please the person who did it? (2) Does it satisfy the person for whom it was done? (3) Does it accomplish the purpose for which it was designed? If it has these three merits it is good. If, in addition, it has virtue in itself, then it is excellent, thereby adding grace to the doer, the recipient, and the work.

Men and women who can do things in that spirit are in great demand. They have the quality of concentrating upon goals attainable in the given situation and solving immediate problems as they arise.

In every walk of scholarly or practical life, and at every level of work, those who get things done are preferred by society to those who do not. The prizes of life go to those who erect buildings, decipher ancient inscriptions, solve equations, build machines, improve farm production , discover a health-giving drug, or govern a province of the nation, rather than to those who convince themselves that these tasks cannot be done because of inevitable difficulties.

In the Olympic Games it is not the most beautiful or the strongest or the most imaginative or the most talkative people who win the crowns, but those who actually enter the lists as combatants and do things. To get from paper plans to action one must commit oneself. It is unjust and unreasonable to be unwilling to pay this price.

Written primarily from the social worker's point of view, this article makes many salient points for special education administrators. Many educators spend a good deal of time apologizing for being administrators and waxing nostalgic about the joy of returning to be a teacher of children. Apparently, administrators in mental health settings do the same thing.

Some Pitfalls in Administrative Behavior

Arthur K. Berliner

Trying to define with precision the duties of an administrator poses some sticky problems. There is, however, at least one component of the role that is not ambiguous. The administrator wields power;[1] he has the capability of influencing the behavior of others. This power is vested in the administrator because he occupies a particular position, the nature of which requires the exercise of authority to direct the work of others. The sources of administrative power, as implied above, are impersonal and

---

[1] The term *authority* might be used instead. Both terms, *power* and *authority*, have been employed interchangeably by social scientists to characterize an essential attribute of leadership. Central to the former (power) is the element of coercion (through the potential application of negative sanctions); for the latter term (authority) the dominant connotation is consent (of those governed). In practice many leadership positions contain elements of both authority *and* power. A footnote cannot adequately convey either the distinctions between or the interrelatedness of these terms and their underlying conceptual bases. For a more systematic discussion, see Walter Buckley, *Sociology and Modern Systems Theory* (Englewood Cliffs, NJ: Prentice-Hall, 1967), pp. 176-207.

From *Social Casework*, November 1971, pp. 562-566. Reprinted by permission of Family Service Association.

objective. They derive from organizational structure and are accessible to the user because of the circumstance of incumbency. The organization is, theoretically at least, immortal; incumbency is transient. "Men may come and men may go, but I (the organization) go on forever."

A generous admixture of subjective elements, however, frequently contaminates administrative behavior. This article is an attempt to identify some of the sources of these subjective elements that interfere with effective transactions between the administrator and his staff.

THE ELEMENT OF APOLOGY

To begin with, there is adminstrative behavior that reflects the feeling: "I really must apologize for doing what I do." This apologetic approach derives from the hierarchy of values shared by many clinicians, which accords highest status to therapy or any other direct-service activity. Other jobs are of secondary importance compared with working directly with the patient or client. After all, is not the latter activity the organization's ultimate reason for existence? It is not unusual to hear one's colleagues justify their movement up the hierarchical ladder largely on the basis of increased financial rewards. This justification may be accompanied by remarks indicating a distaste for "all this paper work" and nostalgia for "working directly with" the client or patient. Relatively rare, in clinical settings, is the person who affirms positive regard for management activities and for the wielding of organizational responsibilities. The preference for involvement in client service may also stem from more subtle sources.[2]

A defensive reaction to being an administrator may also be the outgrowth of a feeling that bureaucracy, if not exactly a dirty word, is at least a regrettable reality. Layered organizations, so the argument goes, make heavy demands on staff time and money (true); involve duplications, overlap, and excessive monitoring activities (sometimes true); impede service delivery (questionably true); and frustrate or delay innovation (sometimes true).

These criticisms should prompt two responses on the part of the administrator. The first is that it is a dubious assumption that innovation is bound to be beneficial. Therefore, it is important to have some built-in brakes on change. It is an important administrative task to say, "No," or

---

[2] This observation was made by Dr. Charlotte H. Wilkie, a member of the center's social work service, in referring to the vicarious gratifications the worker may derive from direct interventive activities. Engaging someone in treatment may be unconsciously experienced as an opportunity to live someone else's life.

"Let's wait a bit," or "Why now?" Most administrators do not enjoy saying no in any of its forms, but maintaining, and helping others maintain, a perspective about change is one of the administrator's important responsibilities. It is even harder to do this if one's identifications with administration are weak because one's heart is in direct service.

The second response is posed as a question. In large, multifunction organizations such as a clinical research center, how does one organize to get the work done? There have recently been some clever, amusing, and pointed criticisms of organizational behavior.[3] Yet no one has come up with a substitute for bureaucracy as a way of organizing and rationalizing work flow and establishing accountability. When our bureaucratic organizations work poorly, the fault may lie not in the structure but in ourselves that things are messed up. Rather than being caused by flaws in organizational arrangements, rigidity may be due to the presence of little men in big jobs.

To return, however, to the basic point of this first section: if the administrator perceives his work as of peripheral significance (non-therapy) and himself as sitting astride an unwieldly pile of bodies, this perception will sabotage his efforts to be effective.

THE FEELING OF POSSESSIVENESS

There is administrative behavior that implies: "Because I am an administrator, people work for me." This feeling of possessiveness on the part of a chief is altogether too common. To refer to other people as "my staff" may be permissible; to consider one's subordinates as extensions of oneself is to deny the unique contribution each person makes to the accomplishment of the organization's mission.

The ends toward which organizational activities are directed are crucial determinants. When one is selling shoes or assembling cards, one may fairly be said to be working for the company, which is personified as the boss or the stockholders. When delivery of a professional service is the organization's reason for being, one is working for the consumer, the recipient of the service, not for the agency.

---

[3] C. Northcote Parkinson, *Parkinson's Law and Other Studies in Administration* (Boston: Houghton Mifflin Co., 1957). Work expands according to the number of people and time available to do it. Laurence J. Peter and Raymond Hull, *The Peter Principle* (New York: William Morrow, 1969). People inevitably are promoted to their level of incompetence. Robert Townsend, *Up the Organization* (New York: Alfred A. Knopf, 1970). Fire all the vice-presidents and the advertising department.

This statement is more than playing with words. When we say "working for the agency," we are referring to the source of income and establishing the fact of administrative accountability. Thus, to work for the United States Public Health Service is to be paid from the federal treasury and to be accountable to an administrative superior who is himself accountable, and so on, all the way up to the United States taxpayer. But one does not work *for* his administrative superior. He works *under* him, under his guidance, direction, or administration. He is working *for* those for whom he is paid to provide services.

Again, the point may be made that this is quibbling over words. But consider how attitudes and behavior may be affected by one's interpretation. It is a truism that members of organizations devote some of their energies toward keeping the organization going, as distinguished from furthering the organization's manifest purposes. Obviously, this is true for service organizations, too. What about that quantum of energy still available to serve the organization's clientele? If one works for one's boss, his interests come first. If one works for the client, the latter's come first. For example, it makes a difference, when considering a change in the institutional staff's work schedule, whose needs are given priority. It also means one does not automatically comply with the stipulations of one's superior if these run counter, in one's judgment, to good patient care. Irreconcilable differences in opinion have to be resolved in favor of one's chief, but until discussion is closed, the boss is not automatically right. The correct view is the one most responsive to patient needs, and wherever one finds himself in the hierarchy of a service organization, this is the only defensible orientation, because one works for (the interests of) the client, *not* the boss.

THE NEED TO BE LIKED

Another pitfall lies in the misconception that one needs to be liked by one's subordinates to assure their loyalty and maximum effort. This is sometimes stated as the pseudoprinciple: "People will work hard for someone they like." Once again, the administrator's premise may be that people are working for *him*. There is also the implicit, demeaning notion that people need to be motivated by such external considerations as approval of someone in authority. The fallacy is the generalized assumption that adults retain such pervasive dependency attitudes that the psychological function of work is to please daddy, rather than to satisfy more mature needs.

Our society may, in fact, breed a large number of dependent people. But if dependency does exist, in latent or overt form, why should the administrator exploit it? Why not assume the existence in one's subordinates of strivings for self-actualizing, responsible performance? They may work in order to express creative impulses, or to feel useful, or for a sense of achievement, or to meet the needs of others. They also work to pay the rent.

It is human to wish to be liked; but if one cultivates popularity as an administrative tool, one is personalizing a relationship that ought to be based on reciprocal performance, not on subjective nuances. If it is based on the latter, the administrator finds it much more difficult to be objective in assessing the functioning of staff members and in confronting them when necessary. The administrator should work toward earning respect, not affection. If he is liked, this fact is at best a fringe benefit, no doubt gratifying, but not to be misperceived as an indication of job competence.

DILUTING LEADERSHIP RESPONSIBILITY

These days we are much aware of the push to support and extend democracy in human relationships. It makes it easier to participate in the fallacy that consensual decisions are invariably to be preferred over unilateral ones. A corollary assumption seems equally in error: Group thinking produces better results than does individual effort. It must have been a thoroughly disillusioned member of some group, however, who defined a camel as a horse producted by a committee. Abraham Lincoln is said to have solicited the opinions of his cabinet concerning promulgation of the Emancipation Proclamation. As the group members were polled, one by one, each voted no. Then Lincoln said, "I vote yes. The ayes have it." One may describe this as enlightened autocracy, or, better still, as leadership. As it turned out, Lincoln, from his solitary vantage point, had the foresight to take the bolder, more enlightened position.

There is often wisdom in numbers, but the majority has frequently been wrong. Sometimes error is introduced into group deliberation because lower-echelon members of the staff lack the facts or the perspective available to the administrator. The latter may have access to information not available to subordinates; he also should have a long-range view by virtue of experience and position, which may not be available to his colleagues. In fairness, however, it should be said that the lower-echelon staff may have an advantage denied the administrator.

Because they are on the firing line, their awareness of the immediate needs or problems may exceed that of their leader.

Perhaps it is a matter of the administrator's identifying which matters call for group decisions because operational problems may be at issue, and which are his to make because they require the perspective of the leader. The Lincoln story, as far as the writer knows, does not include an account of whether the president told his cabinet he simply wished their advice or whether he sought a group decision. It seems essential that the staff be told the ground rules. Is the issue under discussion negotiable? Is the administrator asking for an expression of opinion that may or may not be followed, or is he commiting himself to a consensus or majority verdict? If the decision is to be made unilaterally, the administrator should feel an obligation to so inform his staff members and subsequently identify for the staff the factors that influenced his decision.

THE ROLE OF RESCUER

This incomplete catalogue of pitfalls lists, finally, the administrator's tendency to act as though he is a "rescue merchant."[4] This is the predilection for bailing out or rescuing subordinates who get into predicaments, without regard for the implications of this rescuing behavior.

Many public mental health facilities serve a clientele whom their treatment staffs perceive as deprived, materially or psychosocially. When one considers the enormous cumulative pressure experienced by most inner city residents prior to institutionalization — fragmented family life, underemployment, and poverty — the staff's perception would seem to be a valid one. Given such a premise, some workers' response is to feel the need to give, to undo the deprivation, to make up for alleged parental or societal failures. How does the administrator get in on the act? Perhaps by being a giver to the staff. In this kind of giving there is the danger of suspending critical judgment. Giving becomes synonymous with acceding to requests or demands. To resist or question is to be depriving or punitive.

In losing sight of the fact that giving requires attentive, thoughtful, and intelligent concern about another's strivings for autonomy, the administrator becomes bogged down in a taking-care-of or doing-for syndrome which, in adult-to-adult relationships, is counterfeit giving.

If the administrator is concerned with building a certain image and trying to cultivate "good" staff relationships, he is vulnerable to error. A

---

[4] Professor David Deitch's apt term, which the writer first heard at a seminar for the professional staff of our clinical research center in 1968.

good relationship between administrator and staff is reasonably analogous to a good relationship between worker and client. It involves a contract in which the participants are taking care of business, dealing with the agenda, working on the problems — in brief a relationship that is productive. Sometimes, unfortunately, the use of the term *good* in this context involves dimensions of popularity (the relationship is defined as good because the other person likes me), gratitude (the other person appreciates my efforts), docility (the other person is amenable to direction), or placidity (the other person is well behaved). Nobody is making waves, so things must be good.

The rescue-merchant concept, as a special case of the above, is a pitfall that originates with the administrator's quest for gratification of his own omnipotent strivings or else comes from his desire to justify his existence. Social worker and nurse, or doctor and vocational rehabilitation counselor, have reached an impasse in their efforts to arrive at some decision or carry out some act. The staff member asks for the intervention of his chief in order to have his view prevail. Here is a chance to show loyalty to one's subordinate by extricating him from a lateral impasse through getting together with one's opposite number — the chief of nursing, for example — in order to resolve the problem. There are authentic impasses, of course, in which bucking the problem upstairs may be necessary. Most of the time, however, administrative intervention is ill-advised. It is a response to someone else's dependent strivings, to the person's posture of apparent helplessness. It is sometimes difficult not to be seduced by this appeal to our power and beneficence. We feel impelled to do for the other.

Supportive behavior by the administrator is called for, but it does not mean taking over. Support means helping the person think through the rationale of his position, either toward reaffirmation of his own logic or toward achieving a shift in his stance because of the fresh insights that emerge in discussion. Loyalty to one's subordinate means giving him one's best in the way of tough questions and sustained scrutiny of his ideas. This response is paying the upmost respect to his ability to think and function responsibly. The take-over response is easier, in the same sense that telling someone the answer to a problem is easier than helping him to figure it out, but it offers the other person no opportunity for learning or growth.

Happy is the administrator who has learned the virtues of, and techniques for, sharing of his power. Sharing of power leads to high staff morale, organizational effectiveness, and the on-the-job education of the generation which inevitably must succeed him. The administrator may create subsystems within the larger staff whole — committees, task forces,

249

and so forth — to which responsibility may be delegated. There are organizational tasks to which newer staff members may be assigned. Such arrangements not only lighten the administrator's load; they also help subordinates perform some aspects of administrative behavior. They improve the administrator's view of the whole and thus enhance his capacity to be objective. They make more likely of attainment the leader's use of administration, not as a staircase to status, but as another gateway to service.

Educational administrators continue to disagree over the merits of some organized system of management such as management by objectives. Special educators get caught up in the same arguments. Opinions range from enthusiastic endorsement to the belief that MBO is an exercise in paperwork. This author reviews the problems and shows how MBO can be a positive force in determining priorities.

Management By Objectives (or)
I'll Try To Find Time
To Observe More Teachers Next Year

Robert R. Spillane

"Management" is a concept regarded with intense suspicion by both school workers and the taxpayers to whom they are so immediately accountable. Property owners do tend to accept the need for classroom teachers and even for principals and custodians. But the appointment of curriculum coordinates or assistant superintendents suggests gross waste of public money. To speak of a "management system" implies computers and the year 2001.

To school professionals, the term hints at Babbittry and time-motion studies. Many educators are uncomfortable with the idea of "management" because so much of their life experience has been limited to schools.

How, then, is a classroom normally managed? By dictatorship, of course. If a piece of work is not up to standard, the teacher feels free to comment aloud not only upon the immediate discrepancy but upon the

From *Phi Delta Kappan*, April 1977, pp. 624-626. Copyright © Phi Delta Kappa, Inc. Reprinted by permission.

general character of the student, upon the school record of siblings, upon the probable bearing of that particular misspelling on chances of acceptance at college, or upon any other sins the student seems likely to commit. All orders from the teacher have equal weight: "Complete problems 9-12," "Bring me a chair," "Don't be so stupid." The chances of any order being obeyed (including the last one) depend far more on the personality of the teacher than on any rational system of management.

Most of the people who become teachers do so without ever having done anything else except go to school. Our peculiar system of training means that a new teacher will be locked up in that room with those kids with little more guidance about how to manage a class than memories of how hated or beloved teachers did it. Classroom teachers become certified administrators the same way they became teachers, by taking courses at some institution well removed from the realities of hallway horrors or cafeteria chaos. Management continues to be seen as something done by a combination of charisma, luck, and bluff.

Classroom teachers rarely see the connection between the struggles of the board of education to balance the budget and the rise or fall in third-grade reading scores — apart from their acceptance of the principle that all money spent to meet union demands is good for education. In turn, boards of education can become so involved in budget balancing and attempts to satisfy the demands of particular pressure groups as to lose sight of the purpose of all of those late nights and the neglect of spouses.

Superintendents can become so involved in responding to external and internal pressures as to neglect the planning process.

Other factors make management of the schools difficult. Education has a particular need for systematic and continuous definition of goals. School administrators function under constraints imposed by union contracts, community pressures, state laws, parental desires, student needs, changing revenue sources, and the fluctuating demands that a constantly changing society makes upon those entrusted with the transmission of culture. At the same time, these administrators deal in a particularly amorphous product. The hospital administrator has mortality rates with which to judge effectiveness. The widget manufacturer has the widget sales curve as a check on production-line routines. The schools have their reading scores, but we all know the difficulties inherent in judging either what the reading scores mean or what steps to take to change them.

When I became superintendent of schools in New Rochelle, I had some difficulty in comprehending the actual goals for the district from observation of the management system. Traditional budget methods made it difficult to assess those curriculum areas that were receiving a major share of the taxpayers' dollar. Personnel were not deployed according to urgent priorities. There were districtwide coordinators for music and art, for example, but none for reading or math, although scores in these basics were sliding rapidly downhill.

A major effort of the district since that time has been to develop a budgetary system (PPBS) and a management-by-objectives system that fits the needs of our schools, allows for planning and evaluation of achievement, and involves district personnel at all levels in both formulation and implementation.

Preliminary discussion of these goals uncovered vast layers of paranoia.

Our progress toward an MBO system has been slow because of a consciousness that nothing could work until a great deal of the wariness could be overcome.

Yet MBO offered the district an opportunity. It is a medium for flexible and effective planning and for continuous assessment of the results of that planning. In New Rochelle, management by objectives was presented as a process, not a product; a means, not an end; a pathway, not a destination. The process was presented as one that emphasizes results, not personalities. MBO does not want to know if a teacher (or an administrator) is "energetic, healthy, personable, and cooperative." MBO wants to know what he or she planned to do that semester and the result of that planning.

The task of defining objectives was pursued on several leads. The budget was redesigned, following PPBS guidelines, so that the board of education, administrators, and the public could all see more clearly the commitment of resources and the results. A series of public hearings was held to gather as much input as possible on citizen views of school priorities. The final result of these meetings was a list, "Educational Goals for New Rochelle," adopted by the board as a general statement of purpose. A series of seminars was held for administrative personnel to explore the implications of PPBS and MBO. Speakers were invited from the Harvard Business School and consultants from one of the few districts known to be involved in an MBO system, West Hartford, Connecticut.

These exchanges of ideas continued over many months. Information in the form of reprints of articles and accounts of the meetings was distributed throughout the school system and the community. Steps were taken to establish ways of judging results in the schools. An annual "New Rochelle School Profile" was put together, printed, and distributed to professionals and parents. (We are now heading for the fifth year of publication.) The profile provides a school-by-school report of reading and math achievement in selected grades for all elementary and secondary units, together with educational ability scores, information about the community, number of foster children, ADC cases, etc. It also provides information on such school-related factors as level of staff training, percentage of non-English-speaking pupils, pupil mobility rate, etc.

The introduction states:

> The New Rochelle School Profile has been developed for a single important reason: to provide our schools with the information they need to improve. This it will accomplish by strengthening building-by-building accountability to the public, by improving communications between each school and the people it serves, and by providing a common objective basis for identifying problems, setting priorities, recognizing successful programs in individual buildings that can be transplanted to the others, and reviewing on a continuing schedule the results of our educational efforts.

At the same time that principals were being asked to plan for their own schools, they were also being asked to assume new districtwide responsibilities. Each principal took over a particular area of curriculum or administration as his or her own particular concern. One principal worked with a committee of teachers to redesign the elementary math curriculum and to develop a method of keeping individualized math achievement records for every child in the district. Another introduced a new social studies curriculum.

The New Rochelle Principals Association set up an MBO Task Force. After six months of discussions, the task force drew up a report that, while firmly rejecting the notion of attaching merit pay to any MBO system, was a useful program statement. The report was used as the basis of a superintendent's working paper, "Managing the Schools: Setting Goals and Objectives," which was presented to the principals and other administrators early in the school year.

In that paper I drew upon our years of experience and discussion to state a philosophical base for our own MBO system. I offered guidelines to help each principal draw up his or her own list of objectives and outlined four kinds of managerial objectives:

1. Routine objectives. E.g., hiring of staff, drawing up a budget.

2. Problem-solving objectives. E.g., coping with the rising cost of oil, lowering ethnic tensions.

3. Innovative objectives. E.g., developing new ways of teaching reading at the junior high level.

4. Personal objectives. E.g., developing skills in a particular area, such as budget or community relations.

254

No particular objectives were suggested. The examples were intended purely as examples. The only direction indicated was in the rather broad parameter of the aforementioned list of "Educational Goals for New Rochelle" included in the paper. Our MBO system was intended to develop the initiative and planning skills of each administrator, not to find a more efficient way of imposing central-office directives.

The paper states that "the objectives . . . will be written in such a way as to clearly state the objective and a method of assessing success or failure." Again examples were given of possible formats, such as "The objective is to cut teacher absenteeism by x% in the 1973-74 school year" or "The objective is to increase third-grade reading scores. This objective will be considered achieved when x% of the third-grade students read at yz level."

There were also examples of method, not content, the intent being to clarify thinking on both sides, not to control objectives.

Principals were asked to submit their lists of managerial objectives with their budget requests for the coming year and to meet with the superintendent or his representative to review objectives and reach mutual agreement on appropriate procedures.

The statements of objectives submitted revealed considerable commonality (i.e., strengthening basic math and reading skills), but they also reflected the variety of principals and schools. Our buildings vary. We have a high school for 3,000 students in which an elaborate and up-to-date physical plant provides its own managerial difficulties, such as the care and upkeep of a swimming pool and a planetarium. At the other end of the scale is a 60-year-old elementary school enrolling, at last count, 299 children. An important part of the objectives of the high school principal was to strengthen the managerial skills of his staff. To this end he is planning a series of MBO workshops and seminars of his own.

Some principals had difficulty in formulating objectives in measurable terms — and appreciated the assistance of staff members more familiar with the statistical measurement of achievement. Some areas of endeavor are of course less easily measured than others. On the other hand, difficulties in establishing methods of measurement often indicated the need for rethinking an objective and the means for achieving it. Better community relations were often mentioned as a desirable objective. As is often the case, much of the burden for achieving this objective was placed on community members. The need for systematic evaluation of effort produced the realization that community members are not accountable to the school system. A principal can mandate that teachers invite parents for conferences — but not that parents attend. A principal can even suggest words that a teacher might use at such a conference — but not be able to influence an irate mother's reply.

Some of the objectives that first year were expressed in the hopeful terms of New Year's resolutions ("I will try to find time to observe more teachers next year"). The emphasis on realism and measurability in the working paper, however, seemed to have produced objectives that were, on the whole, useful and achievable.

Principals seemed to have more difficulty in formulating the fourth kind of objective (personal) than any other. Usually this was omitted, which probably indicated the need for clarification of the guidelines. Perhaps there was an assumption that an expression of a desire for improvement implied an awareness of weakness.

Our system of management by objectives has now been operating for four years and has, over and over again, proved its worth. I have always liked to believe that there is an innate connection between clarity of thought and clarity of expression. In this case the need for the terse expression of measurable objectives does seem to have vastly improved the ability of the writers to determine and define desirable goals. Principals and administrators have learned to express their objectives more clearly and to devise more accurate methods of measurement. In the area of staff supervision there has been spectacular growth in the use of more systematic ways of observation and evaluation.

Each person has tended to arrive at his or her own way of writing out the process. One person lays out the plan in two columns headed "Objectives" and "Analysis," with areas termed "Instruction," "Staff," "Students," "Extracurricular," "Personal," and "Miscellaneous."

Inclusion of the "Personal" area is, by now, rare. Most principals and administrators have tended to drop the whole subject as too difficult to analyze — although the continuing general inclusion of "staff development" objectives shows their awareness of the need for personal growth on the part of *other* people. One principal, however, devised such interesting objectives as "To read a minimum of 12 current professional books" and "To write a minimum of five professional articles."

Another principal uses the two-column format, heading the first column "What and When" and the second "How." This allows for the expression of a general — and sometimes vague — idea in the first column and its reduction to specifics in the second. For example:

What and When

Continue close monitoring of honors program all year long.

How

1. Meet with parents of incoming honors students during September.

2. Schedule meetings with chairmen of honors teachers in November, March, and June.

3. Maintain file of any complaints received.

4. Meet with other secondary principals in fall for general discussion.

Another format had three parts, allowing for the inclusion of a vital section of information, "Indicators" (indicating the existence of a problem), followed by "Objectives" and "Action Plan." I must admit that not until I read this detailed account of the life of a school did I realize how necessary it is to know why an administrator thinks there is a problem. The validity of an objective — and its achievement — depends greatly on whether the administrator's awareness came from close observation of students or teachers, from parental complaints, from a desire to conform to the expressed desire of the superintendent, or from a quick reading of a recent journal. "Indicators" would be a useful addition to any list of objectives.

The variety of styles used by administrators in defining their plans suggests that we have achieved one of my original objectives: the development of a flexible system that encourages not only accountability but creativity and adaptability to particular and changing circumstances.

An area of failure was indicated when I met with the citywide Parent-Teachers Association to explain the new management system. The audience listened politely, laughed at the jokes, and admired the neatness of the charts and my dextrous handling of the overhead projector. When question time came, alas, they wanted to talk about homework and the pass/fail marking system at one of the junior highs. And there was the parent who feared that what I had presented was a "mechanistic" approach. She explained that her real concern was whether the students were learning to care about each other.

I knew then that one of my chief management objectives for the coming year is to find ways to make discussions of management as exciting to community groups as sex education or the ethnic origin of administrators. We have to convince mom and dad that effective management is caring management.

This excellent article addresses the thorny issues involved in evaluating employee performance. Levinson's discussion is directed toward employee appraisal in the private sector, but his observations should have real meaning to educators. Though business may be criticized for equating appraisal with results at any cost, educators may be vulnerable at the other extreme for designing evaluation systems that pay little attention to achievement outcomes.

Appraisal of *What* Performance?

Harry Levinson

It may be stretching it a bit to argue that the epigram "It's not the winning or losing that counts, but how you play the game" ought to be strictly followed in designing performance appraisal systems. In business, results are important, few would disagree. What the epigram points out, however, is that some results are not worth the means some take to achieve them. Nonetheless, most performance systems in most companies focus on results of behavior while in reality people are judged just as much on how they get things done. In this article, the author argues that in order for a company to have a performance appraisal system that accounts for the "how" as well as the "what," it will need to establish: job descriptions that are behavior- as well as results-oriented; a critical incident program in which managers write reports regularly on the behavior of their employees; and support mechanisms to help managers honestly appraise the behavior of their employees as well as of their bosses.

A corporate president put a senior executive in charge of a failing operation. His only directive was "Get it in the black." Within two years of that injunction, the new executive moved the operation from a deficit position to one that showed a profit of several million. Fresh from his triumph, the executive announced himself as a candidate for a higher-level position, and indicated that he was already receiving offers from other companies.

The corporate president, however, did not share the executive's positive opinions of his behavior. In fact, the president was not at all pleased with the way the executive had handled things. Naturally the executive was dismayed, and when he asked what he had done wrong, the corporate president told him that he had indeed accomplished what he had been asked to do, but he had done it singlehandedly, by the sheer force of his own personality. Furthermore, the executive was told, he had replaced people whom the company thought to be good employees with those it regarded as compliant. In effect, by demonstrating his own strength, he had made the organization weaker. Until the executive changed his authoritarian manner, his boss said, it was unlikely he would be promoted further.

Implicit in this vignette is the major fault in performance appraisal and management by objectives — namely, a fundamental misconception of what is to be appraised.

Performance appraisal has three basic functions: (1) to provide adequate feedback to each person on his or her performance; (2) to serve as a basis for modifying or changing behavior toward more effective working habits; and (3) to provide data to managers with which they may judge future job assignments and compensation. The performance appraisal concept is central to effective management. Much hard and imaginative work has gone into developing and refining it. In fact, there is a great deal of evidence to indicate how useful and effective performance appraisal is. Yet present systems of performance appraisal do not serve any of these functions well.

As it is customarily defined and used, performance appraisal focuses not on behavior but on outcomes of behavior. But even though this executive in the example achieved his objective, he was evaluated on *how* he attained it. Thus, while the system purports to appraise results, in practice, people are really appraised on how they do things — which is not formally described in the setting of objectives, and for which there are rarely data on record.

In my experience, the crucial aspect of any manager's job and the source of most failures, which is practically never described, is the "how." As long as managers appraise the ends yet actually give greater weight to the mean, employ a static job description base which does not describe the "how," and do not have support mechanisms for the appraisal process, widespread dissatisfaction with performance appraisal is bound to continue. In fact, one personnel authority speaks of performance appraisal as "the Achilles heel of our profession."[1]

Just how these inadequacies affect performance appraisal systems and how they can be corrected to provide managers with realistic bases for making judgments about employees' performance is the subject of this article.

Inadequacies of Appraisal Systems

It is widely recognized that there are many things inherently wrong with most of the performance appraisal systems in use. The most obvious drawbacks are:

- No matter how well defined the dimensions for appraising performance on quantitative goals are, judgments on performance are usually subjective and impressionistic.

- Because appraisals provide inadequate information about the subtleties of performance, managers using them to compare employees for the purposes of determining salary increases often make arbitrary judgments.

- Ratings by different managers, and especially those in different units, are usually incomparable. What is excellent work in one unit may be unacceptable in another in the same company.

- When salary increases are allocated on the basis of a curve of normal distribution, which is in turn based on rating of results rather than on behavior, competent employees may not only be denied increases, but may also become demotivated.[2]

- Trying to base promotion and layoff decisions on appraisal data leaves the decisions open to acrimonious debate. When employees who have been retired early have complained to federal authorities

---

[1] Herbert Heneman, "Research Roundup," *The Personnel Administrator*, June 1975, p. 61.

[2] Paul H. Thompson and Gene W. Dalton, "Performance Appraisal: Managers Review," *Howard Business Review*, January-February 1970, p. 149.

of age discrimination, defendant companies have discovered that there were inadequate data to support the layoff decisions.

● Although managers are urged to give feedback freely and often, there are no built-in mechanisms for ensuring that they do so. Delay in feedback creates both frustration, when good performance is not quickly recognized, and anger, when judgment is rendered for inadequacies long past.

● There are few effective established mechanisms to cope with either the sense of inadequacy managers have about appraising subordinates, or the paralysis and procrastination that result from guilt about playing God.

Some people might argue that these problems are deficiencies of managers, not of the system. But even if that were altogether true, managers are part of that system. Performance appraisal needs to be viewed not as a technique but as a process involving both people and data, and as such the whole process is inadequate.

Recognizing that there are many deficiencies in performance appraisals, managers in many companies do not want to do them. In other companies there is a great reluctance to do them straightforwardly. Personnel specialists attribute these problems to the reluctance of managers to adopt new ways and to the fear of irreparably damaging their subordinates' self-esteem. In government, performance appraisal is largely a joke, and in both private and public enterprise, merit ratings are hollow.[3]

One of the main sources of trouble with performance appraisal systems is, as I have already pointed out, that the outcome of behavior rather than the behavior itself is what is evaluated. In fact, most people's jobs are described in terms that are only quantitatively measurable; the job description itself is the root of the problem.

THE STATIC JOB DESCRIPTION

When people write their own job descriptions (or make statements from which others will write them) essentially they define their responsibilities and basic functions. Then on performance appraisal forms, managers comment on these functions by describing what an individual

---

[3] Herbert S. Meyer, "The Pay for Performance Dilemma," *Organizational Dynamics*, Winter 1975, p. 30.

is supposed to accomplish. Forms in use in many companies today have such directions as:

1. "List the major objectives of this person's job that can be measured qualitatively or quantitatively."

2. "Define the results expected and the standards of performance —money, quantity, quality, time limits, or completion dates."

3. "Describe the action planned as a result of this appraisal, the next steps to be taken — reevaluation, strategy, tactics, and so on."

4. "List the person's strong points — his aspects and accomplishments — and his weak points — areas in which improvement is needed. What are the action plans for improvement?"

In most instances the appraiser is asked to do an overall rating with a five-point scale or some similar device. Finally, he is asked to make a statement about the person's potential for the next step or even for higher-level management.

Nowhere in this set of questions or in any of the performance appraisal systems I have examined is anything asked about how the person is to attain the ends he or she is charged with reaching.

While some may assert that the ideal way of managing is to give a person a charge and leave him or her alone to accomplish it, this principle is oversimplified both in theory and practice. People need to know the topography of the land they are expected to cross, and the routes as perceived by those to whom they report.

Every manager has multiple obligations, not the least of which are certain kinds of relationships with peers, subordinates, and various consumers, financial, government, supplier, and other publics. Some of these are more important than others, and some need to be handled with much greater skill and aplomb than others. In some situations a manager may be expected to take a vigorous and firm stand, as in labor negotiations; in others he may have to be conciliative; in still others he may even have to be passive. Unless these varied modes of expected behavior are laid out, the job description is static. Because static job descriptions define behavior in gross terms, crucially important differentiated aspects of behavior are lost when performance appraisals are made.

For example, in one of the more progressive performance appraisal systems, which is used by an innovative company, a manager working out his own job description prepares a mission or role statement of what he is supposed to do according to the guide which specifically directs him to concentrate on the what and the when, not on the why and the how.[4] The guide instructs him to divide his mission into four general areas: (1) innovation, (2) problem solving, (3) ongoing administration, and (4) personal.

In still another company, a manager appraising a subordinate's performance is asked to describe an employee's accomplishments, neglected areas, goals, and objectives. The manager is told that he is to recognize good work, suggest improvement, get agreement on top priority elements of the task, clarify responsibility, verify and correct rumors, and talk about personal and long-range goals.

In another company's outstanding performance appraisal guide, which reflects great detail and careful consideration, the categories are: work, effectiveness with others, problem solving, decision making, goal setting, organizing and planning, developing subordinates, attending to self-development, and finding initiatives. Each of these categories is broken down into example statements such as: "exhibits high level of independence in work"; "identifies problems and deals with them"; "appropriately subordinates departmental interest to overall company goal"; or "gives people genuine responsibility, holds them accountable, and allows them freedom to act."

Some personnel researchers have advocated role analysis techniques to cope with static job descriptions, and this is a step in the right direction.[5]

But even these techniques are limited because they lean heavily on what other people — supervisors, subordinates, peers — expect of the manager. These expectations are also generalized; they do not specify behavior.

Nowhere in these examples is an individual told what *behavior* is expected on him in a range of contexts. Who are the sensitive people with whom certain kinds of relationships have to be maintained? What are the specific problems and barriers? What have been the historic manufacturing blunders or frictions? How should union relationships and union leaders be dealt with? What are the specific integrative problems to be resolved and what are the historical conflicts? These and many more similar pieces of behavior will be the true bases on which a person will be judged, regardless of the questions an appraisal form asks.

---

[4] John B. Lasagna, "Make Your MBO Pragmatic," *Howard Business Review*, November-December 1971, p. 64.

[5] Ishwar Dayal, "Role Analysis Techniques in Job Descriptions," *California Management Review*, Summer 1969, p. 47.

Static job descriptions are catastrophic for managers. Job proficiency and goal achievement usually are necessary but not sufficient conditions for advancement; the key elements in whether one makes it in an organization are political. The collective judgments made about a person, which rarely find their way into performance appraisals, become the social web in which he or she must live. Therefore, when a person is placed in a new situation, whether in a different geographical site, at a different level in the hierarchy, or in a new role, he must be apprised of the subtleties of the relationships he will have with those who will influence his role and his career. Furthermore, he must be helped to differentiate the varied kinds of behavior required to succeed.

Some people develop political diagnostic skill very rapidly; often, however, these are people whose social senses enable them to move beyond their technical and managerial competence. And some may be out and out manipulative charlatans who succeed in business without really trying, and whose promotion demoralizes good people. But the great majority of people, those who have concentrated heavily on their professional competence at the expense of acquiring political skill early, will need to have that skill developed, ideally by their own seniors. That development process requires: (1) a dynamic job description, (2) a critical incident process, and (3) a psychological support system.

DYNAMIC JOB DESCRIPTION

If a static job description is at the root of the inadequacies of performance appraisal systems, what is needed is a different kind of job description. What we are looking for is one that amplifies statements of job responsibility and desired outcome by describing the emotional and behavioral topography of the task to be done by the individual in the job.

Psychologists describe behavior in many ways, each having his or her own preferences. I have found four major features of behavior to be fundamentally important in a wide range of managerial settings. These features have to do with how a person characteristically manages what some psychologists call aggression, affection, dependency, and also the nature of the person's ego ideal.[6]

Using his preferred system, one can begin formulating a dynamic job description by describing the characteristic behavior required by a job. This is what these terms mean with respect to job descriptions:

---

[6] Harry Levinson, *The Great Jackass Fallacy* (Cambridge University Press, 1973), Ch. 3.

265

1. *How does this job require the incumbent to handle his aggression, his attacking capacity?* Must he or she vanquish customers? Must he hold on to his anger in the face of repeated complaints and attacks from others? Will she be the target of hostility and, if so, from whom? Must he give firm direction to others? Must she attack problems vigorously, but handle some areas with great delicacy and finesse? Which problems are to be attacked with vigor and immediately and which coolly and analytically?

2. *How does this job require the incumbent to manage affection, the need to love and to be loved?* Is the person required to be a socially friendly leader of a close-knit group? Should the person work closely and supportively with subordinates for task accomplishment? Is the task one in which the person will have to be content with the feeling of a job well done, or is it one which involves more public display and recognition? Will he be obscure and unnoticed, or highly visible? Must she lavish attention on the work, a product, a service, or customers? Must he be cold and distant from others and, if so, from whom?

3. *How does this job require the incumbent to manage dependency needs?* Will the individual be able to lean on others who have skill and competencies, or will he have to do things himself? How much will she be on her own and in what areas? How much support will there be from superiors and staff functions? How well defined is the nature of the work? What kind of feedback provisions are there? What are the structural and hierarchical relationships? How solid are they and to whom will the person turn and for what? With which people must he interact in order to accomplish what he needs to accomplish, and in what manner?

4. *What ego ideal demands does this job fulfill?* If one does the task well, what are the gratifications to be gained? Will the person make a lot of money? Will he achieve considerable organizational and public recognition? Will she be eligible for promotion? Will he feel good about himself and, if so, in what ways? Why? Will she acquire a significant skill, an important element of reputation, or an organizational constituency? Will he acquire power?

Individuals may be described along the same four dynamic dimensions: How does this person characteristically handle aggression? How does he or she characteristically handle affection? How does he or she characteristically handle dependency needs? What is the nature of his or her ego ideal?

Once the subtleties of the task are defined and individuals described, people may be matched to tasks. I am not advocating a return to evaluation of personality traits. I am arguing for a more dynamic conception of the managerial role and a more dynamic assessment of an employee's characteristics. And only when a person's behavior is recognized as basic to how he performs his job will performance appraisal systems be realistic.

CRITICAL INCIDENT PROCESS

Having established a dynamic job description for a person, the next step is to evolve a complementary performance appraisal system that will provide feedback on verifiable behavior, do so in a continuous fashion, and serve coaching-, promotion-, and salary-data needs.

Ideally, a manager and his subordinate will have defined together the objectives to be attained in a certain job, and the criteria by which each will know that those objectives have been attained, including the more qualitative aspects of the job. Then they will have spelled out the subtleties of how various aspects of the job must be performed. They will in this way have elaborated the *behavioral* requirements of the task.

In order for performance appraisal to be effective for coaching, teaching, and changing those aspects of an employee's behavior that are amenable to change, an employee needs to know about each piece of behavior that is good, as well as that which for some reason is not acceptable or needs modification. Such incidents will occur randomly and be judged randomly by his manager.

So that there will be useful data, the manager needs to quickly write down what he has said to the subordinate, describing in a paragraph what the subordinate did or did not do, in what setting, under what circumstances, about what problem. This information forms a *behavioral* record, a critical incident report of which the subordinate already has been informed and which is now in his folder, open to his review.

This critical incident technique is not new.[7] In the past it has been used largely for case illustrations and, in modified forms, has been suggested as a method for first-level supervisors to evaluate line employees. Supervisors already record negative incidents concerning line employees because warnings and disciplinary steps must be documented. However, efforts to develop scales from critical incidents for rating behavior have not worked well.[8] Behavior is too complex to be scaled along a few dimensions and then rated.

---

[7] John C. Flanagan, "The Critical Incident Technique," *Psychological Bulletin*, 51:327, 1954, and John C. Flanagan (co-author Robert K. Burns), "The Employee Performance Record: A New Appraisal and Development Tool," *Howard Business Review*, September-October 1955, p. 95.

[8] Donald P. Schwab, Herbert C. Heneman, III, and Thomas A. DeCotis, "Behaviorally Anchored Rating Scales: A Review of the Literature," *Personnel Psychology*, 28:549, 1975.

But instead of scaling behavior, one might directly record the behavior of those being appraised, and evaluate it at a later date. There are other good reasons for adopting this technique as well. At last, here is a process that provides data to help managers perform the basic functions of performance appraisal systems — namely, provide feedback, coaching, and promotion data. Another plus is that recorded data live longer than the manager recording them.

Here is how behavioral data might be put to use in the critical incident process:

1. *Feedback data:* When there is a semiannual or annual review, an employee will have no surprises and the manager will have on paper what he is using as a basis for making his summary feedback and appraisal. Because the data are on record, an employee cannot deny having heard what was said earlier, nor must the manager try to remember all year what have been the bases of his judgments.

Also, as each critical incident is recorded, over time there will be data in an individual's folder to be referred to when and if there are suits alleging discrimination. Critical incidents of behavior, which illustrate behavior patterns, will be the only hard evidence acceptable to adjudicating bodies.

2. *Coaching data:* When employees receive feedback information at the time the incident occurs, they may be able to adapt their behavior more easily. With this technique, the employee will receive indications more often on how he is doing, and will be able to correct small problems before they become large ones. Also, if the employee cannot change his behavior, that fact will become evident to him through the repetitive critical incident notes. If the employee feels unfairly judged or criticized, he may appeal immediately rather than long after the fact. If there are few or no incidents on record, that in itself says something about job behavior, and may be used as a basis for discussion. In any event, both manager and employee will know which behavior is being appraised.

3. *Promotional data:* With such an accumulation of critical incidents, a manager or the personnel department is in a position to evaluate repeatedly how the person characteristically manages aggression, affection, and dependency needs, and the nature of his ego ideal. These successive judgments become cumulative data for better job fit.

When a person is provided continuously with verifiable information, including when he has been passed over for promotion and why, he is able to perceive more accurately the nuances of his behavior and his behavoral patterns. Thus, when offered other opportunities, the employee is in a better position to weigh his own behavioral configurations against those required by the prospective job. A person who knows himself in this way will be more easily able to say about a given job, "That's not for me." He will see that the next job in the pyramid is not necessarily rightfully his. In recognizing his own behavioral limitations he may save himself much grief as well as avoid painful difficulty for his superiors and the organization.

But the most important reason for having such information is to increase the chances of success of those who are chosen for greater responsibility. In most personnel folders there is practically no information about how a manager is likely to do when placed on his own. Data about dependency are noticeably absent, and many a shining prospect dims when there is no one to support him in a higher-level job. Managements need to know early on who can stand alone, and they cannot know that without behavioral information.

4. *Long-term data:* Frequently, new managers do not know their employees and all too often have little information in the folder with which to appraise them. This problem is compounded when managers move quickly from one area to another. For his part, the employee just as frequently has to prove himself to transient bosses who hold his fate in their hands but know nothing of his past performance. With little information, managers feel unqualified to make judgments. With the critical incident process, however, managers can report incidents which can be summarized by someone else.

Some may object to "keeping book" on their people or resist a program of constant reviews and endless reports — both extreme views. Some may argue that supervisors will not follow the method. But if managers cannot get raises for or transfer employees without adequate documentation, they will soon learn the need to follow through. The critical incident process compels superiors to face subordinates, a responsibility too many shirk.

While it might seem difficult to analyze performance in terms of aggression, affection, dependency, the ego ideal, or other psychological concepts, to do so is no different from learning to use economic, financial, or accounting concepts. Many managers already talk about these same issues in other words, for example: "taking charge" versus "being a nice guy"; "needing to be stroked" versus the "self-starter"; "fast track" versus the "shelf-sitter." A little practice, together with support mechanisms, can go a long way.

SUPPORT MECHANISMS

Performance appraisal cannot be limited to a yearly downward reward-punishment judgment. Ideally, appraisal should be a part of

269

a continuing process by which both manager and employee may be guided. In addition, it should enhance an effective superior-subordinate relationship.

To accomplish these aims, performance appraisal must be supported by mechanisms that enable the manager to master his inadequacies and to cope with his feelings of guilt; have a record of that part of his work that occurs outside the purview of his own boss (e.g., task force assignments which require someone to appraise a whole group); and modify those aspects of his superior's behavior which hamper his performance. All of this requires an upward appraisal process.

1. *Managing the guilt:* The manager's guilt about appraising subordinates appears when managers complain about playing God, about destroying people. A great crippler of effective performance appraisal is the feeling of guilt, much of which is irrational, but which most people have when they criticize others.[9] Guilt is what leads to the fear of doing appraisals. It is the root of procrastination, of the failure to appraise honestly, and of the overreaction which can demolish subordinates.

Fortunately, there are group methods for relieving guilt and for helping managers and supervisors understand the critical importance, indeed the necessity, of accurate behavioral evaluations. One way is by having people together at the same peer level discuss their problems in appraisal and talk about their feelings in undertaking the appraisal task. In addition, rehearsals of role playing increase a manager's sense of familiarity and competence and ease his anxiety.

In fact, a five-step process, one step per week for five weeks, can be extremely helpful:

- Week one: Group discussion among peers (no more than 12) about their feelings about appraising subordinates.

- Week two: Group discussions resulting in advice from each other on the specific problems that each anticipates in appraising individuals.

- Week three: Role playing appraisal interviews.

- Week four: Actual appraisals.

- Week five: Group discussion to review the appraisals, problems, encountered, both anticipated and unanticipated, lessons learned, and skill needs that may have surfaced.

---

[9] Harry Levinson, "Management By Whose Objectives," *Howard Business Review*, July-August 1970, p. 125.

2. *Group appraisal:* By group appraisal, I do not mean peer approval of each other, which usually fails; rather, I mean appraisal of a group's accomplishment. When people work together in a group, whether reporting to the same person or not, they need to establish criteria by which they and those to whom they report will know how well the task force or the group has done — in terms of behavior as well as results. Group appraisals provide information that is helpful both in establishing criteria as well as in providing each individual with feedback.

At the end of a given task, a group may do a group appraisal or be appraised by the manager to whom they report, and that appraisal may be entered into folders of each of the people who are involved. It will then serve as another basis for managerial and self-judgment.

3. *Upward appraisal:* Finally, there should be upward appraisal. Some beginning voluntary steps in this direction are being taken in the Sun Oil Company, and by individual executives in other companies. Upward appraisal is a very difficult process because most managers do not want to be evaluated by their subordinates. As a matter of fact, however, most managers *are* evaluated indirectly by their employees, and these evaluations are frequently behavioral.

The employees' work itself is a kind of evaluation. Their work may be done erratically or irresponsibly. Or they may be poorly motivated. Negative behavior is a form of appraisal, and one from which a manager gains little. A manager cannot be quite sure what precipitated the behavior he sees, let alone be sure what to do about it.

If, however, the manager is getting dynamic behavioral appraisal from his employees, then he, too, may correct his course. But if he asks his subordinates for upward appraisal without warning, he is likely to be greeted with dead silence and great caution. A helpful way to deal with this situation is to ask one's employees to define the criteria by which they would appraise the manager's job, not to judge his actual performance.

This process of definition may require a manager to meet with employees weekly for months to define the criteria. By the end of three months, say, the employees should be much more comfortable working with their manager on this issue. And if the manager can be trusted at all, then when he or she finally asks them to evaluate the performance, including specific behaviors, along the dimensions they have worked out together, they are likely to be more willing to do so. Of course, if there is no trust, there is no possibility of upward appraisal. In any event, the upward performance appraisal should go to the manager's superior so that people do not jeopardize themselves by speaking directly.

Under present performance appraisal systems, it is difficult to compensate managers for developing people because the criteria are elusive. With a developing file of upward appraisals, however, executives can judge how well a manager has done in developing his people. The employees cannot evaluate the whole of their manager's job, but they can say a great deal about how well he or she has facilitated their work, increased their proficiency, cleared barriers, protected them against political forces, and raised their level of competence — in short, how the manager has met their ministration, maturation, and mastery needs.[10] A top executive can then quantify such upward evaluations and use the outcome as a basis for compensating a manager for his effectiveness in developing his employees.

When a group of manager peers experiments with upward appraisal and works it out to their own comfort, as well as to that of their employees, then it might be tried at the next lower level. When several successive levels have worked out their own systems, the process might be formalized throughout the organization. Acceptance of the upward appraisal concept is likely to be greater if it has been tested and modeled by the very people who must use it, and if it has not been imposed on them by the personnel department. With appropriate experience, the managers involved in the process would ultimately evolve suitable appraisal forms.

WHAT ABOUT RESULTS?

What does adopting the critical incident technique and the dynamic job description mean for judging a person's ability to obtain results? Does quantitative performance lose its importance?

My answer is an unqualified no. There will always be other issues that managers will have to determine, such as level of compensation or promotability — issues which should be dealt with in other sessions after the basic behavioral performance appraisal.[11]

Some of the performance appraisal information may be helpful in making such determinations, but neither of these two functions should contaminate the performance appraisal feedback process. There can still be an annual compensation evaluation, based not only on behavior, which is the basis for coaching, but also on outcome. Did an employee

---

[10] Harry Levinson, *The Exceptional Executive* (Cambridge, Harvard University Press, 1968).

[11] Herbert H. Meyer, Emanual Kay, and John R. P. French, Jr., "Split Roles in Performance Appraisal," *Howard Business Review*, January-February 1965, p. 123.

make money? Did he reach quantitative goals? Did she resolve problems in the organization that were her responsibility?

No doubt, there will be some overlapping between behavior and outcome, but the two are qualitatively different. One might behave as it was expected he should, but at the same time not do what had to be done to handle the vagaries of the marketplace. He might not have responded with enough speed or flexibility to a problem, even though his behavior corresponded to all that originally was asked of him in the job description and goal-setting process.

Both behavior and outcome are important, and neither should be overlooked. It is most important, however, that they not be confused.

Although this article has been widely quoted and paraphrased ever since it first appeared in 1974, we often haven't taken the time to go back and read it in its entirety. Oncken and Wass tell us how bosses end up with all the problems (monkeys on their backs) and what managers can do to train subordinates to solve their own problems.

Management Time:
Who's Got the Monkey?

William Oncken, Jr. and Donald L. Wass

Why is it that managers are typically running out of time while their subordinates are typically running out of work? In this article, we shall explore the meaning of management time as it relates to the interaction between the manager and his boss, his own peers, and his subordinates.

Specifically, we shall deal with three different kinds of management time.

Boss-imposed time — to accomplish those activities which the boss requires and which the manager cannot disregard without direct and swift penalty.

System-imposed time — to accommodate those requests to the manager for active support from his peers. This assistance must also be provided lest there be penalties, though not always direct or swift.

Self-imposed time — to do those things which the manager originates or agrees to do himself. A certain portion of this kind of time, however, will be taken by his subordinates and is called "subordinate-imposed time." The remaining portion will be his own and is called "discretionary time." Self-imposed time is not subject to penalty since neither the boss nor the system can discipline the manager for not doing what they did not know he had intended to do in the first place.

The management of time necessitates that the manager get control over the timing and content of what he does. Since what the boss and the system impose on him are backed up by penalty, he cannot tamper with those requirements. Thus his self-imposed time becomes his major area of concern.

The manager's strategy is therefore to increase the "discretionary" component of his self-imposed time by minimizing or doing away with the "subordinate" component. He will then use the added increment to get better control over his boss-imposed and system-imposed activities. Most managers spend much more subordinate-imposed time than they even faintly realize. Hence we shall use a monkey-on-the-back analogy to examine how subordinate-imposed time comes into being and what the manager can do about it.

WHERE IS THE MONKEY?

Let us imagine that a manager is walking down the hall and that he notices one of his subordinates, Mr. A, coming up the hallway. When they are abreast of one another, Mr. A greets the manager with, "Good morning. By the way, we've got a problem. You see . . . " As Mr. A continues, the manager recognizes in this problem the same two characteristics common to all the problems his subordinates gratuitously bring to his attention. Namely, the manager knows (a) enough to get involved, but (b) not enough to make the on-the-spot decision expected of him. Eventually, the manager says, "So glad you brought this up. I'm in a rush right now. Meanwhile, let me think about it and I'll let you know." Then he and Mr. A part company.

Let us analyze what has just happened. Before the two of them met, on whose back was the "monkey?" The subordinate's. After they parted, on whose back was it? The manager's. Subordinate-imposed time begins the moment a monkey successfully executes a leap from the back of a subordinate to the back of his superior and does not end until the monkey is returned to its proper owner for care and feeding.

In accepting the monkey, the manager has voluntarily assumed a position subordinate to his subordinate. That is, he has allowed Mr. A to make him his subordinate by doing two things a subordinate is generally expected to do for his boss — the manager has accepted a responsibility from his subordinate, and the manager has promised him a progress report.

The subordinate, to make sure the manager does not miss this point, will later stick his head in the manager's office and cheerily query, "How's it coming?" (This is called "supervision.")

Or let us imagine again, in concluding a working conference with another subordinate, Mr. B, the manager's parting words are, "Fine. Send me a memo on that."

Let us analyze this one. The monkey is now on the subordinate's back because the next move is his, but it is poised for a leap. Watch that monkey. Mr. B dutifully writes the requested memo and drops it in his outbasket. Shortly thereafter, the manager plucks it from his inbasket and reads it. Whose move is it now? The manager's. If he does not make that move soon, he will get a follow-up memo from the subordinate (this is another form of supervision). The longer the manager delays, the more frustrated the subordinate will become (he'll be "spinning his wheels") and the more guilty the manager will feel (his backlog of subordinate-imposed time will be mounting).

Or suppose once again that at a meeting with a third subordinate, Mr. C., the manager agrees to provide all the necessary backing for a public relations proposal he has just asked Mr. C to develop. The manager's parting words to him are, "Just let me know how I can help."

Now let us analyze this. Here the monkey is initially on the subordinate's back. But for how long? Mr. C realizes that he cannot let the manager "know" until his proposal has the manager's approval. And from experience, he also realizes that his proposal will likely be sitting in the manager's briefcase for weeks waiting for him to eventually get to it. Who's really got the monkey? Who will be checking up on whom? Wheelspinning and bottlenecking are on their way again.

A fourth subordinate, Mr. D, has just been transferred from another part of the company in order to launch and eventually manage a newly created business venture. The manager has told him that they should get together soon to hammer out a set of objectives for his new job, and that "I will draw up an initial draft for discussion with you."

Let us analyze this one, too. The subordinate has the new job (by formal assignment) and the full responsibility (by formal delegation), but the manager has the next move. Until he makes it, he will have the monkey and the subordinate will be immobilized.

Why does it all happen? Because in each instance the manager and the subordinate assume at the outset, wittingly or unwittingly, that the matter under consideration is a joint problem. The monkey in each case begins its career astride both their backs. All it has to do now is move the wrong leg, and — presto — the subordinate deftly disappears. The manager is thus left with another acquisition to his menagerie. Of course, monkeys can be trained not to move the wrong leg. But it is easier to prevent them from straddling backs in the first place.

Who Is Working for Whom?

To make what follows more credible, let us suppose that these same four subordinates are so thoughtful and considerate of the manager's time that they are at pains to allow no more than three monkeys to leap from each of their backs to his in any one day. In a five-day week, the manager will have picked up 60 screaming monkeys — far too many to do anything about individually. So he spends the subordinate-imposed time juggling his "priorities."

Late Friday afternoon, the manager is in his office with the door closed for privacy in order to contemplate the situation, while his subordinates are waiting outside to get a last chance before the weekend to remind him that he will have to "fish or cut bait." Imagine what they are saying to each other about the manager as they wait: "What a bottleneck. He just can't make up his mind. How anyone ever got that high up in our company without being able to make a decision we'll never know."

Worst of all, the reason the manager cannot make any of these "next moves" is that his time is almost entirely eaten up in meeting his own boss-imposed and system-imposed requirements. To get control of these, he needs discretionary time that is in turn denied him when he is preoccupied with all these monkeys. The manager is caught in a vicious circle.

But time is a-wasting (an understatement). The manager calls his secretary on the intercom and instructs her to tell his subordinates that he will be unavailable to see them until Monday morning. At 7:00 p.m., he drives home, intending with firm resolve to return to the office tomorrow to get caught up over the weekend. He returns bright and early the next day only to see, on the nearest green of the golf course across from his office window, a foursome. Guess who?

That does it. He now knows *who* is really working for *whom*. Moreover, he now sees that if he actually accomplishes during the weekend what he came to accomplish, his subordinates' morale will go up so sharply that they will each raise the limit on the number of monkeys they will let jump from their backs to his. In short, he now sees, with the clarity of a revelation on a mountaintop, that the more he gets caught up, the more he will fall behind.

He leaves the office with the speed of a man running away from a plague. His plan? To get caught up on something else he hasn't had time for in years: a weekend with his family. (This is one of the many varieties of discretionary time.)

Sunday night he enjoys ten hours of sweet, untroubled slumber, because he has clear-cut plans for Monday. He is going to get rid of his subordinate-imposed time. In exchange, he will get an equal amount of discretionary time, part of which he will spend with his subordinates to see that they learn the difficult but rewarding managerial art called, "The Care and Feeding of Monkeys."

The manager will also have plenty of discretionary time left over for getting control of the timing and content not only of his boss-imposed time but of his system-imposed time as well. All of this may take months, but compared with the way things have been, the rewards will be enormous. His ultimate objective is to manage his management time.

GETTING RID OF THE MONKEYS

The manager returns to the office Monday morning just late enough to permit his four subordinates to collect in his outer office waiting to see him about their monkeys. He calls them in, one by one. The purpose of each interview is to take a monkey, place it on the desk between them, and figure out together how the next move might conceivably be the subordinate's. For certain monkeys, this will take some doing. The subordinate's next move may be so elusive that the manager may decide — just for now — merely to let the monkey sleep on the subordinate's back overnight and have him return with it at an appointed time the next morning to continue the joint quest for a more substantive move by the subordinate. (Monkeys sleep just as soundly overnight on subordinates' backs as on superiors'.)

As each subordinate leaves the office, the manager is rewarded by the sight of a monkey leaving his office on the subordinate's back. For the next 24 hours, the subordinate will not be waiting for the manager; instead, the manager will be waiting for the subordinate.

Later, as if to remind himself that there is no law against his engaging in a constructive exercise in the interim, the manager strolls by

279

the subordinate's office, sticks his head in the door, and cheerily asks, "How's it coming?" (The time consumed in doing this is discretionary for the manager and boss-imposed for the subordinate.)

When the subordinate (with the monkey on his back) and the manager meet at the appointed hour the next day, the manager explains the ground rules to this effect:

"At no time while I am helping you with this or any other problem will your problem become my problem. The instant your problem becomes mine, you will no longer have a problem. I cannot help a man who hasn't got a problem.

"When this meeting is over, the problem will leave this office exactly the way it came in — on your back. You may ask my help at any appointed time, and we will make a joint determination of what the next move will be and which of us will make it.

"In those rare instances where the next move turns out to be mine, you and I will determine it together. I will not make any move alone."

The manager follows this same line of thought with each subordinate until at about 11:00 a.m. he realizes that he has no need to shut his door. His monkeys are gone. They will return — but by appointment only. His appointment calendar will assure this.

Transferring the Initiative

What we have been driving at in this monkey-on-the-back analogy is to transfer initiative from manager to subordinate and keep it there. We have tried to highlight a truism as obvious as it is subtle. Namely, before a manager can develop initiative in his subordinates, he must see to it that they *have* the initiative. Once he takes it back, they will no longer have it and he can kiss his discretionary time good-bye. It will all revert to subordinate-imposed time.

Nor can both manager and subordinate effectively have the same initiative at the same time. The opener, "Boss, we've got a problem," implies this duality and represents, as noted earlier, a monkey astride two backs, which is a very bad way to start a monkey on its career. Let us, therefore, take a few moments to examine what we prefer to call "The Anatomy of Managerial Initiative."

There are five degrees of initiative that the manager can exercise in relation to the boss and to the system: (1) *wait* until told (lowest initiative); (2) *ask* what to do; (3) *recommend*, then take resulting action; (4) *act*, but advise at once; (5) *act* on own, then routinely report (highest initiative).

Clearly, the manager should be professional enough not to indulge himself in initiatives 1 and 2 in relation either to the boss or to the system. A manager who uses initiative 1 has no control over either the timing or content of his boss-imposed or system-imposed time. He thereby forfeits any right to complain about what he is told to do or when he is told to do it. The manager who uses initiative 2 has control over the timing but not over the content. Initiatives 3, 4, and 5 leave the manager in control of both, with the greatest control being at level 5.

The manager's job, in relation to his subordinates' initiatives, is twofold; first, to outlaw the use of initiatives 1 and 2, thus giving his subordinates no choice but to learn and master "Completed Staff Work"; then, to see that for each problem leaving his office there is an agreed-upon level of initiative assigned to it, in addition to the agreed-upon time and place of the next manager-subordinate conference. The latter should be duly noted on the manager's appointment calendar.

CARE AND FEEDING OF MONKEYS

In order to further clarify our analogy between the monkey-on-the-back and the well-known processes of assigning and controlling, we shall refer briefly to the manager's appointment schedule, which calls for five hard and fast rules governing the "Care and Feeding of Monkeys" (violations of these rules will cost discretionary time):

Rule 1: Monkeys should be fed or shot. Otherwise, they will starve to death and the manager will waste valuable time on postmortems or attempted resurrections.

Rule 2: The monkey population should be kept below the maximum number the manager has time to feed. His subordinates will find time to work as many monkeys as he finds time to feed, but no more. It shouldn't take more than 5 to 15 minutes to feed a properly prepared monkey.

Rule 3: Monkeys should be fed by appointment only. The manager should not have to be hunting down starving monkeys and feeding them on a catch-as-catch-can basis.

Rule 4: Monkeys should be fed face to face or by telephone, but never by mail. (If by mail, the next move will be the manager's — remember!) Documentation may add to the feeding process, but it cannot take the place of feeding.

Rule 5: Every monkey should have an assigned "next feeding time" and "degree of initiative." These may be revised at any time by mutual consent, but never allowed to become vague or indefinite. Otherwise, the monkey will either starve to death or wind up on the manager's back.

CONCLUDING NOTE

"Get control over the timing and content of what you do" is appropriate advice for managing management time. The first order of business is for the manager to enlarge his discretionary time by eliminating subordinate-imposed time. The second is for him to use a portion of his new-found discretionary time to see to it that each of his subordinates possesses the initiative without which he cannot exercise initiative, and then to see to it that this initiative is in fact taken. The third is for him to use another portion of his increased discretionary time to get and keep control of the timing and content of both boss-imposed and system-imposed time.

The result of all this is that the manager will increase his leverage, which will in turn enable him to multiply, without theoretical limit, the value of each hour that he spends in managing management time.

Dr. Feldman's article focuses on management of mental health organizations, but many of his points apply with equal force in special education. The director of special education is not the only one involved either. Supervisors of program units such as school psychology and social work services run into essentially the same dilemma as Feldman described in his abstract of the article:

Clinicians promoted to middle management positions have a good deal of difficulty coping with the use of power and with a variety of other unfamiliar and uncomfortable dilemmas. Among the most difficult of these is their responsibility for supervising the work of the professional staff. This article identifies the values on their behavior, and the problems these cause for middle managers in mental health organizations.

The Middle Management Muddle

Saul Feldman

Despite what is frequently expressed as strong disinclination toward management, sooner or later many mental health professionals spend time as middle managers in community mental health centers, hospitals, clinics, and other organizations. Lured by the prospect of higher salaries and for a variety of other reasons — to bring about change, self-expression, boredom, and status — they accept positions for which they are frequently ill suited by training and perhaps by temperament. Not surprisingly, they often have difficulty coping with the conflicts and problems that are so inherent in middle management jobs.

From *Administration in Mental Health*, 1980, *8*(1), 3-11. Reprinted by permission.

At least in part, the problems of middle managers result from too little knowledge about management and the dynamics of organizational behavior. The education of mental health managers rarely includes course work designed to enhance their understanding of organizations, particularly those things that will affect them most directly. While part of mental health training does take place in organizations, it is almost exclusively related to the diagnosis and care of patients rather than the organization itself. The way organizations function, the interplay between individual and organizational goals, formal and informal groups, organizational change, communication patterns and the like are not ordinarily dealt with, at least not heuristically.

The benign neglect of training for mental health managers is strikingly different from our attitudes about training mental health professionals who work directly with patients. Their training is widely discussed and tightly prescribed. Psychiatrists, psychologists, psychiatric social workers, and others not trained in accordance with generally accepted standards have difficulty finding employment. This is not true of mental health managers. Are we to assume from this that the degrees of difficulty and knowledge required to care for individual patients are greater than those needed for the care of the organization? I think not.

Organizations have a common set of characteristics that dominate or at least strongly affect the behavior of their members. These characteristics include a power hierarchy and leadership process; rules and procedures that prescribe at least some degree of uniformity; defined responsibilities; a division of labor; supraordinate goals either latent or manifest; a staff responsible for maintaining the organization; and a structure that may be informal or collegial but nonetheless requires some accountability to other individuals or groups.

While these characteristics vary, they typify most formal organizations, including those engaged in widely diverse activities. Even less formal ones, or those that appear less formal (e.g., mutual benefit associations), have similar features. They all require some uniformity and some lessening of individual autonomy. Or phrased somewhat differently, even when a group of anarchists gets together, someone has to call the meeting to order.

While sharing these characteristics, mental health organizations have an array of others that create special problems for middle managers. As Mechanic (1973) has pointed out, "Mental health agencies by their very character bring into sharp focus many of the complexities of organizations. The goals of such organizations are usually multifaceted and ambiguous. They normally encompass some concept of treatment, rehabilitation and consultation. They frequently combine such functions as providing service to clients, training professionals and other personnel, and some research. These functions would be difficult enough under the best of circumstances, but problems are compounded at almost every point by the absence of agreed upon technologies, by differences in ideologies among varying professional groups, by disagreements on basic intervention approaches, and by continuing situational pressures involving community support, funding, staffing, and the like." These characteristics are most prevalent in community mental health centers and have caused me to describe centers as "organized anarchies" though some of my colleagues take issue with my use of the word "organized."

As a result, mental health organizations are very complex and difficult to manage. Of all the problems, there are none more difficult, more characterized by conflict and hostility, or more important for middle managers than those having to do with managing professional staff. The discussions at meetings and other places where mental health professionals gather abound with criticism of the organizations in which they work and attest to the low esteem with which these organizations and their managers are viewed. Indeed, few things seem to inspire greater camaraderie among mental health professionals than their dislike, if not their vilification, of organizations and managers, except perhaps for government. Budget inequities, salaries that are too low, misplaced priorities, restrictive policies, excessive rules and regulations, insensitivity and a general criticism of organizations as not sufficiently responsive to either the needs of clients or of staff are among the many complaints.

In good measure, these complaints and hurt feelings stem from the values of mental health professionals and the effects of these values on their behavior as well as on the organizations in which they work. While some of the values are associated with professionalism in general, others are more specifically related to the mental health field. Acquired during training and through the professional socialization processes to which the members of the mental health disciplines are exposed, these values result in behavior that generates considerable tension between mental health professionals, middle managers, and the organizations in which they work. Not infrequently, they cause the typical mental health organization to resemble a Navy with more admirals than ships. The tensions may not always be dysfunctional — under certain circumstances they may actually enhance the functioning of mental health organizations. But dysfunctional or not, they almost invariably involve the middle manager as a key party to the process of getting the organization's work done.

AUTONOMY

While every organization requires some conformity with an authority structure as well as compliance with uniform rules and policies, mental health professionals seem to value just the opposite — autonomy. Webster defines autonomy as "functioning independently without control by others." It is among the values most highly cherished by mental health professionals and, therefore, most troublesome for middle managers. Autonomy is manifested as the ability (or divine right) to be free of external controls on professional behavior. The idealized role-model is that of the private practitioner who may consult with colleagues but whose sovereignty is inviolate. The sanctity of this self-image is emphasized, at least by implication, in the training of mental health professionals and is considerably reinforced by the nature of their relationships with patients.

Patients with emotional problems or those who are mentally ill may, in the course of their treatment, become highly dependent and endow mental health professionals with virtues they do not always possess. While well-trained clinicians recognize and are able to cope with this process, it may inflate their self-image, strengthen their feelings of autonomy, and affect their relations with the "nonpatient world." Within organizations, these values may be expressed as an unwillingness to comply with requests, a need to have everything explained so that "reasonableness" is assured, hurt feelings, and an insistence upon being involved in all decisions that may in any way affect one's life within the organization.

As Whittington (1973) has written, the mental health professional "frequently receives enormous ego gratification from patients who see him as all powerful. It is difficult to move from a position of such great authority and status to a position of an employee of an agency. The mental health professional simply does not want to fit into a system . . . " In effect, his work with patients "reinforces and encourages his strivings toward independence and special status."

In addition to this autonomy, mental health professionals also appear to have a strong sense of entitlement stemming from long years of study and sacrifice as well as a keen sense of the privileges attached to their credentials, particularly to the title "doctor." As such, they are often impatient with routine, highly selective about the activities in which they choose to engage, resistant to supervision and invariably alert to their "special status" in other ways as well. I use the term "M. Deity" to describe this attitude in psychiatrists although it is shared by other mental health professionals as well.

ORGANIZATIONAL LOYALTY

The conflicting loyalties of mental health professionals also cause difficulties for middle managers. Many mental health organizations operate without clear goals except perhaps at a high level of abstraction. As a result, individual staff members may view their relation to these goals quite differently. That this difficulty also exists outside the mental health field is illustrated by the three brick layers, each of whom was asked what he was doing. The responses of each were laying bricks, building a wall, and helping to erect a great cathedral.

But even in the absence of specific goals, most organizations have an ethos that characterizes them, helps shape their programs, and defines their priorities. These comprise an organizational identity, a set of values and ideas to which, at least theoretically, its members should subscribe.

Professionalism, on the other hand, requires allegiance to a particular set of standards and values that help define acceptable modes of behavior. With mental health professionals, these values are an integral part of professional training and are reinforced afterwards through relationships with colleagues and membership in professional associations. Often the originators and enforcers of professional standards, these associations are a source of external support for mental health professionals in organizations and a continuing validation of their professionalism. As a result, psychiatrists, psychologists, psychiatric social workers, and others often become strongly identified with the values of their profession. To the chagrin of managers, this identification is not always consistent with the goals and values of the organizations in which they work. According to Blau and Scott (1962), "A professional orientation is inversely related to organizational loyalty." They indicate that "professionals tend to assume a 'cosmopolitan' orientation and willingness to move from one employer to another, whereas those less committed to professional skills are usually 'locals' with strong feelings of loyalty to their organization." Similarly, in a study of mental health professionals, Wagenfeld and his colleagues (1974) found that "agency policy is seen as expendable to professional standards." In the event of a real or imagined conflict between the two, professional standards tend to dominate.

In a field like mental health where truth is elusive and values are more compelling than facts, professionalism is a major determinant of the staff's perceptions, beliefs, and modes of behavior. The opinions of staff about what is professionally correct, opinions that are often quite emphatic, sometimes self-righteous, and almost invariably influenced by personal and professional values, contribute to the classic dilemma of a professional organization — how to maximize the effectiveness and

287

objectivity of needed professional expertise while reducing the subjective effects of the process through which such expertise is acquired and retained. Gouldner (1957) has described this dilemma as the "tension between an organization's bureaucratic needs for expertise and its social system needs for loyalty."

While the conflicting loyalties of the professional staff manifest themselves in several ways, they may appear to the managers of mental health organizations as self-serving, disloyal, and dysfunctional to the well being of the organization and its clients. In such a context, the boundaries between disloyalty and constructive criticism are not easily defined. Of course, the extent to which organizational loyalty may have positive or negative effects is highly situational. Is dissent disloyal and the refusal to go along insubordinate? Under what conditions is it proper or even essential to work against the objectives of one's own organization, to not follow the leader? Rarely loath to express a point of view and never lacking the verbiage to do so, mental health professionals are particularly well suited for the adversarial process implied by these questions. And, of course, middle managers with their own conflicting loyalties are in the eye of the storm.

COLLEGIALISM

Collegialism is another strongly held value of mental health professionals. It represents the more personal and fraternal aspects of professional loyalty. It is a particular problem for middle managers who must prescribe and supervise the behavior of colleagues with whom they share professional and, not infrequently, personal bonds. The problem here is how to reconcile the need for affection or at least acceptance by one's colleagues while at the same time critically reviewing their behavior and making decisions that may adversely affect their welfare.

The collegial and personal bonds between middle managers and staff may erode the utility of organizational rules and procedures when middle managers are more identified with the needs and values of the staff than with those of the organization or the director — a not uncommon occurrence. No wonder that such accountability processes as supervision and review are sometimes less than effective instruments to ensure the quality of professional performance.

IMPLICATIONS FOR QUALITY

But why is all this important? Why should we care about the tension between the needs and values of mental health professionals and those of the organizations in which they work? Because there appears to be some evidence that suggests a correlation between the way mental health professionals feel about the organizations they work in and the quality of their performance. As Sarata (1976) has written, "Staff morale and attitudes affect the quality of services provided in mental health and other human service settings. High staff morale contributes to the social climate within which the client is served. Highly satisfied staff display greater task involvement and more cooperative attitudes. Absenteeism and turnover among staff who provide treatment services are negatively correlated with job satisfaction and morale."

In his case study of a large psychiatric hospital, Rogers (1975) made a similar point. He wrote that both "staff and patients to a large extent believe they are victimized by an unidentified 'them,' those in control . . . The result is a feeling of powerlessness and the need to exercise one's wits, to play up to the 'power structure' in order to be able to do 'one's own thing.' While carefully testing the limits of institutionally acceptable behavior, staff and patients seem routinely to behave in an apathetic manner. Yet, close to the surface, there is a lack of security and strong feelings of frustration, discontent, rage, and guilt."

ADMINISTRATIVE STYLE

For middle managers there are several special attitudinal issues. Mental health is a helping profession in which the values of caring, support, and therapy are dominant. These values are sometimes inconsistent with the exercise of power — the directive and perhaps authoritative stance sometimes necessary in management.

As a result, middle managers are not always comfortable with the use of power in organizations. Levinson and Klerman (1972) have indicated that, "Often the clinician-turned-executive is hindered in the exercise of authority by his feeling that an interest in power is intrinsically immoral; that it is antithetical to truly noble interests in being a healer or a scientist. Indeed, the predominant view of power . . . in the mental health profession is much like the Victorian view of sex. It is seen as vulgar, as a sign of character defect, as something an upstanding professional would not be interested in or stoop to." This reluctance to use organizational power contrasts with the "professional" power derived from the "doctor-patient" relationship discussed earlier. One is expressed as a disinclination to exercise control; the other as an aversion to being controlled.

This anxiety about power may lead middle managers to over-emphasize collective decision-making or participatory management and a hesitancy to make decisions. On the other hand, a sensitivity to the psychological needs of staff and the value of a supportive environment may improve the psychological "climate" of an organization and result in improved performance. The middle manager who is able to blend the use of power with this sensitivity is likely to be extremely effective.

There are other difficulties specific to middle managers, difficulties that are almost inevitably part of the transition from staff to management roles. They include:

a. The self-image that accompanies a shift in loyalty from profession to organization and in identity from clinician to manager;

b. The new manager's need to be liked, to be seen as "nice" in contrast to his or her own image of organizations and managers as "hurting rather than helping people." (Bailey & Jensen 1965);

c. Anxiety about relying on other people to get work done, and dependence on others for one's own success;

d. New dilemmas about such previously alien things as efficiency, budgets, costs, order, rules, and the like;

e. Feelings of loss about less personal and perhaps less congenial contact with colleagues, and less involvement with direct clinical work;

f. Discomfort with authority and status;

g. Conflicts arising from multiple and frequently conflicting allegiances to subordinates, to superiors, to personal and professional values;

h. Feelings of isolation — Webster defines middle as "equally distant from all sides."

Among the most important and perhaps most subtle effects of the middle management role on mental health professionals is their tendency to forget what it feels like to be a patient — to be on the other side of the fence, to feel bewildered, powerless, dependent, depersonalized, ashamed. To forget that those who need help most generally have the most difficulty reaching out for it and when they do, to forget how tentative and fragile the reach is.

It is easy to forget what it feels like to be a patient — to become captives of the contexts in which we work, the processes for which we are responsible — and of our personal needs. It happens to many of us, well-meaning and well-trained as we are. We become numb, desensitized, distanced from the very people and feelings that are supposed to be the reason for our existence. We begin to think of our patients as "cases," as somehow very different from ourselves, we grow detached from them, and we no longer ask such questions as, "Is this the kind of mental health service I would want my family to use?"

I believe this numbing to be one of the most important but least recognized problems for middle managers in mental health organizations, a problem whose etiology and treatment are uncertain, one with barely recognizable yet pervasive and deadly effects, one that demands attention. We now know enough about organizations and the life cycles through which they move to understand that at some time in their lives, they inevitably begin to emphasize internal processes — rules, conformity, procedures, discipline, and control — to such an extent that these become values in themselves. The organization's attention shifts away from the purpose for which it was formed and moves toward preserving and securing its funding base.

In effect, the organization "forgets" what it's there for. In mental health organizations this problem is compounded by the size to which we have permitted (if not encouraged) our organizations to grow, the elusiveness of our success criteria, and the lack of a competitive market. Because it is so difficult to assess how well or poorly mental health organizations are doing, it is not unlikely that at least for some their survival and even growth may be inversely related to their value.

As one possible remedy for this numbing, I believe that mental health managers should in their training and periodically thereafter be required to spend some time as patients or pseudo patients in mental health organizations — to experience what it's like to be a patient, to remember, and to reflect that experience in their work. I do not mean by this that all mental health managers need psychotherapy or should be psychoanalyzed, though I know many of them have heard such suggestions from their staffs and I'm not sure it would be such a bad idea. I do mean that the pseudo patient experience — spending a week as an inpatient, calling the emergency service at 2:00 in the morning, sitting in the waiting room periodically, participating in a day care program — may be among the few things we can do to help mental health organizations continue to care about and meet the needs of the people they serve.

291

The personal characteristics of middle managers are very important too. Among the most important of these I would include a good sense of humor, honesty, a high tolerance for ambiguity and frustration, ability to anticipate the unintended effects of decisions, distrust of power, and an irreverence toward the things most people take too seriously, particularly themselves.

To a considerable extent, the effectiveness of mental health organizations is dependent upon the skill and vitality of their middle managers — program chiefs, unit heads, assistant directors, and the like. Clinicians promoted to such positions face a variety of new and somewhat bewildering problems. Some of these problems are attributable to subject matter deficiencies — lack of knowledge about such things as personnel administration, budgeting, planning, and other management processes. Others have more to do with discomfort about the role shifts that are an inevitable part of the transition from clinician to clinician-manager, shifts that are often incompatible with the self image and values of clinicians.

There are pitifully few training opportunities for middle managers in mental health organizations despite what appears to be a considerable interest in such training. To be effective, new training programs should include the basic management processes of most importance to middle managers; should reflect the ways in which these are modified by the particular characteristics of the mental health organization; and should help mental health professionals cope with new value and ethical dilemmas inherent in the middle management role.

REFERENCES

Bailey, R.E., & Jensen, B.T. The troublesome transition from scientist to manager. *Personnel*, 1965, *42*(5).

Blau, P., & Scott, W.R. *Formal organizations.* San Francisco: Chandler, 1962, p. 69.

Gouldner, A.W. Cosmopolitans and locals. *Administrative Science Quarterly*, 1957-1958, *2*, 466.

Levinson, D., & Klerman, G. The clinician-executive revisited. *Administration in Mental Health*, Winter 1972, pp. 64-67.

Mechanic, D. The sociology of organizations. In S. Feldman, *The administration in mental health services*, Springfield, IL: Charles C Thomas, 1973.

Rogers, K. State mental hospitals: an organizational analysis. *Administration in Mental Health*, Fall 1975, *3*(1).

Sarta, B. Improving staff satisfaction through job design. *Administration in Mental Health,* Fall 1976, *4*(1).

Wagenfeld, M.O., Robin, S.S., & Jones, J.D. Structural and professional correlates of ideologies of community mental health workers. *Journal of Health & Social Behavior,* 1974, *15*, 199-210.

Whittington, H.G. People make programs: Personnel management. In S. Feldman, *The administration of mental health services.* Springfield, IL: Charles C Thomas, 1973, p. 64.

Index